MENTORS AND FRIENDS

Two Hundred and ten numbered copies of the first edition signed by the author have been reserved for the subscribers, author and publisher.

This copy is number: _____

MENTORS AND FRIENDS

*Short Lives of Prominent
Publishers and Booksellers
I Have Known*

Ian Norrie

Elliott & Thompson
London

Also by Ian Norrie

Publishing and Bookselling (with Frank A. Mumby), 1974
Mumby's Publishing and Bookselling in the Twentieth Century, 1982
Sixty Precarious Years: A Short History of the National Book League, 1985
A Hampstead Memoir: High Hill Bookshop, 1957–1988, 1989
Next Time Round in Provence (with drawings by Michael Floyd), 1993
Next Time Round in the Dordogne (with drawings by Michael Floyd), 1989
Next Time Round in Tuscany (with drawings by Michael Floyd), 1998
Hampstead: London Hill Town (with photographs by Dorothy Bohm), 1981
A Celebration of London (with photographs by Dorothy Bohm), 1984
Sabbatical: Doing Europe for Pleasure, 1983
The Book of Hampstead (co-editor with Mavis Norrie;
illustrated by various hands), 1960, 1968
The Book of the City (editor; drawings by Ronald Saxby;
photographs by Edwin Smith), 1961
The Heathside Book of Hampstead and Highgate (editor;
drawings by RonaldSaxby; photographs by Edwin Smith), 1962
The Book of Westminster (editor; photographs by Edwin Smith), 1964
Writers and Hampstead (compiler; calligraphy by George Simpson;
photographs by Keith Wynn), 1987
Hampstead, Highgate and Kenwood: A Short Guide, 1966,
1967, 1968, 1972, 1977, 1983

NOVELS
Hackles Rise and Fall, 1962
Quentin and the Bogomils, 1966
Plum's Last Tour, 1978
Brought to Book, 2002

SUBSCRIBERS

The author and publishers are indebted to the following whose generous support has made publication of this book possible. The list includes not only authors, booksellers, librarians, literary agents, printers and publishers but also personal friends with no professional trade connections apart from their lifelong willingness to buy books:

Brian Alderson
Anonymous
Naim Attallah
Robert Balyuzi
Richard Barker
Hazel Bell
Eric de Bellaigue
Bryan Bennett
Francis Bennett
Kip Bertram
Philip Blackwell
John Bond
Booksellers
   Association
   of the United
   Kingdom & Ireland
Michael Bott
Peggy Bowyer
Sue Bradbury
Clive Bradley
Sue Bradley
Peter Buckman
Piers Burnett
Jane Carr
Sir Charles
   Chadwyck-Healey
   BT, DL
Ian Chapman
James Chesterman
Serafina Clarke
Nicholas Clee
Peter Cochrane

Jill Coleman
Jeff Cooper
Leo Cooper
Robin C. Cortie
Lady Nora David
Mike Davies
Judith Davis
Giles de la Mare
Anne Dolamore
Michael Dugdale
John Edmondson
Marilyn Edwards
Professor Simon
   Eliot
Charles Elliott
Michael J. Ellison
John & Margaret
   Elsley
Beryl Ennion
Patricia Eve
Maureen Everett
Julian Fall
Klaus Flugge
Colin Forbes
June Formby
Anthony Foyle
Christopher Foyle
John Foyle
Anthony Frewin
David Gadsby
Robert Gavron
Alan Giles

Richard Gisborne
Ben Glazebrook
Martyn Goff
Gordon Graham
Tim Graham
Graham C. Greene
Jane Hamlyn
Jan Hampden
Norman Hart
Andrew Hayward
Ernest Hecht
Nicholas Heffer
Tim Hely
   Hutchinson
Brenda Herbert
Frank Herrmann
Andrew Hewson
David Hight
Geoffrey Hill
Professor Jocelyn
   Hillgarth
John Hitchin
Penelope Hoare
Michael Holman
David Hooper
Miles Huddleston
Bruce Hunter
Simon Huntley
John Hyams
Robin & Inge Hyman
Delphine & Gerald
   Isaaman

MATTHEW J. JACKSON
PATRICK JANSON-
    SMITH
DEREK JOHNS
JOSEPH'S BOOKSTORE
MICHAEL JOSEPH
PHILIP JOSEPH
SHEILA JUDD
JOYCE & TONY
    JUDKINS
PHILIP KOGAN
KARL LAWRENCE
MARK LE FANU
MICHAEL LEGAT
LEILA & ROBERT
DAVID LEONARD
LIONEL LEVENTHAL
RUBIO LINDROOS
JONATHAN LLOYD
JO LUNT
HAMISH MACGIBBON
DAVID MACHIN
CHRISTOPHER
    MACLEHOSE
TIM MANDERSON
SIMON MASTER
SARA MILLER MCCUNE
    SAGE PUBLICATIONS
    INC.
CHRIS MEADE
    BOOKTRUST
IAN C. MILLER
TREVOR MOORE
DONALD MORRISON
P. A. MOUNTAIN
SALLY MUNTON
JOHN R. MURRAY
ANDREW & GLYNIS
    NAIRN
FRED NEWMAN

NIGEL NEWTON
ALASTAIR NIVEN
TRISHA NUNN
ANDREW NURNBERG
CATHERINE &
    MICHAEL
    O'DONNELL
PROFESSOR   MICHAEL
OLIVER CBE
HELEN PAIBA
JOHN PARKE
DIETER PEVSNER
MARTIN PICK
KATE POCOCK
MICHAEL POUNTNEY
PRISCILLA
THE RANDOM HOUSE
    GROUP
THE RANDOM HOUSE
    GROUP ARCHIVE
    & LIBRARY
DIANA RAYMOND
JOHN RICHARDSON
PROFESSOR PAUL
    RICHARDSON
TIM RIX
JOHN ROBERTS
    SCANVIK BOOKS
    COPENHAGEN
NICK ROBINSON
T. G. ROSENTHAL
ANTHONY ROTA
EVE ROY
MRS MICHAEL
    RUBINSTEIN
CHRIS S.
KEITH SAMBROOK
BILL SAMUEL
PER G. SAUGMAN
PAUL SCHERER

TANYA SCHMOLLER
MICHAEL SEVIOUR
GEORGE SIMPSON
    RMS, HS, SLM
CHRISTOPHER
    SINCLAIR-STEVENSON
ROBIN SMEETON
GEOFFREY SMITH
ROGER SMITH
F. C. SWEETEN
JOE TANNER
BING TAYLOR
EMILY TAYLOR
JUDY TAYLOR
AINSLIE THIN
SUE THOMSON
ION TREWIN
MRS C. L.
    TURBERVILLE SMITH
MICHAEL TURNER
CAROL M. UNWIN
DAVID UNWIN
MERLIN UNWIN
MAGGIE VAN REENEN
ED VICTOR
NIGEL VINEY
SIMON WARD
JOHN WELCH
CHRIS WELLER &
    MARGARET LALLY
RONALD WHITING
DAVID WHITAKER
SALLY WHITAKER
COLIN WHURR
KEN WILDER
JON WYNNE-TYSON
MICHAEL ZIFCAK OBE

CONTENTS

SOME ABBREVIATIONS USED IN THE TEXT:

AB – Associated Booksellers of GB & Ireland, The
ABA – American Booksellers Association, The
BA – Booksellers Association of GB & Ireland, The
BSP – Blackwell Scientific Publications
DNB – Dictionary of National Biography, The
FEL – Foyle's Educational Limited
HEB – Heinemann Educational Books
LSE – London School of Economics
IPC – International Publishing Corporation
NBC – National Book Council, The
NBL – National Book League, The
NBA – Net Book Agreement, The
OUP – Oxford University Press
PA – Publishers Association, The

ACKNOWLEDGEMENTS

My original, main motive was to get the facts right. That has remained throughout a primary aim but I know, and the reader knows, that absolute truth is unattainable. One source often contradicts another; two persons' recollections of the same event are usually different. That something may be stated, in black and white, on a sheet of paper in an archive does not necessarily make it true, even when it is signed and dated. I hope that with the much valued assistance of those named below we have together achieved a high percentage of accuracy in facts and, equally important, a correct degree of emphasis where characteristics and personality are concerned.

The following kindly read and commented upon particular chapters with whose subjects they had enjoyed a working – and in some cases a family – relationship: Kip Bertram, Philip Blackwell, Piers Burnett, Mike Butler, Peter Cochrane, Christopher Foyle, Robert Gavron, Michael Hamburger, David Hill, John Hitchin, Jeremy Lewis, Christopher Maclehose, Hamish MacGibbon, Bill McCreadie, Trevor Moore, Penny Mountain, John R. Murray, Patricia Nunn, Dieter Pevsner, Paul Richardson, Keith Sambrook, Bill Samuel, Sue Thomson, Lynette Turberville-Smith, David Unwin and Ronald Whiting.

A smaller number of good friends nobly read the entire typescript. They were Martyn Goff, Gordon Graham, Ernest Hecht, Andrew Hewson, Robin Hyman, Jeremy Lewis and David Whitaker. To them and to all mentioned in the previous paragraph I am greatly indebted for their help and enthusiasm. They corrected me on many points; any errors which remain are my fault, not theirs.

I would like also to single out the genial, patient Michael Bott, who presides over the ever-growing archive of publishing, bookselling and related subjects at the library of Reading University, where, with too little assistance in terms of finance and staff, he preserves order on the very verge of chaos, extending the same loving care to that which is expertly categorised as he does to those items still awaiting classification.

I should like to thank *The Bookseller*, its editor-in-chief, Neill Denny and his colleagues Anna Kafetz and Mark Guest for making its photographic archive available and permitting me to reproduce the illustrations of Elsie Bertram, André Deutsch, Paul Hamlyn and Allen Lane; Kip Bertram for the photograph of Elsie Bertram and himself; Lady Nora David for kindly loaning the photograph of Ian Parsons; Christopher Foyle for permission to use photographs of Christina and William Foyle; John Foyle for permission to use the photograph of Gilbert Foyle; David Hill for making available the photograph of Alan Hill and Jock Murray; the Merton Blackwell Collection and Rita Ricketts for permission to reproduce the photograph of Sir Basil Blackwell; John R. Murray and the Murray archive for the photograph of Jock Murray; Trisha Nunn for kindly providing the photograph of Alan Steele and Merlin Unwin for making available the photographs of Sir Stanley, Philip and Rayner Unwin. Where an acknowledgment has not been recorded I have made every effort to trace the copyright holder.

INTRODUCTION

This book was born partly from a need I felt to correct and extend published obituaries. Many had been written in haste, suffered from the exigencies of subbing and, for the sake of not hurting grieving relatives, tactfully omitted reference to the less admirable characteristics of the deceased. It is also influenced by two book-trade histories I undertook. In 1967, Graham C. Greene of Jonathan Cape invited me to update F. A. Mumby's *Publishing and Bookselling*. Instead I spent six years rewriting it from 1870, six years when Mavis, my late wife (who features often in the lives which follow), and colleagues were required to be more than usually supportive while I teetered on the edge of nervous breakdown. I had recovered by the time Robin Hyman contracted with Cape to publish (1982) my further revisions confined to the twentieth century. These two modestly successful books established my permanent interest in the lives of fellow publishers and booksellers.

In the late 1990s, David Whitaker and I founded but soon abandoned the Graveyard Press to perfect and slightly to extend obituaries. He warned me that his written contribution would be slight; in fact it was nil, which suited me because I like to write my own books. (He likes to rewrite them; we are still close friends.) While working on Christina Foyle I felt an inclination to include more about her father and her uncle, the two men who started the Charing Cross Road business. I had similar reactions when I began to write about Stanley Unwin and Basil Blackwell. In addition to recording the facts, I found it put them into perspective if I noted what others had said about them and also to relate my own experiences. (Gilbert Foyle excepted, I met them all and some were my friends over long periods.) In addition, it seemed appropriate to add brief sketches of some of those who worked beside my main characters, colleagues without whose support and expertise none of them could have achieved and maintained their dominant status.

There were major figures on both sides of the trade who are not included because they died or retired before I became active; others whom I met only once or twice; yet more who are still alive. There were also the marginals. I couldn't include all those I had known. It is better not to name names.

Writing at far greater length than the customary obituary, I became aware that the background to the lives was complementing my Bell &

Hyman volume and becoming an outline history of the British book trade
in the twentieth century. It could prove of value to those entering it in the
present one and interest older colleagues who will be at least aware of the
illustrious names of my subjects, most of which are still found on newly
published title pages or on fascia boards. What I hope may emerge too is a
record of the close companionship we enjoyed in the last century when we
were still, for much of it, a cottage industry. To write 'we all knew everyone else in the trade' would be an exaggeration, but it was a small world
and most of us at least knew of most of the others.

It may seem that I am attempting to portray a golden age in which the
book trade was peopled by Olympians, the like of whom will not be at
work in a new, lacklustre century. That is not my intention. It is natural for
the old to veer towards the belief that everything was better ordered in their
younger days. At almost all periods of history this has been untrue, just as it
is equally inaccurate to suppose that things are bound to improve. The only
certainty is that they will change. I will not labour the point beyond
reminding readers that for at least 95% of the working lives of my subjects
(and in half of the cases 100%) the Net Book Agreement operated and
books were not sold on the Internet.

There is no reason to suppose that this century will fail to come up with
its own Allen Lanes, Christina Foyles and Paul Hamlyns and it is probable
that women will feature more formidably than in my selection. I am proud
of the fact that some of those who were employed in my one small (for
nowadays) bookshop currently hold senior positions in publishing conglomerates, literary agencies and at Book Trust. When I speak with them I
find a similar deep involvement in the trade and in literature to that which
I experienced in my time.

Three institutions, the Society of Bookmen, the National Book League
(later Book Trust) and the Garrick Club, are frequently mentioned because
they figured prominently in the lives of some of my subjects and also in
mine. The reader should not infer that they were the most influential or the
only centres of power in the book trade; they were not. That lay with the
Publishers' Association (hereafter, the PA) and the Booksellers' Association
(hereafter, the BA), and with particular companies and groups, while the
Garrick has no ties with any profession apart from the stage.

Ian Norrie
Sutherland Close, Barnet, April 2006

One

BASIL BLACKWELL

('The Gaffer')

In the twentieth-century, although there were corporate booksellers with more branches than his company owned and publishing imprints larger and more influential than his, there was no more distinguished bookman/businessman than Basil Blackwell. A few publishers may have had greater learning, some booksellers greater profitability, but none could equal his achievement of matching high cultural standards with economic viability. He was a scholar at ease in the market place.

In contrast to the Foyle dynasty, which migrated to Shoreditch from Hampshire, a Blackwell left London's East End, where his family were tailors, in the mid-nineteenth century to earn a living in Oxford. Benjamin Harris Blackwell (1813–55) opened a bookshop in St Clement's High Street, outside the city limits (inside, only freemen were permitted to trade without paying a fine), in 1846. He also became the city's first librarian. The dual occupations resulted in overwork and an early death. His widow closed the bookshop but determined that her son, Benjamin Henry, should follow his father's profession – or one of them. In due course, he was apprenticed to an Oxford bookseller, and while working for him, applied for a job as a librarian in Cardiff. Turned down, he stuck to bookselling, opening premises on his own account with a loan of £150 in Broad Street in 1879. The stock was valued at £126 with a selling price of £190. His mother lived with him and remained when, in 1886, he married Lydia, known as Lilla, a teacher who came from farming stock in Norfolk. They had two children, Dorothy in 1887 and Basil Henry, who was born on the second floor of 51 Broad Street, two years later.

Basil and Dorothy were not allowed into the bookshop except on Sundays when they used it to play at hide-and-seek. By then the sales area had increased from the original twelve square feet because the adjoining shop had been rented. Before that it was so small that Fred Hanks, the apprentice, had to vacate it if more than one customer was present. One of his duties was to ensure that Basil, in his pram in the yard, was secure. This same Hanks served Blackwell's for his entire working life, which he ended as a director of the company.

When Basil was seven the family moved to a large house in North Oxford, halfway to Summertown. From there he attended a nearby dame school. On Sundays the family, non-conformists and teetotallers, continued to worship in the city centre. Cycling on the sabbath was thought wicked so they walked the mile to chapel, with Basil dressed in 'Eton suit, stiff collar and dicky with a brief "bum-freezer" jacket'. At chapel they often heard an address by a Blackwell worker, so that Basil learned early to respect those on the family payroll. As an adult he recorded, 'Mr Vincent was the employee who preached at me.' His early relations with Hanks and Vincent guided him towards good management and he grew up with firm convictions that it was not only the gap between town and gown which needed closing but also that between employer and worker. The family later worshipped at the newly built St Andrew's Church, where father Blackwell became a warden; in due course he was elected a city councillor for North Oxford in the Liberal interest.

Benjamin Henry, with little formal education, had learned his trade as an apprentice and saved sufficient from his small wages to tour England by rail buying stock for his bookshop. Determined his son should have a better start, he sent the twelve-year-old to Magdalen College School from where he won a scholarship to Merton. Basil was the first of his family to go to university, exchanging the security of home for rooms in college, a transition made all the more traumatic because he was twelve months younger than most of his fellow undergraduates. At Merton he enjoyed rowing – he was dubbed 'the engine of the boat' – and playing rugger. It was there he met Adrian Mott ('the brother I never had'), who was to become a publishing colleague.

Basil was a dedicated classicist, preferring Greek to Latin – Greek being, he avowed, 'the more expansive literary vehicle'. He disappointed his tutors by achieving only a second in Greats, possibly because he had allowed himself to become distracted by attending Lady Ottoline Morrell's house parties at Garsington, where he listened to Bertrand Russell and other radicals. It was a time when he also became aware of the political situation in Europe. He joined the university OTC (Officer Training Corps), but his extreme short-sightedness, legacy of an attack of measles as a boy, exempted him from military service in the slaughter to come. Merton influenced him profoundly; he remained closely associated with it all his life.

When in 1911 Basil came down, Benjamin Henry decided that his son should develop Blackwell's publishing. This had existed from 1879, when he had placed his imprint on the first of many anthologies of undergraduate verse, but it remained very much a sideline during the decades when he developed both new and secondhand bookselling and helped to form the Oxford Branch of the recently founded Associated Booksellers of Great Britain. He decreed that Basil was to be the publisher of the family and sent him for a post-graduate year to Oxford University Press's London office. There the young man's first task was to edit a volume of the World's Classics series. The year was extended to sixteen months to allow him to hand over to the next trainee – one Geoffrey Faber. This was the only time of his life that Basil worked outside Oxford.

On 1 January 1913, he returned to Broad Street and to Blackwell's publishing. In the early years there was intense activity but little profit due to Basil's concentration on novice undergraduate poets. Many, later to become famous, were lured away by London publishers. 'His' authors included Edith Sitwell and Wilfred Owen (neither of them students), J.R.R. Tolkien and Dorothy L. Sayers, who also became his first editorial assistant. He admired Sayers for her 'witty, lively, gallant mind', but her religious convictions, attested to by the crucifix on her desk, made him '… provocatively sceptical', prompting him to observe that 'it was not fair to expect her to become a steady efficient publisher. It was like harnessing a racehorse to a plough.'

Despite having published both Edith Sitwell and Dorothy L. Sayers, he maintained that women, 'frippets' as he sometimes called them, 'were not great readers, not kindly disposed to books, which lie about and harbour dust … ', but there could have been a twinkle in his eyes as he said it. Certainly, much later he recorded of his secretary Eleanor Halliday, who died of cancer after working for him for forty years, that she had taken with her 'half his competence'.

One of his secretaries found 'he was full of quips and jollity … He had a quotation, a story, a joke for every occasion.' Whatever his pretended attitude towards them, many women admired him. Graham Greene's wife Vivienne likened him to Sayers' character Lord Peter Wimsey, because of his 'light-hearted, high spirited … debonair personality … his pointed nose, fair, flat hair … and a tendency to quote from *The Hunting of the Snark*;' Christine, his wife, saw him as 'in a frenzy of ideas and activities, someone of irrepressible physical and mental energy'.

In 1914 Basil had married Marion Christine Soans, a graduate of London University who had worked with Gilbert Murray on translating Greek classics. Though her scholarship matched his, she accepted domestication, devoting her life to Basil and bearing him three daughters and two sons.

Both boys were expected to enter the family business but there never seemed to be any question of the same being required of the girls. Christine seems not to have demurred on this issue but proved as firm as her mother-in-law had been with Dorothy in ensuring that her daughters received every possible educational opportunity.

During the First World War his Merton chum Adrian Mott joined Blackwell's editorial department. In addition to poetry, they published children's books and a magazine whose contributors included G.K. Chesterton, Hilaire Belloc, Rose Fyleman and Enid Blyton.

The Gaffer (as he was later labelled by the educationist and publisher John Newsom) always cared for fine editions, having since schooldays admired the craftsmansip of William Morris, whose biography, by J.W. Mackail, he had chosen when awarded a prize. His enthusiasm was shared by the printer and scholar Bernard Newdigate, who worked with the Shakespeare Head Press at Stratford-upon-Avon. This was owned by A.H. Bullen who, in the aftermath of war, was near to bankruptcy. Blackwell bought the imprint and encouraged Newdigate to preserve the Morris/Kelmscott Press tradition for the next twenty years. That was in 1920, the same year in which Basil Blackwell & Mott Ltd became a publishing company separate from the bookshop. Basil is quoted in Norrington's history of Blackwell's as stating of himself during his first decade at work that he had 'spoken, understood and thought as a publisher'. It was his father who was the bookseller. The Gaffer was determined that the publishing should become profitable while honouring high standards of text and production and that its books should also be cheap enough to attract new readers. He produced fiction at 3s. 6d., including Graham Greene's first novel (*Babbling April*, April 1925), and investigated the educational market. He bought several school textbooks for £1 and was appalled by their poor quality. This led to his commissioning Marten and Carter to write a famously successful history series.

Despite losing his star poets to London publishers, Blackwell continued to bring out annually, or periodically, anthologies (*Oxford Outlook, New Oxford Outlook*) and slim volumes of verse by Aldous Huxley and others. At the same time he found himself increasingly alienated by much contemporary verse. To a friend he wrote, 'I am ashamed to have dropped out of the current of modern poetry'; later he was to lament, 'How many poets now submit themselves to the disciplines of the sonnet?' Yet, as a publisher he believed implicitly in the right of the author to choose how to express himself. His enjoyment of this role led him to call on London booksellers two or three times a year to subscribe new books. 'And then,' he recorded,

'I went out into the country, to the West country, the Midlands, equally good experience.' But his destiny was to involve him more closely with bookselling. For all that he was ever eager to be first and foremost a publisher and, as a bookseller, preferred the antiquarian trade to the new, he was sidetracked by the call of duty. In 1924, his father died.

There seems never to have been any doubt in Basil's mind that the bookshop would thereafter provide his principal role. He revered his parents, rejoiced that his father, 'apparently reclusive', was 'so highly esteemed by his friends and fellow citizens', and was much influenced by his mother's indomitable qualities, especially her wish to remove the barrier between town and gown. It was his task to preside over Blackwell's retailing, taking a positive, innovative approach though he never ceased to interest himself in its publishing.

One of Basil's earliest outside involvements as overall head of Blackwell's was as president of the Antiquarian Booksellers' Association (ABA). In 1925–6 the infamous 'Ring' came into prominence. This was an unofficial group of dealers who attended sales and, in their own interests, kept bidding down by agreeing not to offer beyond a certain figure. After the sale they met again and purchased among themselves the items they particularly wanted at less than they would have paid at open auction. Blackwell ended this practice by working out an optimum price for each item and outbidding them all. The strategy worked and a ring did not re-emerge until 1955, when Blackwell was again instrumental in suppressing it, at least for some while. In the twenties public indignation against the Ring was so marked that the recently instituted BBC found it newsworthy. Blackwell, ever sensitive to the good name of the trade behaved in a typically honourable manner. His firm had bought a book for £40 which, 'according to "Book Auction Records", had seemed a fair price at the time'. In a London saleroom it was knocked down for £330, a deal broadcast to the nation. Next day, the lady who had sold it to Blackwell's arrived in angry mood at Broad Street, asking, 'Was this fair?'

The Gaffer enquired politely if she had left home before the post had been delivered. She had. He advised her to return at once. She did so, to find a cheque from Blackwell's for £100. It should happen only in fairy tales; it illustrates how the Gaffer could, and did, combine good behaviour with good business.

In his 1931 J. M. Dent Memorial Lecture, delivered at Stationers' Hall, Blackwell said 'the good antiquarian bookseller has some indefinable quality which enables him to know a book when he feels it … my father had it *AND* a long memory'; his address, however, dealt primarily with the new-book trade and commended the 1928 Committee draft report (see next chapter) as 'one of the most enlightening and stimulating documents in [our] archives … ', analysing, as it did, 'book trader methods in Holland and Germany'. He also championed cooperative advertising, thus placing himself in a small minority which continued, unsuccessfully, to advocate it well into the 1960s. The Gaffer thought it should be aimed by 'a sane and scientific method … at the UNREADING public'.

In this same Dent Lecture he referred to the necessary toughness of fibre which was the essential accompaniment to his achievements. He asserted that 'without some commercial adroitness' he could not have survived. He did indeed exude love and tolerance but there was also a streak of ruthless commonsense which enabled him to cope better than most with the thorny side of business.

In 1929 Basil and Christine moved, with their five children, to the village of Appleton, near Abingdon, into Osse Field, a house which he partly designed. It took its name from the river flowing through the garden. Daughter Corinna recalled in old age, 'We were brought up to be tough, with bedroom windows open, no matter what, and put out into the garden after breakfast however foul the weather.'

Basil and his wife dwelt at Appleton for the remainder of their lives, with the house becoming, on occasion, a retreat for members of staff. Employees and their families came as guests, having access to the swimming hole and the squash courts and eagerly devouring Christine Blackwell's home-baked cakes. The former scholar was also an ardent gardener and found time occasionally to index a book. Husband and wife became integral members of the community, with the Gaffer serving as chairman of the parish council, churchwarden and school manager; every year at the Bell Festival on 4 March Blackwell-archivist Rita Ricketts recorded, 'he could be heard chanting (he could never sing) his favourite mantra: "There's a hole in my bucket".' In 1940, he commanded the Appleton Home Guard.

At Appleton, Basil would rise at 5.30, take a dip in the Osse Dyke Brook, walk in adjacent woods and, in clement weather, exercise naked on the lawn while attempting to outshout the dawn chorus. Then he made his breakfast before setting off for Broad Street where he reckoned to arrive by 7.15. It was at Osse Field that he entertained Allen Lane during a Ripon Hall Conference (see below) and legend has it that Penguin Books was born while they sat beneath an apple tree. (This has a distinct Old Testament ring.) The occasion is 'authenticated' by a poster displayed in the Gaffer's former office at Broad Street. At less formal meetings book-trade

guests joined in gardening and attended evensong at Appleton church with
the family.

Also a resident of Appleton was Cuthbert White, the Blackwells' 'right-
hand man', who helped Christine with the garden and chauffered the
Gaffer, even to the extent of being made to transgress the Oxford one-way
system which his master – sometime Justice of the Peace – abhorred. Basil's
work in the garden was confined to obsessive scything of grass and chop-
ping of wood, an occupation beloved of generations of Blackwells.
(Younger son Toby once admitted to me he would like to have become a
lumberjack in Canada.)

From Osse Field the Blackwell family holidayed in Anglesey or Cornwall,
in rented accommodation or hotels, with Basil often following on later due
to pressure of work. There are few obvious instances of this paragon behaving less than perfectly, so it is a relief to record that he more than once, perhaps regularly, left Christine to cope with the family holiday while he
'looked after the shop'. Absence on business trips she did not have to endure.
He went only once to the USA and once in 1961 to South Africa.

In the 1930s, prompted by the belief that 'a man should serve the trade by
which he lives' (a dictum attributed to both his colleague Henry Schollick
and to bookseller David Roy and echoing Francis Bacon's 'I hold every
man a debtor to his profession'), the Gaffer became much involved in the
affairs of the Associated Booksellers of Great Britain, which, as distinct from
the ABA, mainly represented retailers of newly published books. He served
on its council and as its president in 1934 and 1935, a period which partly
overlapped with Stanley Unwin's presidency of the Publishers' Association.
Blackwell and Unwin (q.v.) were members of the Society of Bookmen, a
private dining club founded, in 1921, by the novelist Hugh Walpole to promote the sale and use of books. Both supported the Joint Committee of the
two associations mentioned above on Book Trade Organisation. They
were equally concerned with the health and status of the book trade and
lunched regularly (each at his own expense, Unwin being famously stingy)
to discuss common problems. One result of these meetings was Blackwell's
suggestion that, during 1934, they should jointly host an informal weekend
conference at Ripon Hall, Oxford, to be attended by fifty publishers and
booksellers. The Gaffer further recommended discussion of a theme: The
New Reading Public. The occasion was so highly approved that it was
repeated in 1935. One of the delegates was John Hampden, of Thomas
Nelson, who accepted the proposal that he should edit and publish a
symposium to be called *The Book World*. He chose eleven contributors,

including the Gaffer, whose subject was bookselling in the provinces. He listed the Seven Deadly Paradoxes of his calling, commencing with, 'The better the bookseller and the more representative his stock, the less chance has he of thriving.' He attacked the daft system under which the retailer who had sold all copies of a book subscribed by the publisher's rep, and therefore carrying preferential terms, could only reorder at this lower discount if he waited until the rep's next quarterly visit. He quoted his Cambridge counterpart Ernest Heffer's epitaph for a provincial bookseller – DIED WAITING FOR THE TRAVELLER TO CALL.

The Gaffer was ever conscious of the advantages that Blackwell's enjoyed in operating at a centre of learning, even though he said that 'generations of undergraduates have done their reading at [Broad Street] without cost'. Through his work for the AB he became aware of the struggles of smaller booksellers everywhere. Some of those in financial trouble, such as Parker's of Oxford, received his help; others, like George's of Bristol, were taken over, heralding a much wider development of an academic chain in the 1960s.

Blackwell's were represented on the Joint Committee by Fred Hanks. This illustrates the extent of the role of the 'apprentice-directors' and also of the Gaffer's willingness to delegate. The men who reached the top at Blackwell's were no holders of sinecures. They were expected to work for both the trade and the company and some were permitted to buy shares in the latter. 'Without them,' the Gaffer told A.L.P. Norrington, Master of Trinity College, who wrote the official history of the firm, 'the burden of running the companies would have been intolerable.'

The Blackwell's were also pioneers in introducing pension schemes for staff (in 1923), allowing three weeks' paid holiday, and other benefits, long before they became customary or legal requirements. The Gaffer himself played a leading part in ensuring the success of Book Tokens, the brain child of publisher Harold Raymond, who proposed their inception at a Society of Bookmen dinner. Basil rightly forecast that an unexpected source of wealth for the trade would come from unredeemed tokens. His colleague Henry Schollick was to become a long-serving director and chairman of Book Tokens Ltd.

In 1932, as a young graduate looking for work, Henry Schollick was impressed by the Gaffer's courtesy 'to an unknown and unsponsored applicant'. The temporary job he was given became permanent when the man responsible for publishing had a breakdown and died. Then Schollick became a close friend, colleague and an honorary member of the family, known as 'Uncle Henry' both to Blackwellians and to the trade at large.

Schollick recalled of the Gaffer, 'He had a sort of radiance to which people reacted wherever he went … he had no use for confrontation … was a marvellous negotiator [who] got the cooperation of every bookseller', and he believed in delegation. 'Far too many booksellers,' he quoted him as saying, 'allow themselves to be caught in the web of detail … Never do a job that a cheaper man can do for you … '

'With such a man to guide me,' wrote Schollick, 'and his constant allusions to literary works ranging from Langland to *The Bab Ballads* … I came to see English Literature as a way of life and not as an academic principle.' He soon discovered that he was 'in the very centre of trade affairs. There was change in the air. Basil gathered round him a group from both sides of the trade … . It is hard now to imagine the secrecy which at that time covered the affairs of booksellers and publishers. Basil's personality did much to break this down.' His fortnightly meetings with Stanley Unwin '… led to the restructuring and alignments of the constitutions of the PA and AB which were to serve the trade nobly in … the early years of World War II.' (The AB did not, in fact, become the BA until 1948.)

'Uncle Henry' said that the Gaffer was a lifelong obsessive reader who, early in his married life, had determined to read the best of the English corpus of literature which he collected not for its market-place value but in order to have at hand the best edition of each writer. (A particular favourite was George Eliot's *Middlemarch* which he considered had 'an immortal quality'.)

It was around the time of Schollick's advent that the Gaffer concerned himself with the one-volume Shakespeare, designed by Bernard Newdigate. He used it as a weapon against the newspaper barons who were giving away vast quantities of books in a circulation war. To make a selling price of 6s. viable Blackwell bravely ordered 50,000 copies, and had them printed in the best traditions of the Shakespeare Head Press. Such was the demand he ordered a reprint. His ability to appraise a mass market foreshadowed Paul Hamlyn.

Blackwell came off less well when he was forced to pay commercial homage to his idol William Morris. He had long been friendly with Morris's daughter May, for whom he offered to publish anything of her father's writing not previously printed. May presented him with some half-a-million words which Basil tried, unsuccessfully, to persuade Longmans (Morris's publishers) to accept. He then suggested a compromise over which May took umbrage. She accused him of going back on his word. Her companion, a Miss Lobb, attacked him. 'I hate old William Morris – dreadful old bore – but I'll not have May worried.'

The Gaffer agreed to publish every word.

• • •

Perusal of the minute books of what were known as 'Friday Meetings' offers intimate glimpses of Blackwell's at work. These gatherings of the directors and departmental heads lend credence to some form of worker-management control, although I suspect that they were actually a safety valve for the operation of a genuinely benevolent dictatorship. A study of them, for the early and mid thirties, shows that 'Mr Basil' usually took the chair and the subjects under discussion ranged from the financial health of the business to the vexed matter of who should dust the stock and when.

Figures for turnover and annual staff BONI (as they were designated) were often written in code. Thus the sales for February 1933, against the same month for 1932, are shown as '£ s s t s' and '£ s y e o', while, to make them more meaningless to prying eyes, one is given gross and the other net. It is more instructive to learn that in the following month the figures were £5,022 compared with £4,500, or would be if one could interpret them in inflationary terms. A more comprehensible statistic is that for the number of letters received during a twelve-month period, 1932–3, which was 73,705, up nearly two thousand on the preceding year; another shows that 92,459 parcels of books and magazines were despatched during 1934.

Over-staffing in the advertising department caused concern: 'The Chairman thought it possible to transfer one of [its] four maidens [elsewhere]'. The same luminary was also congratulated, in July 1933, for having collected some £10,000 of debts 'since April 1932'. 'Mr Basil' features, too, in the briefest of entries: 'FLOSSIE. The Chairman reported he had dealt with this case.' (Does this refer to a company pet, a shoplifter or what?)

Two months later (7.4.34), there is another conundrum: 'LEAKAGES: Suggestions needed for a "tightening up".' Is this a euphemistic allusion to the pilfering of stock as an inside job? And, if so, does it follow on from 2.2.34, when the committee discussed a tendency of 'staff staying late of an evening, even up to 10 p.m.' concluding that, unless given exemption by a Director, 'all staff must leave premises by 8 p.m.'?

The chairman frequently reports on his visits to George's of Bristol, while proposals concerning the 'Dispensary' are discussed at meeting after meeting. This immensely important issue of the time involved the cooperation of Trinity College, owners of much of the land on or around the Blackwell Broad Street site. On 9.12.32, it was believed that this Dispensary should be widened. A few months later the cost of the work was estimated at £283 10s. 0d. Another two months on, Trinity objected to 'the hole in the wall' this necessitated. Was it about creating an area where goods-in and goods-out could be conveniently conveyed? It is difficult to believe that this was not a matter for higher management decision. Similarly with the many references to applications from university libraries, colleges and schools, all over Britain and the English-speaking world, to be supplied by Blackwell's. The minutes give the percentage discount agreed to be offered them, but surely it was a senior manager, or a director, who decided this on the spot and then, diplomatically, had it rubber-stamped by the committee? A business expanding as fast as Blackwell's could not have been effective and succesful if it had to endure such bureaucratic democracy.

DUSTING was another matter altogether. There the management could afford to give the workers their heads. On 21.3.30, 'It was agreed a certain amount of "dusting" should be undertaken this Easter vacation commencing with the history section.' By 28.7.33, the situation must have worsened. 'All the staff,' it is recorded, 'should participate to get the work done quickly.' Three months later, 'Boyd and Alder had taken 62 hours to complete the task. They received £4 each' – and the wages of Alder, an apprentice, 'went up to £2 10s. 0d.'. Alder, in due course, is observed to have completed his apprenticeship and to have been made 'an Improver'; he remained with Blackwells for the rest of his working life, not achieving director status, but having secure employment and in retirement being found accommodation, with his wife, at the Booksellers' Retreat in Hertfordshire.

Other matters discussed by the 'Friday Meeting' were the installation of a fire extinguisher in the basement and the possibility of 'a hot-water tap being affixed to our system'. There were references sending 'the usual mortician's letter to the executors of the late Prof. Giles of Cambridge, and to the Revd D. S. Haygate of Eton' (presumably to solicit the opportunity of purchasing their libraries), the delivery of a new Bedford van, a decision not to open a branch in Manchester and ruling that 'accounts for undergraduates must be paid "terminally" '. (The latter conjures visions of a repeat *Zuleika Dobson* situation – but how would Blackwell's have got their dues from the students drowned in the Isis?)

Underlying all the entries in these minutes is concern for the dignity and wellbeing of the staff. They were involved at as many points along the way as was practical with the conduct of a commercial enterprise.

Near the end of the 1930s, Blackwell's, as booksellers, had a sizeable export trade dealing with academic institutions, including medical colleges, worldwide. This, plus the generous endowment by Lord Nuffield of a Medical School Trust in the city, led to the formation, in 1939, of Blackwell Scientific Publications. Nuffield, then W. R. Morris, had brought prosperity to Oxford when he established his motor-vehicle factories there, an enterprise not initially welcomed by some members of the faculty. The Gaffer, who had a decade earlier played a part in bringing town (as represented by Morris) and gown (by an ex-vice chancellor) together, gave his blessing to the formation of BSP. Nothing could illustrate better his understanding of what would be beneficial to the community as a whole – to businessmen, workers and academics. The establishment of BSP was suggested in a memorandum submitted to the board by John Grant, a young assistant at Broad Street.

Per Saugman, the Danish-born bookseller who became head of Blackwell Scientific after WWII, wrote in his memoirs, 'I do not think by any stretch of the imagination it could be suggested that scientific literature interested him greatly but he [B.B.] gave a young manager encouragement and self-confidence.' Saugman praised Blackwell's chairmanship of BSP. Commenting on his management qualities, he wrote, 'The Gaffer kept his door open – anybody could approach him at any time. He walked around the bookshop at least once a day and spoke to as many staff as possible … Everybody found exchange of ideas easy and nobody was afraid of making a fool of themselves. He used to advise that if a man had been cornered, he should be left room to get out.'

Hitler's Luftwaffe did not bomb Oxford, which is surprising when you consider that Nuffield's factories must have been turned over to war work. There were fewer undergraduates than in peacetime but business in books was brisk, thanks in part to the new demand envisaged by the convenors of the Ripon Hall Conferences and of the advent of Penguin Books. The Shakespeare Head Press received, like other publishers, a paper quota, but given the conditions of wartime austerity production there was no question of issuing books in fine editions; sensibly its allocation went to textbooks for one of the other Blackwell companies.

Part of the Gaffer's war work included writing to friends and customers in America, urging them to buy books to boost the nation's exports, and to serving members of Blackwell's staff, twenty-one of whom were in uniform on overseas fronts, telling them how things were in Broad Street. Even more welcome, for the latter, than the sight of Blackwell's handwriting was the news that their pensions contributions were being paid.

It was during the fourth year of war that the Gaffer addressed the Society of Bookmen, on 29 January 1943, on the subject 'A New Order in the Book Trade?' There was growing confidence that the allies would be victorious and many were looking towards a brave new world. Despite his opening remarks concerning the 'febrile output of novelists, travellers and biographers' during the decades between the two world conflicts, a period he named as 'among the most barren of creative genius in the history of English Literature', it was a thoughtful dissertation. He dared to suggest that a National Book Trade Association, over and above the PA and the AB, should be formed 'to judge, to plan and to speak for the good of the trade as a whole', with every member paying a subscription which would go partly to the National Book Council (shortly to become the National Book League). It was not implemented.

The Gaffer's wisdom was further in evidence when Richard, his elder son (born 1918), returned in 1946 from war service with the Royal Navy. As he had spent only a short time with the company before being called-up, Basil sent him on a roving commission 'to familiarise himself with every part of the firm's operations' and to make recommendations for its future structure. He gave Richard his head while he was still young, before his initiative could be sapped by spending too long playing second fiddle.

Richard, who became known as 'the Guv'nor', recommended and carried through a massive expansion of Blackwell's export department at both personal and institutional levels, developed library-supply and the periodicals-subscriptions departments, purchased the Copenhagen-based academic-bookselling business of Munksgaard, inaugurated Blackwell North America Inc., when the Richard Abel company in Oregon failed, and co-founded UBO, University Bookshops Oxford (see below).

As the volume of business transacted at Broad Street grew, separate premises were taken for children's books, art books and for a music shop. There was also a basic change in policy which did not at first please some older employees. Instead of all staff being expected to know a little about everything so that they could work in any department that needed them, the Guv'nor argued the desirability of individual expertise in an increaingly specialised world. He was an intelligent, educated man whose arrogance and superiority complex enraged many – not least when he exchanged Latin tags at Bookmen dinners with the few classicists present – but he understood the changed and power-charged world of international business. This substantially increased Blackwell's market share of it. Between 1946 and 1979 annual turnover rose from £165,000 to £27m. 'That,' wrote the company's historian, 'was the measure of Richard's achievement.'

Richard was a Wykehamist and, on his father's assessment, a snob. He adopted a drawling, upper-class accent and often wore a pained look when addressed by a fellow shopkeeper, of lower caste, one accustomed actually to serving customers over a counter. (It is unlikely that he ever similarly exposed himself to the public.) Nevertheless he served the trade well both in his work for the BA, of which he was president in 1966–8, and in enhancing the standing of bookselling generally by developing Blackwell's. He was not markedly literary or academic, although he became a Fellow of St Cross College, Oxford in 1978: in *Who's Who* he listed his recreations as 'Sailing, shooting, swimming'. I crossed swords with him occasionally when I criticised the very existence of the Booksellers' Association which, in the 1960s, did little for its members apart from giving them the right to sell and exchange book tokens. Richard phoned me one day and asserted, in his languid, commanding-officer manner, 'You're a sore in the side of the BA. The trouble with sores, Ian, is that they sometimes fester,' and into that last word he invested extra syllables so that it sounded like 'fiesta'.

One feature of Blackwell's which was not changed by Richard's policies was the famous sign laid out almost as verse on a wall at 50 Broad Street:

> When you visit Blackwell's, no one will ask you what you want.
> You are free to ramble where you will; to handle any book;
>> In short to browse at leisure.
> The assistants are at your service when you need them,
> But unless you look to them they will leave you undisturbed;
> You are equally welcome whether you have come to buy or
>> to browse.
> Such has been the tradition at Blackwell's for fifty years.

Equally sacrosanct was Muirhead Bone's 1950 pastel drawing of the interior of the shop, showing it crowded with browsers and buyers.

The Gaffer's younger son joined the company in 1952, at first specialising in its spatial expansion. It was he who had charge of the bold, imaginative scheme to create, below the existing bookshop, the vast Norrington Room, occupying ten thousand square feet and having two-and-a-half miles of shelving. Julian (known as Toby) also played his expected role in the Booksellers' Association, serving on its council for long periods and becoming president (1980–2). Blackwell's, in two capacities – as Basil Blackwell & Mott and as Blackwell Scientific Publications, were also members of the Publishers' Association, but none of the family sat on its council, nor was the Gaffer, as stated in Rita Ricketts's book (see Sources), ever its president. The brothers were markedly different. Toby, though hankering to be a lumberjack, remained firmly implanted in the book trade and friendly, even to the untouchables. I shall not write more of him here because my self-imposed terms of reference are to deal not with the living but the dead. Many times, over almost fifty years, I enjoyed his company.

• • •

When first I met the Gaffer in 1956 (the year in which he was knighted), he commented approvingly upon the American custom of announcing one's name on being introduced. Clearly enunciating his he prompted me to do the same. Handshaking and goodwill abounded while he filed mine in his memory for future reference, if necessary. I was visiting Blackwell's with my then employer, Hubert Wilson, to observe their accounting system. Wilson's was on the verge of bankruptcy partly because Hubert had spent too much of his time absorbed in BA matters and in writing pseudonymous articles for *The Bookseller* telling the book trade how to organise itself. The Gaffer, who never failed in his duty to either the Association or his own company, liked Hubert but recognised his shortcomings. When Hubert, forgetting the purpose of our visit, rabbited on about the need for better training for booksellers' assistants, the Gaffer smiled and said rapidly, 'Hubert, when young people start at Blackwell's I want them to come here with their heads empty, so that they can then be filled with the names of authors, the titles of books and the imprints which publish them.' Hubert sniggered nervously at this practical approach. Years later, when I had been leading off on the same subject in *The Bookseller*, the Gaffer wrote to me, 'How absurd of you to pronounce that the best way of teaching a duckling to swim is to throw it in the water. I agree with you.'

He regularly attended Society of Bookmen dinners at Kettner's in Soho but, even while he was chairman, he left early with other Oxford members and guests to catch a convenient train from Paddington. The Blackwells and followers silently left the room as the meeting proceeded. This withdrawal became known as the Oxford Movement. At one Christmas meeting he was the judge at a mock trial and found me guilty of Failing to be a Bookseller Pure and Simple. At the golden jubilee meeting at Stationers' Hall in September 1971, when I was chairman, he was one of four distinguished speakers on the theme 'Now Let Us Praise Famous Men'. His speaking voice, mellifluous and low but always audible, would have been treasured by any actor. He employed a dying cadence which brought tears to listeners' eyes; he even hushed an audience of members of the Book Publishers' Representatives Association at their raucous annual dinner in London's Connaught Rooms.

The Gaffer once declared that 'books themselves are more important than people', a statement he might well have withdrawn if challenged – and he most certainly would not have allowed it in the case of *Last Exit to Brooklyn*, Hubert Selby Jnr's novel, which he found so distasteful that he gave evidence for the prosecution when its publisher was tried at the Old Bailey for obscenity. Blackwell, who read the book at his son Richard's request, confessed to Henry Schollick that in doing so he had felt soiled. In court he said he was 'corrupted'. In 1969, he told a journalist, 'It was so horrid, just like stepping in a dog's turd … it haunts my memory.' (The prosecution lost.)

David Holloway, sometime literary editor of the *Daily Telegraph*, recorded that the Gaffer's disapproval of *Lolita* made it unavailable at Blackwell's, 'for a time, at any rate', but this seems questionable. Schollick said that despite his objection to *Last Exit*, the Gaffer did not ban it. 'He did not advocate censorship. He was claiming the Miltonic "liberty to know, to utter, to argue freely according to conscience".'

Despite much delegation, the Gaffer remained chairman until 1969, when he handed over to Richard (already MD since 1966) and became president. This allowed for some relaxation of his strict regime. He delayed daily arrival at Broad Street until 9.15, and in very old age, visited only four days a week. While it is fair to state that the greatest expansion came under Richard Blackwell's chairmanship, Basil himself remained president, and actively interested, until the week before his death. And it was during the Gaffer's chairmanship, although at Richard's instigation, that, in 1964, Blackwell's jointly with Oxford University Press formed University Bookshops Oxford (UBO), and purchased existing bookshops in red-brick university towns to enable them to meet the needs of enlarged campuses. It was a bold step leading to total ownership by Blackwell's when OUP withdrew.

In 1973, Basil became an honorary member of the Worshipful Company of Stationers and was enrolled with due ceremony at that same hall where we had celebrated the Bookmen's golden jubilee. When the Master of the Company commanded, 'Fetch Sir Basil Blackwell from the stockroom', the clerk, who was lame, made his halting way to a side doorway through which the enrobed Gaffer made a noble entrance. In dulcet tones he gave a moving address of acceptance; some of us invited to be present felt it was we who were being honoured.

A degree of retirement allowed the Gaffer to devote more time to voluntary work in Oxford where, at various periods, he was a Justice of the Peace, chairman of the Juvenile Court and prison visitor, work which won him the freedom of the city and an honorary doctorate of civil law. He took a special interest in juvenile delinquency, believing that it was parents who were to blame for much of it. He became a fellow of Merton College, an LL D at Manchester University, president of the Classical Association, 1964–6 and of the English Association, 1969–70 and an officier d'Académie française. The honour which meant much to him was the freedom of his native city; he took it, as Henry Schollick recorded, as much on behalf of his father as for himself.

Following Christine's death in 1977, the Gaffer embarked on rereading the whole of Shakespeare. Schollick recorded that 'it took him six months and that he then read some of it again, plus the Shakespeare Head Chaucer twice, and much casual reading'.

For his 90th birthday in 1979 I was commissioned by *The Bookseller* to spend a day with him in Appleton and Oxford. We met at Osse Field which, since the death of Lady Blackwell, he shared with younger son Toby and daughter-in-law Jennifer.

> The front door [I wrote] opens on to a wide, thickly carpeted hall, giving vistas through various rooms to the grounds beyond. Away on the right is the library, 33 by 16 feet, shelved on most of three of its sides with several windows overlooking the garden and wood beyond. There is an open grate with logs burning … In the spacious room are two lecterns, on one of which *Il Purgatorio* lies open. On the other is Barbara Tuchman's recent account of the 14th century which the Gaffer has regretfully abandoned because the details of man's inhumanity to man are more than he has appetite for at his age …

On his desk were notes for a *DNB* entry he was writing about John G. Wilson of Bumpus. Later we were driven by Cuthbert into Oxford and delivered at the birthplace-bookshop in Broad Street.

'The Gaffer, clasping an empty briefcase, pushes busily up the steps and through the shop, greeting customers and staff, and makes for the stairs leading to his office … ' There his daughter Corinna awaited him, gave him phone messsages and cautioned me to watch him as we crossed roads because he tended to ignore cyclists, a practice particularly dangerous in a university city. (Corinna had become his part-time secretary but her sisters, even this late into the twentieth century, although now directors, did not work in the business. One, Dame Penelope Jessell, was a prominent member of the Liberal Party.)

The Gaffer took me to lunch at Merton. It was in no way a business lunch such as I was accustomed to take with London publishers. We served ourselves from a hot buffet, I was given a glass of beer, introduced to several academics who were rapidly clearing what was on their plates and then marched upstairs (the Gaffer took them two at a time) to take coffee in a reading room. The meal lasted less than twenty minutes.

(Merton's influence on Basil cannot be exaggerated. When made a fellow he commented that this had been his dearest wish. To his college he left valuable books printed in Italy in the late fifteenth century by Aldus Manutius, revered by the Gaffer as 'the man who cut the folio down to pocket size ... ' and gave us ... 'the Dolphin which preceded the Penguin'. At Merton there is a room named after him in Fellows' Quad; elsewhere in the complex the Blackwell Collection is housed.)

After lunch we visited the Fellows' Garden where he told me of a monstrous scheme to construct a relief motorway in the famous meadows. '"No one," he reflects, his wispy white hair taking the wind, as he looks upon a scene he has known for most of his life, "at the official inquiry, apart from myself, made the point that it would destroy the silence. THE SILENCE!" He repeats ... the words shimmering, tremulously across St Alban quad.'

Before returning to Broad Street, we visited other parts of his empire including Blackwell's Music Shop, which was officially opened by his near contemporary the conductor Sir Adrian Boult. He was not himself musical, he told me, beyond a certain prowess at the penny whistle. Before ascending again to his office he accosted a member of staff to tell him he needed a crib for *Il Purgatorio*. There were three such, he was told, but unluckily none was in stock. A cashier who overheard the exchange commented, 'He always asks for something we haven't got.'

I was invited to sign the visitors' book and, as it transpired, had my final meeting with Richard Blackwell, who had just returned to work after an operation for cancer. I was glad we parted in friendship; in the Gaffer's civilising presence we behaved benignly to each other.

> Back at Osse Field he makes me a cup of tea because the home helps have departed and Jennifer is engaged in social work ... in the library we have a final gossip about friends past and present ... He is regretful that his sight, never good, is giving him trouble. He wears a hearing aid ... he does not, as do some elderly people, dwell constantly on the benefits of the past ...

It must have been on this day that the Gaffer told me that he longed to revisit Chartres, with Henry Schollick, to see the stained glass at the cathedral. He and Christine, who usually took the wheel, had motored together in Europe many times, especially in Spain and France. He said that her knowledge of the classical world enhanced these holidays, which were among his happiest memories. There are no references in the archives to these travels or any evidence of his attending concerts, or the theatre, even to see the plays of his beloved Shakespeare. Corinna remembers being taken to performances in schools and out of doors and thinks her parents may have sometimes booked seats at Stratford but grandson Philip suggests that the Bard came to life for him mostly on the page. Sport seems not, after his rowing days, to have been a major relaxation although he enjoyed watching rugger on television and occasionally led staff outings to Twickenham. Philip recalls that he was much excited by the boxer Muhammad Ali's visit to the bookshop to sign books.

Though aware of what was occurring on the world stage the Gaffer was never politically active. He believed that European integration was imperative and supported the Oxford pro-European lobby in the 1974 referendum. He blamed Margaret Thatcher for reinventing the old divide between 'them' and 'us' and disliked the machinations of both the Wilson and the Heath governments. Decades earlier, in his J.M. Dent Memorial Lecture, he had described Capitalism and Socialism as being 'two faces of a coin'. When well into his eighties he became a life member of the short-lived Social Democratic Party. Fifty years before he had tried to promulgate a naïve idea for world peace by suggesting that the Pope should recite the Lord's Prayer over international radio but the outbreak of WWII intervened. He was not a Roman Catholic but, as an adult, an Anglican. He regarded bureaucracy as only slightly better than dictatorship.

Further bereavement came in 1980 with Richard Blackwell's premature death, a loss which, said his father, 'was the only real misfortune the company ever suffered'. The Gaffer survived the Guv'nor by nearly four years, dying at his son's former residence Tubney House, near Abingdon.

Basil Blackwell was buried at Appleton church where he had worshipped for more than half a century. He was survived by his three daughters, Corinna, Penelope and Helen, by his younger son and by many grandchildren. He published books, he sold books (he printed and bound them, too) with enormous success; he also spent a lifetime reading them. This may be why there was not an autobiography, although he made many notes for what might have been one.

The obits were adulatory and warm. The superlatives came naturally and abounded in affection. *The Times*, naming him 'a legend in his lifetime' noted his 'awesome reputation of being one of the best-read men in Britain', and quoted from the Dent Lecture the Gaffer's view of 'the book-seller par excellence': one who 'must have the proficiency of a bibliographer of universal range; [and] of a librarian whose library is of unlimited scope', plus 'business ability', thus neatly permitting him to record succinctly his own epitaph.

In the *Oxford Times*, Hugh Williamson, retired printer and publisher, named him 'the greatest bookman of his time ... always young in heart and never immature in wisdom ... An indomitably lively spirit ... He observed people, events, books and institutions with a clarity that transcended eyesight. His spoken and written comments ... were apt, terse and memorable ... His conversation was light-hearted, cogent, precise and witty ... ' Williamson commented that even in the midst of work the Gaffer 'had time for unexpected visitors. Up would go both arms in cheerful welcome, paperwork would be set aside ... ' To which should be added an anecdote from Rita Ricketts's *Adventurers All*, relating that when the Gaffer received American visitors he liked to lead them to his office, walking deliberately slowly, while enquiring, 'What becomes of all the time you save?'

I wrote the Gaffer's factual obituary for *The Bookseller*. Some of it has already been included here: another long tribute, in the same journal, appeared the following week, written by Henry Schollick. I have quoted from it earlier and from his moving address at the memorial service, held at the University Church on the 31 May 1984. Adrian Mott, like Henry Schollick, thought he had 'urbane dignity', while his son Toby described him as, 'a tallish, very slight good looker, with endless charm who engendered [sic] a sense of mischievousnous.'

The obituaries convey much of Basil Blackwell the man, but do not do justice to the depth and breadth of the Blackwell companies. The Gaffer saw his father's simple shop grow into a massive worldwide business, always capitalised from within, and almost totally owned by the family. After his death, it remained so into the twenty-first century, making it remarkable, possibly unique, among major commercial entities of its size. It had taken over its 'rival', Heffer's in Cambridge, had bookshops in most major cities of England and Scotland, including a branch in London's Charing Cross Road, and remained a major exporter and the owner of Blackwell Publishing, as the two former companies had become. All honour to the three generations which achieved this and to a fourth which was maintaining it, albeit with some internal squabbling, but particularly to the Gaffer who, though seldom during his ninety-three years straying far from his birthplace, enjoyed a vision which was always more global than provincial.

Sir Basil Henry Blackwell, Kt, JP, born Oxford, 29 May 1889, son of Benjamin Henry and Lydia Blackwell. Married Marion Christine Soans, 1914, two sons and three daughters. Died Tubney House, near Abingdon, 9 April 1984.

Two

STANLEY UNWIN

Batsford, Penguin, Mills & Boon, became household names. Allen and Unwin along with most imprints did not. Its founder, Stanley Unwin, unlike Paul Hamlyn, had not become a millionaire almost overnight by entering a previously untapped market. He did not, as Collins, Heinemann, Macmillan and other larger competitors did, enter bids for likely bestsellers. He travelled the world to familiarise himself with potential customers for his broad-based list, and became, in the process, better known to foreign and commonwealth publishers and booksellers than any of his contemporaries.

Unwin had an influence on national and international publishing out of all proportion to the medium-sized imprint over which he ruled and which, until Tolkien took wing, featured only an occasional outstanding seller. He was not primarily literary or academic and might have succeeded as well in insurance, in banking or as a City merchant. That his destiny was publishing was due to his father's commercial misfortune and the fact that his uncle, who was childless, was already in the business.

Stanley was the seventh son of Edward and Elizabeth Unwin. He led a sheltered, middle-class life in the South London suburb of Lee Green until he was fifteen. The family were congregationalists and strict teetotallers. Edward gave a percentage of his earnings to 'good works' and displayed missionary fervour; Elizabeth tended towards Quakerdom. Family prayers were held every day. Edward was a printer, Elizabeth had been born into the Spicer family, well regarded as manufacturing stationers. Stanley believed he inherited his business acumen from her more than from his father, whose printing works in Chilworth, Surrey, was destroyed in a fire soon after the poor man had fallen behind in his mortgage payments on moving house to the nearby suburb of Shortlands.

Stanley was taken out of Abbotsholme, his private, progressive, boarding school in Derbyshire, one term after the disaster struck. At Abbotsholme he was taught by one Dr Reddie, the eccentric headmaster, who included on the curriculum, practical haymaking, the value of hygiene and duty towards others. He learned to swim and to be obedient; he was impressed by

Reddie's contempt for learning facts by rote. Reddie was a great influence on Stanley who would, almost forty years on, publish a biography of him.

In 1900 the boy Stanley went straight from school to join a shipping and insurance-broking firm in Crosby Square in the City at 10s per week, working almost six full days (on Saturdays they finished at 3 p.m.). He wore a silk hat and frock-coat, with an orchid in the button hole. For several weeks his daily lunch was sausage and chips. It cost 6d. His wages were doubled when he became a chartering clerk dealing with the commissioning of ships and claims for damaged vessels. This work led to a lifelong interest in insurance, but it was not sufficiently strong to deter him from accepting an invitation to join his uncle T. Fisher Unwin's publishing company.

Stanley, by then earning £52 p.a. made the provision that he must first be permitted to spend one year in Germany and six months in France. His older brothers, as part of their education, had finished their schooling learning German, which, at that time, was thought desirable. It is not clear who paid for Stanley but his wish was granted and he went in September 1903 to a school in Haubinda, Sachsen Meiningen, with which Abbotsholme was associated. Possibly Fisher Unwin was financing his nephew because, at the end of only one term, by which time Stanley could converse without difficulty in German, he insisted that the young man should go as a 'volunteer' to the theological bookseller, J.C. Hinrichsche in Leipzig. Here, for six days a week (Stanley declined to work on the seventh, stating his parents would object on religious grounds) he had an unrivalled opportunity of discovering how the efficient German book trade operated, and became acquainted with the *Borsenblatt*, its daily newspaper. He remained for three and a half months, after which he agreed to travel German bookshops for his uncle who sent him £10 for the purpose. Half of this meagre allowance went on rail fares to all the principal German cities, plus Prague, Salzburg, Innsbruck and Basel, in neighbouring countries. He returned to Leipzig with 4d. in his pocket, having spent some nights on trains to save booking a bedroom, to be Fisher's guest at the Easter Book Fair. He attended a banquet lasting several hours, refusing all offers of alcohol. The party continued at various beer cellars where he was dubbed by the Germans Herr Wasser-Trinker. They drank his health in water, which became a ritual in the years ahead whenever he visited the fair.

During his German visit Stanley obtained the British rights on Baedeker's celebrated travel guides, a deal which more than covered the tiny amount allowed for his expenses, yet Fisher still insisted on reducing his time on the Continent to nine months. So he did not visit France but he was allowed three months' experience at his father's resuscitated printing works, now situated near Ludgate Hill station in the City. This was to Fisher's advantage because, while there, the young man learned much of the technicalities of a closely allied trade.

S.U.'s official publishing career began on 1 September 1904 at Fisher's offices, 11 Paternoster Buildings, close to St Paul's Cathedral. He worked first as an invoice clerk, then went on the road selling to booksellers before returning to the capital to take over the rights and export departments. Even then he continued to go twice a year to Cambridge and Oxford, making the acquaintance, at the latter city, of B.H. Blackwell, Basil Blackwell's father, to Leipzig for the fair and also, in 1907, to the United States. While at home he pursued his interrupted education at evening classes at the London School of Economics until his family persuaded him that this was injurious to his health. Each year Uncle Fisher leaned more heavily on his industrious nephew but did not pay him commensurately. Indeed when Stanley was absent with appendicitis Fisher said he must regard the required period of convalescence as his annual holiday. The outraged young man instantly resigned, and refused to be wooed back when uncle doubled his salary because with that peace offering went a contract which would have barred him from ever setting-up independently as a publisher.

'When I left in 1912 the business of T. Fisher Unwin had worldwide fame. Today,' wrote Stanley Unwin, in 1960, 'it is nearly forgotten.' (Forty years on, there was a parallel.)

Unwin, out of work and courting Mary Storr, suggested to Rayner, his future father-in-law, that he should go on a world tour – though not with his fiancée. Instead, he invited her brother Severn to accompany him. 'To embark on matrimony at that moment would have wrecked my career,' he recorded, adding, 'I used, laughingly, to tell my wife I fell in love with my father-in-law before I fell in love with her.' Somehow, despite the low salary he had received from Fisher, Stanley had saved sufficient to fulfil his boyhood ambition of travelling the world. The story of his first global trip, reconstructed from the letters the young men wrote home, was published long after by Allen & Unwin. The highlights of his life combined travel with business. On this initial journey he began the card index of world booksellers which he kept updated throughout his career. 'My business is my pleasure,' he wrote.

The momentous year 1914 was of personal significance to Stanley. He founded George Allen and Unwin Ltd on the day in August when the First World War began; later, on his birthday in December, he married Mary Storr at Lyndhurst Congregational Church in Hampstead, taking extra value from the ceremony by commissioning a book in the vestry from the officiating vicar. The marriage proved lasting and happy; Stanley and Mary had two sons, David and Rayner, and a daughter, Ruth. There is a touching note of domesticity in the father's recollection of pushing David in his pram up Haverstock Hill towards the Heath whilst reading Tawney's *The Sickness of an Acquisitive Society*, a book about which S.U. was so enthusiastic that he *bought* copies, to give to friends.

The formation of Allen & Unwin from the already merged imprints of George Allen and Swan Sonnenschein was far from simple. An official receiver had been appointed for the company which had originated partly with the list inspired by John Ruskin, whose warehouseman, George Allen, became his publisher. Business was desperately poor, turnover no more than a few hundred pounds per month. Sonnenschein, a highly creative publisher, had long since departed to run Routledge & Kegan Paul; Allen had died. There were three debenture holders who were determined to receive preferential treatment. Stanley Unwin, approaching thirty, was anxious to become a publisher on his own account. Paradoxically, he achieved this by paying the receiver far less than his original offer but at the same time saddling himself with three joint managing directors. One of them was an army officer on the reserve list, another was a lawyer, the third, a trainee solicitor. Unwin demanded that none of them should receive more than £300 p.a. in salary and that his appointment was for life.

He got his way because the other managing directors knew little about running a publishing house. They left it to S.U., at the same time as insisting that two of them must sign every contract. The outbreak of war assisted Unwin because Colonel d'Albiac (chairman) was recalled to the army, E.L. Skinner took a job at the War Office and C.A. Reynolds was deemed fitter for the front line than himself. Under wartime regulations one director was not liable to be called to the colours. Stanley, who at that time was a pacifist, was the one.

The new company made sufficient impact for Stanley's uncle to publish an announcement in the December 1914 issue of his monthly penny newsletter *Mainly About Books*:

> Mr T. Fisher Unwin desires to inform his clients that he is the sole proprietor of the publishing business carried on under his name … and he is no way connected with any other firm carrying on the business of publishing, printing and bookselling.

Fisher's staff were not permitted to redirect orders intended for Stanley's company; they had to be returned marked 'not known'. S.U. behaved honourably, always forwarding orders received for his uncle's books and refusing to filch any Fisher Unwin author who offered him a typescript.

Unwin soon became identified with books about conscientious objection to the war, one of which, Mrs Henry Hobhouse's *I Appeal unto Caesar*, was spurned by the trade despite a demand so large that more than one thousand copies were sold direct to members of the public at the Allen & Unwin offices. S.U. was rightly proud of this but held it against booksellers ever after that, initially, they had not supported this title. A prominent figure in the anti-war camp was the philosopher Bertrand Russell who became a natural on the Allen & Unwin list and was to remain on it all his life. The aristocrat Russell was imprisoned; Unwin became a nurse with the Voluntary Aid Detachment (VAD) but calls on his time were not heavy and, in the welcome absence of the other managing directors, he set about building on the back list inherited from Swan Sonnenschein. The company moved to 40 Museum Street in Bloomsbury, where the premises were named Ruskin House; therein was Stanley Unwin's office for the next fifty-four years. In the early part of them at least it was situated in a pokey ground-floor room from which he had first view of anyone entering the building. His was of necessity a cloak-and-dagger version of publishing until he succeeded in ousting his fellow managing directors, all of whom returned unscathed from WWI.

In the early years Unwin set out deliberately to represent the best literature in all categories. Though a lifelong teetotaller that didn't inhibit him from issuing a book about brewing. 'I have always maintained,' he wrote, 'that if it was by a recognised authority, and was the best on the subject, my firm would publish any book regardless of whether it was particularly in our line or not.' So he brought out fiction, poetry, philosophy, scientific and technical volumes, children's books, art books.

Of his list the book-trade historian, Frank Mumby, wrote, 'In proportion to its size the firm of George Allen and Unwin Ltd has probably done more than any other to add to the common store of knowledge.' To assist him Stanley Unwin employed, among others, as editors, Charles Furth and his nephew Philip Unwin, who had also begun his career with Fisher, his great-uncle.

In appearance Unwin was of medium height. He had blue eyes, a pointed beard and was bespectacled, in early days wearing pince-nez. He had a sprightly walk. Philip Unwin, arriving home in Surrey for a late Saturday lunch in the early 1920s, after working in the morning for Fisher, found Stanley and Mary already seated at table:

Stanley, clad as usual in his brown, double-breasted suit and square-toed shoes, jumped up smartly from the table and shook me vigorously by the hand. He gave his number one greeting, 'Very pleased to meet you,' which my etiquette-conscious sister Joyce had told me one should not say … Talk veered round to our Uncle Fisher. I raised a laugh … by recounting one of his eccentricities … Stanley held forth on one of his T.F.U. memories, and I realised at once that we had a bond …

It was a bond which led, following the sale of Fisher Unwin's list to Ernest Benn, to employment for Philip at Ruskin House, where he started on the first day of March 1927, at a salary of £14.00 per month. Philip spent more time working alongside 'the Chief' (as he came to refer to him) than either of Stanley's sons. He was able to write uninhibitedly, though fairly, about the experience after the patriarch's death. 'Personal modesty,' he noted, of his uncle, 'was not one of the virtues inculcated in his youth,' but he had admired his shrewdness, 'his compelling, almost mesmeric, force in argument', and he appreciated the training he received. Anyone in line for senior management was given every opportunity of observing the minutiae of the daily routine. He would sit with S.U. at the morning ritual of opening the post and be given certain letters to deal with himself, plus advice on how this should be done. More followed when 'the Chief' came to vet the replies because he saw every item of outgoing correspondence. 'He was so full of his subject,' wrote Philip,' and recollected so much case history that there was a danger of being overwhelmed by his warnings, examples and object lessons.' He watched 'lynx-eyed, taking personal care to see that every nut and bolt of the business was tightly screwed together … ' Philip pinpointed S.U.'s habit of gesticulating throughout every verbal exchange:

> No telephone conversation of any importance went through without his free hand doing circular receding chops into the air. No reference could be made to another department without a quick stab in its direction; and, after my forty years in Museum Street, when he looked into my office to say 'Can you come through to my room?' he would still point over his shoulder to indicate where it was.

Rayner noted that although Philip became responsible for more than half the annual list his father never wholly trusted his judgments and he was the target of S.U.'s occasional petulant attacks; for his part, Philip admitted that sometimes 'he fussed, irritated, provoked argument and could arouse all one's aggression'. He added that his colleague Malcolm Barnes, a senior editor and director, once confessed, 'He makes you so mad sometimes, you want to go home and kick the cat.'

While making the list saleable and enviable, S.U. by no means neglected his duty to the book trade and to literature. He was always a public-spirited man – it was part of his upbringing. He regarded 'the international inter-change of literature as an outstanding part of his life's work'. To that end he sought to be influential within the Publishers' Association, the British Council, the National Book Council and the Society of Bookmen. His presence was not always welcomed. When, on forming Allen & Unwin, he applied to join the PA he was turned down for allegedly having acted unfairly to George Allen's son. He was advised to reapply but his dignity would not allow that so, a decade later, it was the Association which wooed and won him. In his memoirs he claimed, characteristically, he was unaware of having acted unfairly against Allen.

Allen & Unwin not only became a member of the PA, Stanley himself was to prove one of its leading lights – as he was of the International Publishers' Congress. This body, moribund by 1918, became the International Publishers' Association and was revived mainly due to Unwin's efforts.

A neighbour in Hampstead, in the 1920s, was the first Labour prime minister, Ramsay MacDonald, who had been a fellow pacifist in the Great War. They often walked together on Hampstead Heath of a morning before the working day began. Despite their friendship, and indeed, with MacDonald's blessing, Allen & Unwin published Trotsky's attack on the Labour leader.

S. U. was a supporter of and publisher for the League of Nations but found this role financially unrewarding. He thought it a more effective organisation than the United Nations, which was formed after WWII, although, in his memoirs, he did not explain why.

He was a founder member (1921) of the Society of Bookmen which held monthly dinners to discuss problems of the book trade and became influential as a sounding board for innovative proposals. From its delibera-tions arose the National Book Council (later the National Book League), Book Tokens and the first Book Trade Working Party. Unwin was active in all of them. He allowed the NBC, which he described as 'his child', rent-free accommodation in a building he owned adjoining Ruskin House. This could be reached across a flat roof from his office so that Maurice Marston, secretary of the Council, frequently had the disconcerting experience of being visited by Sir Stanley through the window. Initially the NBC administered Book Tokens before handing over to the Associated Booksellers, a solution which embittered Unwin because it gave the book retailers' organisation more financial clout than he thought desirable. He would have liked Book Tokens to be jointly owned by the two trade associations, a point of view shared, curiously, by Basil Blackwell.

In addition to these activities, in 1926, mostly while on holiday, he wrote *The Truth About Publishing*, the first textbook designed to help entrants to the profession and allied trades. It went into numerous editions and was translated into at least twelve languages.

Unwin's practical experience of the German book trade led to his suggestion that our own should be anatomised. He headed a delegation to Holland and Germany, visiting Amsterdam and Leipzig, as a result of which, the 1928 Committee, comprised of publishers and booksellers, including himself, was formed. Its report, edited by Frank Sanders, secretary of the Publishers' Association, was published by Allen & Unwin but not until 1939. By then both Unwin and Basil Blackwell, as respective presidents of their trade associations, had made a significant move towards cooperation between the two bodies by jointly hosting the Ripon Hall Conferences (see preceding chapter). At a more social level this was what the Society of Bookmen had been doing, with some success, for fourteen years. Unwin claimed that he and Blackwell arranged for their presidencies to overlap so that 'the wolf and the lamb fed together' but did not indicate which of them was which.

As well as writing his textbook, S. U. made one of the earliest broadcasts on the same subject for the BBC and published pamphlets about other trade matters. On air on 17 December 1930 he coined the phrase, 'Trade follows the book.' It also, in his case, followed the ski. One year, in search of slopes, the doughty little skiier went not to Switzerland but to Scandinavia where, of course, he also sought out publishers and booksellers. Pamphlets about the Swedish and Norwegian book trades followed. In the 1930s he concerned himself with the plight of publishers in countries coming under Nazi domination, arranging for Dr Bela Horowitz, of Vienna's Phaidon Press, to take on the protection of Allen & Unwin's name in order to transfer its assets to London.

Unwin resisted opening a New York office, believing publishing on the western side of the Atlantic to be extravagantly managed. He preferred to nurse his resources, buying and selling American rights from Museum Street. He was ever conscious of the fact that his company never had an overdraft; each night he calculated how much should be added to or withdrawn from the interest-earning deposit account.

In the 1930s a few titles of major potential came on to the Allen & Unwin list, notably Lancelot Hogben's *Mathematics for the Million* and *Science for the Citizen*. Meanwhile the status of Bertrand Russell was growing yearly and J.R.R. Tolkien made his first appearance with *The Hobbit*. Stanley had paid his son Rayner a modest fee of 1s. for a highly favourable reader's opinion.

At this time Philip noted that 'the Chief' created a myth that A & U was the largest of publishers whereas he was actually employing a mere twenty-five people and importing as few as 250 copies of some American titles on his list. The myth was believed and became 'the Truth'.

It was also in the thirties that Unwin rid himself of Skinner, the only remaining joint managing director, became owner, with Cape and Dent, of the ailing Bodley Head after its proprietor, Allen Lane, had successfully launched Penguin Books, and saved his neighbour, the small bookselling business of W.J. Bryce, from bankruptcy. Its later proprietor, Ivan Chambers, observed of his landlord, 'We daily see him, not walking by, not hurrying by, but progressing by what can only be described as an Unwinian gait, a species of elegantly running motion …'

Stanley Unwin believed positively in everything he did. Travel was second nature to him and made triply virtuous by being easily combined with both holidays and work. Also, every sensible person exercised, so he walked and he played tennis. Especially he played tennis, often on the court attached to his Hampstead home, always on Saturday and Sunday afternoons. *The Times* obituarist noted that he played 'a skilful game', also that in the very last year of his life, such was his enthusiasm for it, that in Washington, during a tournament, he was heard giving international players 'advice about the exact place on the court where it was best to receive certain deliveries'. Philip Unwin quotes one of his partners at the Hampstead house as saying 'there was in him a "careful" streak so far as tennis balls were concerned … he once produced a box … that must have been ten years old … it was like playing with blancmange'. The literary agent Graham Watson recorded that when fellow publisher Billy Collins was invited there were new balls, but only three were used. His partners/opponents were seldom invited indoors either before or after games, although in the thirties domestic staff served tennis teas in a garden summer-house. He was hospitable towards only his family and visiting foreign booksellers.

• • •

The Unwins all wrote books as well as publishing them.

S.U.'s characteristics, his strengths and weaknesses, receive much attention from nephew Philip and both sons. Rayner is observant, respectful but more detached than his brother, yet he it was who contrived to work with his father (provided they did not live in the same house) and who left this comment on the nature of office life under the autocrat:

> … because so many decisions had to be agreed by father he needed to be easily available. Opening the post was one place to catch him, another was in the directors' lavatory. He never locked the door, and there was enough space to stand behind him and state one's case …

Elder son David's stance veers between love and exasperation, with much guilt thrown in. David saw himself as a pawn on his father's chessboard. He found him 'inflexible, adamant, VEHEMENT, a formidable autocrat' … yet … 'He may have had his limitations but he was a well-intentioned man.' He believed that 'those who did not know my parents were apt to underestimate' the power that Mary had over her husband. She laughed gently at him. 'It was her way of coping with him. He had very little sense of humour.'

David, who became a writer of novels and children's books, much to his father's horror (S.U. knew just how little most authors earned), reveals many of his characteristics – he had a sweet tooth and drank ginger pop, he hated evening dress, liked open-neck shirts, collar outside a Norfolk jacket and wore each of his many suits for thirty or forty years. (This led to a joke among junior staff: 'What does Sir Stanley do with his old clothes?' 'He *wears* them.') Browning was his favourite poet, the Latin countries were anathema to him (he was happier in 'the antiseptic north'), he seldom bought a book from a bookshop, had no enthusiasm for organised worship but often resorted to prayer, had a thirst for recognition (he adored all the honours which came his way), lamented the lack of servants when WWII broke out, having been 'born into a world when menfolk were not expected to lift a finger', and was 'too confident, too full of the pleasure of being himself, too involved with his own personality to relate effectively to other people'. Despite which, David endured travelling with his father on one of his global trips, acting as his secretary and even drawing the older man's praise in a letter written to Mary. He also remembers his father awaiting him at Victoria Station when, as a young man, he was returning from a vacation:

> ... a smallish figure in a neatly buttoned overcoat, his beard neatly
> clipped, hands clasped in front of him; so spruce, so organised, so
> together; ... his gaze so sharp, so direct, so artless ...

On an earlier occasion David noted that S.U.'s beard was 'copper red' and
that he had one shoulder higher than the other. Decades after, the publisher
John St John, writing in *Books and Bookmen*, saw him with '... pointed
beard, sharp blue eyes and long thin arms ... it is hard to avoid thinking of
some powerful, eccentric bird – a cross between a stork and a buzzard'.

David's experience of office life came in two phases. After a childhood
during which his education was much interrupted by illness, he joined Allen
& Unwin as assistant to the office boy, the lowliest of all jobs. His health
broke down again. Then, being unfit for military service in WWII, he was
employed in the production department. That became his war work from
which he escaped into authorship. Thereafter, he was his own man, daring
to drink a glass of beer at his father's table, and contemptuously paying S.U.
one halfpenny as a contribution to the household electricity bill when
accused of allowing a forty-watt light bulb on the landing to burn all night.

In his autobiography, S.U. admitted that the time he spent in the 1930s on
PA and IPA business, six years with the former, all ten with the latter, plus
the burden of dealing with several deaths in the family, had a 'devastating'
effect on his firm's profit-and-loss account. Nevertheless, he survived to take
on renewed public activity when war broke out. He played a prominent
role in fighting for fair allocations of paper and in campaigning against a possible purchase tax on books.

His singleness of mind is illustrated by a letter he wrote to *The Times* on
19 October 1940. He complained, at a time when London was being
bombed nightly, about 'telephone, telegraph and postal delays'. His bank,
in the centre of the capital, had been asked to ensure that a letter posted to
him in Hampstead should arrive sometime on a Saturday. 'It was not delivered until the second post on Tuesday ... it thus took a day for each mile
of its journey.'

On the day this letter was printed he made a broadcast speaking com-
forting words on the benefits of air raids, which, '... bring to many of us
increased opportunities to indulge in the pleasures of reading ... ' As the
blitz raged he played Dvorak loudly on his gramophone.

Two months later, many publishers lost their offices in the fire blitz on
Paternoster Row; 1,400,000 Allen & Unwin books ranging over 2,100 titles
were destroyed in one warehouse alone and the PA was bombed out of

Stationers' Hall. S.U. offered the latter temporary accommodation in his overflow premises at 28 Little Russell Street – '... Not free but at less than the economic rent,' he proudly recorded.

In 1944 he addressed the Royal Institution, a body founded in 1799, on 'Publishing in Peace and War', using the occasion to denounce Churchill's coalition government for 'the mean and deplorable way in which paper for books has been handled'. His address, plus further notes on *The Status of Books*, appeared as a pamphlet, a copy of which he sent to the newspaper baron Lord Beaverbrook, then in the government, nagging him to use his influence in Downing Street. His hopes, he recorded, 'were not fulfilled in the ensuing ten years'.

Partly to acquire a greater allocation of paper, Unwin bought the assets of the Murby imprint when its proprietor died and of other companies which went into liquidation. Many publishers resorted to similar tactics in an attempt to keep their lists going because the rules governing paper supply tended to favour newcomers.

In 1945, Unwin had an honorary LL D conferred upon him by Aberdeen University, followed, six months later, by a knighthood in the New Year's Honours List. Many awards, from various countries, also came his way and in 1966 he was made KCMG.

After six years of total war a return to peacetime conditions was inevitably gradual. Sir Stanley tended, as did others, to take the slow transition personally, feeling that his company had been 'affected ... cruelly' in connection with Bertrand Russell's *History of Western Philosophy*, a title with which he hit the bestseller stakes. By the time his biggest successes – Thor Heyerdahl's *Kon-Tiki Expedition* and Tolkien's *Lord of the Rings* trilogy – were published the situation had eased and his chief complaint had become the burden of tax.

In 1949 S.U. embarked on a second world tour, accompanied by his wife. This took them to New Zealand, via North America, then home through the Indian subcontinent and Suez. Three years later, this time with David, he covered 26,000 miles by air visiting the Far East and Japan. On the return journey he took in Athens and Rome. Everywhere he went he called on booksellers as well as on political heads and British Council offices. He discussed sales taxes with prime ministers and governors and gave them his advice, his mission when in Indonesia being, in his own words, 'to secure the removal of the many obstacles to the free flow of British books to a country where English has been substituted for Dutch as the second language'; in Japan, he was concerned with the rebuilding of bridges following the upsets of war. He was an ambassador for the entire book trade, as he never failed to remind his fellow publishers.

As a traveller S.U. was indefatigable. His senior colleague, Charles Furth, who was responsible for educational books, was dragged round Africa and Asia with him. Once, at a lunch in London, they heard a speech about the developing book market in West Africa. 'S.U. decided suddenly that he wanted to go to Nigeria,' Charles Furth told Philip, 'and a shift in the firm's policy had to follow.' Philip recorded that 'there was no market research, no discussion by the board … in a very few weeks they were off, S.U. taking care to see that the British Council offices were alerted in any city he visited. This usually ensured that he was met at airports and had the use of the Council's cars.'

David wrote to his wife from the Far East:

> He is EXACTLY the same man who took me to Germany when I was a child and who drove me nearly scatters when I was a young man … He induces a sense of isolation, for casual acquaintances do not exist as far as he is concerned and he pays no attention whatever (not a 'good-morning') to any other passenger on this aeroplane …

David found himself expected to cut costs by sharing a bedroom with father. He resolved this situation by keeping a fan whirring all night until the old man finally booked separate rooms. From Japan he wrote, also to his wife:

> 'He has nearly a thousand pounds here … in blocked currency but is reluctant to use taxis even in Tokyo and will walk miles rather than spend 100 yen (2/-) … I was reprimanded for being over hasty in purchasing a newspaper it turned out we didn't want. Cost: not quite twopence. ('Ah, but you've never had difficulty in earning a few pence, etc.') He should be made to tear up and throw away at least five pounds daily …

Rayner went on many trips by himself for Allen & Unwin but not often, if at all, with his father. He refers to an incident he was told about:

> Once, on his way to New Zealand, his ship called at Melbourne. It was a Sunday but, quite regardless, father busied himself ashore, going from shop to shop posting his visiting cards through their

letter-boxes with expressions of regret that, although he had called, they were not open.

They, of course, were in the wrong.

In 1950, thanks to Thor Heyerdahl's *Kon-Tiki Expedition*, Allen & Unwin hit the big time. The book came to the list through Philip Unwin happening to take a holiday in Norway. Philip also understood that business and pleasure were not separate undertakings; it came naturally to him to call on publishers when he was in Oslo. There he was offered the book about six men who had sailed a raft across the Pacific, east to west, to prove an anthropologist's theory. He had no difficulty in persuading his uncle to take it on. There are differences of opinion about just how convinced S.U. was that he had a bestseller on his hands but Philip and the company's salesmen had no doubt. Reactions from the retail trade were encouraging, the Book Society made it their Choice of the Month (a first for A & U) and a buzz of excitement passed through the firm. The London reps Leslie Berry and Ronald Whiting (in those days there wasn't a sales manager) became so taken with the book's potential that they went to see S.U. They dared to suggest that the first print order should be for 30,000 copies. S.U. poured cold water on this, thanked them for their enthusiasm but dismissed *Kon-Tiki* as just another travel book. He thought that the agreed initial run of 5,000 was probably excessive and expressed doubt about 'so many illustrations'.

To S.U.'s credit, once the orders began to pour in he changed his attitude and later claimed the book was never out of stock. In fact, for one week it was. By then, Unwin, typically, had issued an edict that booksellers wishing to place repeat orders must take six copies to get full trade terms. Eventually it sold seven hundred thousand copies in that edition. One result was that Whiting's wages increased from £6. 10s .0d per week in 1948 to £9.00 in 1951, while, in the long term, staff received bonuses. Company cars were introduced, Leslie Berry being granted (on medical grounds because he had war wounds) an ancient Jowett which had once been Philip Unwin's. He was also appointed sales manager.

At this time Collins also had a winner with a wartime escape story, *The Wooden Horse* by Eric Williams. It and *Kon-Tiki* were attracting the public into bookshops in numbers previously associated only with Churchill's war memoirs. The two companies had fun in the trade press with cartoonists depicting a race between the horse and the raft for the greatest sales, each boasting its prowess over the other.

It was a new situation for Unwin and his staff. Collins was accustomed to massive sellers; at Museum Street, despite Hogben and Russell, business was not conducted at razzmatazz level. Now the company took a leap into the mid-twentieth century. *Kon Tiki* was followed, more modestly, by the delightful French fantasy, *The Red Balloon*, aimed at both children and adults. For this title Stanley Unwin threw a party at which the film on which the book was based was shown. Many bookseller guests were astonished when alcoholic drinks were served.

Then came *The Lord of the Rings* trilogy. Rayner Unwin had joined the company and was so impressed by Tolkien's first volume that he dared to ask his father if he might pay a thousand pounds for the trilogy which, in Museum Street, was an unheard of sum for an advance. Father said, yes, if he really thought the book was worth it, an astonishing reaction from one who had built his list piecemeal with rigorous frugality. It showed shrewdness, or faith in his son, or the weakness of a parent (which seems unlikely in this case). It could not have paid off better, especially as the profit-sharing agreement with Tolkien, which would have made any literary agent shudder, was beneficial in cash-flow terms to the publishers, just as an earlier unaltered arrangement with Bertrand Russell, who didn't receive advances, had been for decades (but, see below). In his memoirs, Rayner states that Tolkien did not feel at ease with his father, who never read any part of *The Lord of the Rings*.

Then, to the directors' surprise, they were offered through an agent, Curtis Brown, James Pope-Hennessy's official life of Queen Mary (wife of George V). Allen & Unwin could be said to have joined the top league, which was endorsed when they acquired another bestselling author in Roald Dahl, whose children's books, published in the last year of S. U.'s life, achieved instant success.

In 1954 there had been a lull in his travels to allow for celebrations of Sir Stanley's first fifty years in the book trade. A dinner for 130 was held at Cutlers' Hall in the City, where he was presented with a book of tributes by some of his most distinguished authors – Bertrand Russell, Gilbert Murray and Radhakrishnan. 'Gaffer' Blackwell sent a personally written one recalling that he had been entrusted with initiating David and Rayner into the mysteries of bookselling and adding, '… You twit me sometimes for invading the field of publishing while you refrain from bookselling … IT IS NOT TOO LATE … ' The gauntlet lay where it was flung although S.U. could have retaliated by pointing out he had been a director of W.J. Bryce for twenty years. Other festivities, organised by the Publishers' Circle and the Booksellers' Association, followed. In a profile in the *Sunday Times*, a contributor stated that few of his fellow publishers loved Sir Stanley but he was personally respected. 'His progressive ideas, his fearless dicta and his efficient planning ... have during almost the whole of the century acted upon other publishers and booksellers like a series of cold baths ... ' Hamish Hamilton may or may not have felt that an appropriate description of what Unwin inflicted upon him one weekend.

For many years after everyone else not engaged in the service industries had gone on to a five-day week, S.U. chose to drive down from Hampstead in his Daimler, or take the tube, to his office on Saturday mornings to open the post. On one occasion he phoned Hamilton, whose offices were in nearby Great Russell Street, to say, 'I thought I should tell you your place is burning down. I've phoned the fire brigade. I know *you* don't work on Saturdays.' (There are various printed versions of this episode.)

He was less acerbic in an encounter with another publisher, as Robert Lusty, still in the early 1950s a director and commissioning editor at Michael Joseph, revealed. He received a phone message from Unwin asking if he might call. Recognising the pecking order, Lusty said that it should surely be for him to call on S.U. Stanley insisted otherwise and explained when he arrived at Joseph's that he was acting as unoffiicial agent for his son David's novel. 'No publisher,' he proclaimed, 'should call upon a literary agent. It has to be the other way round.' (He sold Lusty *The Governor's Wife* which became a Book Society Choice.) Agents reciprocated S.U.'s feelings about them. David Higham, in his memoirs, refers to 'The Half-Truth About Publishing', and claims that Unwin, from the viewpoint of a professional navigated in 'something like a backwater'.

About ths time Oskar Kokoschka was commissioned to paint a portrait of S.U. The artist agreed that his sitter's work must not be interrupted so a platform was erected above his desk on which Sir Stanley perched, for several weeks, while dictating letters, interviewing authors and answering phone calls. The portrait was used on the front of the jacket of his autobiography, *The Truth About a Publisher*.

In 1955 Unwin was off again around the world, this time by ship. By now he was very much the Grand Old Man of publishing, a respected figure worldwide and one who remained firmly independent in a business climate already veering towards mergers and takeovers, internally and internationally. Allen & Unwin stood aside from this. It was not on offer, it had long been under the control of its founder although his younger son was on the board and, unofficially, its first sales *director*. Rayner, also a scholarly author, was to wait all too long before becoming head of the firm; in the interim period, while also editing Tolkien, he organised the removal of the warehouse to Hemel Hempstead, in Hertfordshire, inaugurated Unwin paperbacks and followed his father's example by taking a leading part in trade affairs.

S.U. did not involve himself much editorially but one author with whom no one but he dealt was Bertrand Russell. The philosopher would deliver a typescript personally in the afternoon, the publisher took it home to read that evening, 'then, as no further view needed to be taken and no copy-editing was considered necessary, a contract was made out (the terms of which were never queried by Russell) and the script was handed over to production for estimating next day'. Rayner believed that 'like the Victorian aristocrat that he was Russell regarded my father as a tradesman who knew his job'. There was no ritual entertaining of an important author. The widowed Lady Russell wrote, in 1970, of the relationship between the two men as 'rare and precious … they both, I think, drew much satisfaction from it'. Once, while S.U. was abroad, Russell delivered a new book to Philip who supposed he was behaving correctly in giving the author a four-figure advance. Russell was pleasantly surprised; Sir Stanley's reaction is not recorded. It was possibly during the same absence from Museum Street that S.U. called on a Nigerian bookseller to collect a debt of £25.00. He was so moved by his customer's evident ill health that he reduced the sum owing to £5.00, explaining, 'he thought he had not the moral right to release the man from all sense of obligation'.

Unwin once attended an International Publishers' Congress at Florence from where delegates went to Rome to meet the Pope. On the coach returning Unwin sat himself next to Robert Lusty who asked, 'Did you have a nice talk with the Pope?' 'No, no, Lusty, I didn't. You see, he knows me, so I pushed one or two of the others forward.' (I wonder if it was S.U.'s nonconformist origins which led him to avoid a meeting with the pontiff?)

Lusty who was a friend of Philip Unwin's asked him for a proof of *The Truth about a Publisher* to read on a trip to New York. Half the book trade wanted early sight of Unwin's autobiography; proofs were rationed. The request was granted by Stanley on condition that he agented the book for him in New York, thus redeeming the situation years earlier over David's novel. Lusty seems to have been successful; certainly the book was published there.

Sir Stanley's alleged meanness was legendary in the book trade. His family report on it conflictingly. Philip is precise: 'His frugality … extended to such little things as the famous stubs of pencil with which he did all his writing'. Once Philip was in the embarrassing situation of being in the middle of a dispute between 'the Chief' and Ronald Whiting, the junior London rep, a young married man with two children, working for a low wage. Whiting was entitled to ten shillings weekly expenses for bus fares. Finding himself hard-pressed, he asked Philip to intercede for a 25% rise to twelve shillings and sixpence. Philip put it to S.U. who, after due deliberation, offered 20% – twelve shillings.

Whiting, on a tape I made with him for the National Life Story Collection (NLSC) at the British Library, records handing in his notice when he was offered another post ... S.U.'s door was always open unless he had a visitor.

> ... 'Yes, yes, what do you want?' ... Whenever I saw Sir Stanley in his office I was never, ever, offered a seat, and he was nearly always drinking tea and nibbling a biscuit ... 'What do you want, Whiting, what do you want? ... You can't give in your notice, you've been here since you left school ... Are you sure you're not casting away the substance for the shadow?' ... I replied, 'This shadow is worth four quid a week more.'
> ' ... Get out, get out,' shouted Unwin.

Half an hour later, Whiting was told by Philip, who locked the door of his office and fished a packet of cigarettes out of his desk drawer (smoking was strictly forbidden at Ruskin House), he could have a £200 p.a. rise. When he refused it Philip asked, 'Was there one particular thing which made you take this decision?' 'Yes,' he was told. 'Sixpence.'

Ronald Whiting, who in wartime, had joined The Bodley Head from school, found himself re-employed by S.U. while he was waiting to be demobilised from the army. He was stationed in London and virtually unoccupied. He learned of a government initiative which permitted essential tradesmen, such as electricians and plumbers, to be given extended leave, while waiting release, so that they could be useful in the community. Whiting persuaded his commanding officer that repping for Allen & Unwin came into this category, so for a while he worked for S.U. for nothing, apart from meagre travel expenses, and changed into uniform every seventh day to collect his army pay. Sir Stanley would have thought it the height of extravagance for anyone to pay a man twice for working the same hours.

Bookseller Ivan Chambers, who has also recorded that his sometime employer, later partner, William Jackson Bryce turned down his own appeal for a rise with the words, 'You will get your reward in heaven', excused S.U.'s parsimony on the grounds that as a youth he had been obliged to look after the pennies. He maintained that it was simply habit and that Unwin could be generous when persuaded a petitioner had an indisputable case.

There was disagreement about Sir Stanley's sense of humour. Many alleged he had none, although Philip noted that he 'could be a vivid and amusing raconteur'. S.U. himself claimed that Goncharov's comic novel *Oblomov*, which he published, was one of his favourite books, Ivan Chambers said that he was 'a concise and incisive speaker and could be a witty one', while son David maintained he had 'no ability whatever to look at and to laugh at himself'. Sir Basil Blackwell, on the other hand, at an eightieth-birthday celebration, said, possibly tongue in cheek, 'I have never known Uncle Stan decline any innocent frolic.' Robin Denniston, in the *DNB*, while praising *The Truth about Publishing* as a great textbook, said, 'It set down all the facts but left out all the fun.'

On that particular quality there were conflicting views; on two others, his rectitude and his obstinacy, all were in accord. Of the first the most famous but possibly apocryphal instance is recorded by Denniston and was mentioned by obituarists. Philip was invited by S.U. to offer an opinion on reading the typescript of 'the Chief's' autobiography. Daringly he responded with, 'Don't you think, uncle, that you might somewhere give an instance of where you were wrong?' 'My dear boy,' Stanley replied, 'I can't start writing fiction at my time of life.' (But, was he making a joke?)

S.U., unlike most resident Hampstead publishers, seldom visited my bookshop and certainly never bought a book, but one evening long after we had officially closed, he rapped on the door because he wished to purchase a long-playing record for Lady Unwin's birthday. He instantly complained because the door was locked. On another occasion I tried to persuade him to reprint Barratt's lavishly illustrated three-volume *Annals of Hampstead* which had become a collector's item. I suggested he might publish it as a labour of love and a symbol of fifty happy years spent in Hampstead. He borrowed the volumes one at a time. When he brought back the third, he handed it over, glared at me accusingly, and said, 'You didn't tell me this one was longer than the others. It completely upsets the costing'. (Barratt was later reprinted by Lionel Leventhal as a facsimile boxed-set and the edition sold out.) Another local book which Unwin could have had he passed on to me – Helen Bentwich's *The Vale of Health on Hampstead Heath*. My company made a modest profit on a small edition and it was subsequently reprinted in paperback by the Camden History

Society. Even on publishing matters 'Uncle Stan' was not always right, although it could be argued in these instances that Allen & Unwin's larger overheads might have made both titles uneconomic.

The Unwins lived in Oak Hill Park on a prime site near the highest point of Hampstead Heath. He sold most of it in the 1960s, building for himself a new house and tennis court on what remained. The Unwin Trust, destined to become hugely beneficial to the book trade, was then inaugurated.

On one of his rare visits to my shop Sir Stanley dropped in late on a Saturday morning having heard that the Rhodesian bookseller, Victor Tarica, whom I had met at a conference, was proposing to visit me prior to calling on him. S.U. had a proprietorial attitude about Commonwealth booksellers – they were his clients. Rhodesians, he informed me, usually preferred tea to coffee. I ungenerously suspected that he was hoping to get out of serving this one with either.

Although S.U. did not buy books from me, his daughter Ruth and her family, who lived in a house on the Oak Hill Park estate before it was developed, did. Rayner, when at Hampstead for a dental appointment, also looked in. On one early January visit, in those fruitful years when an independent bookseller endeavoured to sell everything he could by Christmas Eve, Rayner cast his eyes around my emporium and, with a sales-director glint in them, remarked, 'Ian, you don't have enough books.' 'No, Rayner,' I replied, 'I have too many shelves.'

I met Sir Stanley more often at Society of Bookmen meetings. He was its first president, from 1921 until 1968. On the whole he allowed the other officers to run it but when he chose to make a ruling his word was law. He could be stubbornly unforgiving. At a Jerusalem Book Fair, André Deutsch had beaten him to a book or committed some similar solecism, as from a youthful publisher to a GOM. Periodically at Bookmen committee meetings André would be proposed for membership. Sir Stanley would have none of it. If that man were put up he, the president, would resign. The Glasgow bookseller, Ross Higgins, said his attitude was ungenerous and demeaned his stature. Sir Stanley never gave way; a few months after he died, with Rayner's approval, we elected André.

In the mid-sixties, the Society organised a reception for visiting Commonwealth booksellers at the Banqueting House, Whitehall. There was very nearly a diplomatic crisis when Sir Stanley, who had spent much of his life cajoling overseas booksellers to buy British books, and who, indeed, regarded them as his company's life blood, said he must that afternoon be at Wimbledon because the Queen Mother would probably invite him to her enclosure for a strawberry tea. We thought he had got his priorities wrong. Finally, he made both events. A year later when Robert Lusty and I, as chairman and secretary of the society, were arranging his eightieth birthday lunch at the Connaught Rooms, he cast doubt on his ability to attend because the date, which he had already agreed with us, conflicted with the AGM of the insurance company on whose board he sat. He could be ungracious to a degree but he did turn up for the lunch, an occasion when his characteristics were neatly and humorously summed-up by Sir Paul Sinker, director general of the British Council, who read a letter allegedly from one of his representatives in Ruritania. Sir Stanley, he reported, had dropped in to spend 36 hours on his way elsewhere . . .

> ... He visited eight publishing houses and sixty-seven bookshops in Zenda, Strelsau and Tarlenheim, and before leaving he inspected British Council libraries in all these towns and made some helpful suggestions. He regretted that there was not time for him to climb the Ruritanian Alps but he consoled himself by playing six sets of tennis with the Third Secretary of the embassy – all of which he won. I have just seen Sir Stanley off at the airport. I am writing this in bed.

Sir Paul was greeted by an ovation for this witty tribute; it was actually written by his director of books, John Hampden, a fact not disclosed to the audience at the time.

Unwin attended most committee meetings and dinners of the Bookmen but rarely brought a guest. He was not inclined to wine and dine much with fellow publishers and booksellers. He played tennis with some of them who were good enough to stand up to him on court. Beyond that he was a private man. Although a member of the Reform he was not essentially clubbable.

For the 1964 birthday, in addition to the Bookmen lunch, Allen & Unwin gave a reception at Stationers' Hall. For this occasion there was issued an 84-page, stiffly bound paperback, in a limited edition of 50 copies, comprising tributes to the great man. I did not receive one until nearly four years later when Sir Stanley sent me copy number 42, along with two other books to assist me in the book-trade history I was writing. He informed me ... 'Dear Norrie ... ' that it had been produced, on their own initiative, by the printers, Tinling of Liverpool, adding, 'Few even know of its existence'. I was welcome to keep all three volumes. S.U., copy 42, is one of the rarest items in my library. (See Sources, under Anon. for full title.)

Unwin stayed in harness for another four years after its publication, continuing to visit book fairs in many countries and to take a keen interest in all trade matters. He died in 1968 after a short illness and while still head of an apparently prosperous company. He was not to know that great changes in the publishing world were to bring about a decline in Allen & Unwin's fortunes and lead to the virtual disappearance of the imprint by the end of the century.

Despite the abrupt ending to his formal education, and although he did not attend university, S.U. had a clear, logical mind and a formidable capacity for being right. Kingsford's history of the first fifty years of the Publishers' Association, the report of the 1928 Committee and other official documents confirm the extent to which he was involved in book-trade affairs worldwide. To the end of his life he retained an interest in the City where he had had his first employment, and, from 1950 until his death, he was on the board of the Equitable Life Assurance Society.

He was widely obituarised in Britain, the United States, Germany, Japan and other countries. *Publishers' Weekly* named him 'an Olympian figure in a time when book publishing seems increasingly dominated by organisation men', the *New York Times* gave him generous space, as did *Frankfurter Allegemeine Zeitung*. At home, in the *Daily Telegraph*, literary editor David Holloway, (then chairman of the Bookmen) wrote that the world of books had lost 'its most colourful figure'; Ian Parsons wrote to Philip Unwin, '… the thought of there no longer being an "Uncle Stan" for us to defer to, to consider, and even occasionally to mock affectionately, is one we shall find difficult to accept … '; while *The Bookseller* obituary, unsigned but probably by the editor, Edmond Segrave, who had never been well disposed towards his subject, outlined his career accurately and quoted him as saying:

> If I have shown in such matters undue and possibly un-English enthusiasm for my job, I hope that I may be forgiven, and that there will be, at any rate, some who will be inclined to say with Ecclesiastes, 'I perceive that there is nothing better than that a man should rejoice in his own works; for that is his portion.'

More to the point, and more caring, had been Philip's comments, writing of himself and Charles Furth:

> We both started from scratch, fired to enthusiasm by the same exciting chief; we knew tough times, occasionally we rebelled

jointly or severally, but we had the supreme satisfaction of seeing the little acorn firm grow to a sizeable oak. We knew originally the adventure and simplicity of S.U.'s 'one-man show'; thanks to him we always had reasonable security, but with the minimum of formality and organization. It was a full and interesting life with fair rewards ...

Philip, in fact, played a much larger role editorially in Allen & Unwin than did Sir Stanley. Along with Charles Furth and Malcolm Barnes he had been a major commissioner of new books and it must not be forgotten that it was entirely due to him that *Kon-Tiki* was offered to the company. After lunching one day with him he remarked to me with intense pleasure, and beaming eyes, 'Now I'm going back to the office to do some real publishing ... to see an author.' He was a witty and urbane chairman of the Society of Bookmen; it was my good fortune, as secretary, to overlap with the end of his term of office. He was patience personified in his dealings with 'the Chief' and popular with his colleagues. He became Master of the Stationers' Company, an honour not accorded to his twice-knighted uncle; he died in 1981, leaving a widow, two daughters and hosts of friends.

Stanley Unwin had few close friends in the book trade – W.G. Taylor, of Dent's, who features in his autobiography, was one – but he was a devoted family man. I had a touching instance of this when I reviewed David Unwin's book in the *Ham & High*. I referred to the fact that in 1968 I had been asked by the editor to write an obit of Sir Stanley but had declined because although 'I had tried hard I could not prevent myself from recalling anecdotes about his meanness and self-righteousness ... ' which ... 'had seemed unsuitable and I did not wish to offend Lady Unwin.' I had withdrawn pleading a bad case of 'King Charles's Head'. In the issue after my review appeared there was printed a dignified letter written by one of S.U.'s grandchildren saying what a dear he was and how much she had adored him.

In his book *George Allen & Unwin: A Remembrancer*, Rayner Unwin honestly assessed his own failure to guide the company effectively into a changed world of takeovers and mergers. He was scholarly, literary, an intellectual. As Tolkien's editor alone his contribution to the health of the list was invaluable. He had a quick sense of humour and enjoyed the social life of the book trade; in the fifties and sixties he was part of an amorphous group of publishers and booksellers who wined and dined together in Soho after trade meetings. I served with him on several committees and admired his practicality and intelligence. Alas, when he took the reins at Museum

Street he did not fit easily into a role which, had his father died or retired a decade earlier, might have suited him. He appointed various chief executives but the recipe did not work. In 1985 Allen & Unwin lost nearly £1m.; in the next year it joined forces with the smaller but profitable Bell & Hyman. Unwin Hyman, in which Robin Hyman through his banker backers was the dominant financial partner, traded successfully until the 1990 recession, when it was sold to HarperCollins. Rayner was not happy about this solution but was pleased that the name of Allen & Unwin was retained by the Australian branch of the company which was not part of the deal. His son Merlin, who had for a while been MD of Allen & Unwin, for which his cousin Corydon (David's son) also worked, set-up as an independent publisher in Ludlow.

As administrator of the Unwin Trust, Rayner authorised generous financial support for the National Book League (later Book Trust), the Book Trade Benevolent Society (of which he was sometime chairman) and the National Life Story Collection's oral history project, Book Trade Lives. Those of us involved in the latter attempted in vain to persuade him to make tapes; he insisted that he had 'written it all down' and that what he wanted to have recorded were the ordinary lives of those who had worked in publishing as packers, production assistants, secretaries, etc.

Rayner inherited from his father a love of travel which sent him more than once trekking in the Himalayas; he also took time away from publishing to write a deeply researched account of *The Defeat of John Hawkins* (Allen & Unwin, 1960). He died in 2000, survived by Carol, his wife, their four children and by brother David. His particular niche in publishing history is assured by his Tolkien association; he and his father, his entire family from Fisher onwards, stamped their personalities upon the book trade, bestowing riches, literary and monetary.

Sir Stanley Unwin, Kt (1946), KCMG (1966), Hon. LL D Aberdeen, born Lee, London SE, 19 December 1884, seventh son of Edward and Elizabeth Unwin. Married Mary Storr, May 1914, two sons and one daughter. Died, London, 13 October 1968.

Three

ALLEN LANE

No publisher has been more documented than Allen Lane; no imprint more recorded than that of Penguin Books. Any account of him must also be a history of the illustrious imprint he founded and of the array of remarkable people who assisted and sometimes guided him. He has been named a popular educator, the creator of a cultural revolution, the most influential publisher of the twentieth century, attributes suggesting that if he was not actually a saint (which he wasn't) he was undeniably touched with greatness.

The founder of Penguin Books was born Allen Lane Williams into a lower-middle-class family in Bristol near the start of the Edwardian decade. His ancestry was partly Welsh, partly Devonian. Samuel his father worked in the architects' department of the city municipality; Camilla his mother was a second cousin of the publisher John Lane. None who knew him as a boy, or as a young man, would have expected him to be destined for fame and certainly not in a cultural context. He was educated at Bristol Grammar School where he shone at neither academic work nor sport, but although said by many commentators to be totally unmusical, A.L. was in the choir and sang solo. He also belonged to a madrigal society. One of the few positive benefits he derived from his undistinguished school career came through the influence of his headmaster, J.E. Barton, who 'opened Allen's eyes to the significance of design and form'. It may have been this awareness which was detected in him by John Lane, a friend of Barton's who, seeking temporary refuge in Bath from the Zeppelin raids on London during the First World War, visited his West Country friends and relations.

John Lane, a man of humble birth, was a railway clerk who became the entrepreneurial founder of The Bodley Head, a publishing company which dazzled London in the 1890s. He brought out the sensational *Yellow Book* and knew Oscar Wilde, Aubrey Beardsley, Max Beerbohm and other fin-de-siècle notables. Twenty years on his list was still strong in saleable authors such as Stephen Leacock and Saki and featured two future bestselling novelists, Agatha Christie and C.S. Forester. But Lane, married since 1898, had no children; his publishing flair was drying up; he was looking for a successor. The sixteen-year-old Allen was invited to join The Bodley Head when he left school on one condition – that he change his surname to Lane. The youth accepted, although in later life he claimed that going into publishing had thwarted his desire to be an architect and anyhow he would have preferred farming which on his mother's side was in the blood. (His first biographer described him as having come like 'uncle' John on to the publishing scene 'as raw, hesitant and rustic … a businessman in gum boots'.)

It was not only Allen who agreed to change his name. His family – father, mother, younger brothers, Richard and John, and sister Nora – all did.

Allen started work at the offices in Vigo Street, London WI, on 23 April 1919 at twenty-one shillings a week, and was soon lodging with John and Annie, who was American by birth, in their prestigious home in Lancaster Gate Terrace. Through them he was introduced to several strands of society, but by day he was required to learn publishing from the packing floor upwards. He made rapid progress, mastering all menial tasks. John Lane, who was convinced that 'books must please the eye, no less than they satisfy the mind', sent him to visit printers to study techniques of production, after which he was put on the road with the company's reps to sell the list. He was a perfectly groomed, presentable, sociable young man.

By 1925, when John Lane died, Allen was an experienced publisher, who had joined the board of The Bodley Head the previous year. He understood about sales, production, coping with authors, bank managers, controlling staff; he gave a convincing impression of knowing what a book was about even if he hadn't read it. Also he had the gift of listening intently, at least until what he heard became tedious or irrelevant, an attribute I noted in him at our first meeting and on which others who knew him better than I commented.

His fellow directors, two of whom had invested £10,000 each in the company, were unenthusiastic about Allen. They saw him as a product of nepotism who might bankrupt an already tottery business. They had to tolerate him because he had the support of Annie Lane, the largest shareholder until her death (c.1927). She left her interest to Allen, who was soon to become managing director and who had brought Richard Lane, previously a fruit farmer and briefly an actor, into the company. Both lived at Annie's house from where they moved first into Albany and later to Talbot Square, Paddington, where brother John joined them. The Lanes were always interested in interior decoration relating to where they happened to live, and especially to bathrooms, which they thought of as the most important feature of a house. It became their custom to take morning ablutions together while discussing the previous night's revelries – they were young bloods about town – and making business plans.

While Allen inherited the shares in The Bodley Head, his brothers and sister received legacies, which Annie believed to be the fairest way of interpreting the wishes of her late husband. This enabled the brothers, when the time came, to work for Penguin for nothing and for Richard, in 1936, to supply the £100 capital needed to form Penguin Books Ltd.

It is surprising that A.L. spent ten years attempting to retrieve the fortunes of The Bodley Head. He was notoriously impatient, disliked committee meetings, had the lowest of boredom thresholds and, according to a close colleague, read very little, had no love of music and was said to consider that what were known as the Aldwych farces, written by friend and author Ben Travers, the highest achievement of the drama. (Although Hesketh Pearson, Shaw's biographer, relates that he attended the first nights of GBS's plays, and A.L. himself says he enjoyed Wilde and Coward.)

In attempting to find bestsellers Allen made an early mistake by taking on a spoof biography by the said Hesketh Pearson entitled *The Whispering Gallery*. It landed them both in court on libel charges but they were acquitted, following which Pearson sued the publisher with some success. Allen next turned to a book of cartoons by the American Peter Arno, which the board of the Bodley Head refused to finance. So the young director underwrote publication himself. Then, more daringly, he proposed to publish James Joyce's *Ulysses* which none of his competitors would touch for fear of being prosecuted. The only edition in English came from the Odyssey Press in Hamburg, who had taken over the rights formerly held by those gallant women Sylvia Beach and Harriet Weaver. Allen bought a copy and posted it to himself in England with a note on the package saying what it contained. It passed through customs and reached him at Vigo Street. Meanwhile the book had been published in the United States by Random House and survived prosecution. Joyce would have liked Faber & Faber to publish it in Britain, but T.S. Eliot, a director of that company, was wary of the law so it went to The Bodley Head. But again A.L.'s fellow directors, and also Western Printing Services, refused to go ahead without a £20,000 bond guaranteeing them against legal costs. A limited edition of one thousand with a hundred copies signed by Joyce was published and the law did not intervene. Following which something still needed to be done to save The Bodley Head, so it could be said that Penguin Books was born out of desperation more than a desire to enlighten the masses. The stories surrounding its birth are many, some of them legendary.

Allen emulated his 'uncle' in enjoying a social life and cultivating contacts with authors. Agatha Christie, destined to be an oustandingly successful writer of plays and detective fiction, and her archaeologist husband Max
Mallowan became friends and remained so long after she had taken her
books to another publisher. It was after visiting them in the West Country
that Allen found himself browsing at W.H. Smith's bookstall on Exeter station. One story has it that he noted a lack of cheap editions for travellers
and saw a gap in the market. Another is that one H.A.W. Arnold, working in a minor, lowly paid position at The Bodley Head, yearned to own
books and begged his employer to introduce a cheap series for the likes of
himself. A.L. turned down the idea because, he pointed out, the firm
already produced 9d. paperback reprints of novels which weren't selling.
However, a seed was sown and one day, months later, although no reference was ever made to his suggestion, Arnold was instructed to work out
the production costs on a 6d. series. There is a third, the Blackwell version,
which maintains that it was under an apple tree in the Gaffer's Oxfordshire
garden, during a Ripon Hall Conference weekend in 1934, 'that the idea
came to' Lane. The three stories are not mutually exclusive, but the likely
origin of the actual name is that recorded by Joan Coles, who was Allen's
secretary at the time the series was planned. She overheard a discussion,
which had lasted for hours, about what the books should be called. It had
got to the stage where it had been decided to name the series after a bird
because of the admirable Albatross Modern Continental Library of English-
language books published in Germany. As the argument was getting
nowhere Miss Coles called out from an adjoining room, 'Why not
Penguins?' At which point, junior employee Edward Young, who confirmed this version in old age, was despatched to the London Zoo to make
drawings of the birds for use as colophons. For years after she had left his
employment Miss Coles received Christmas cards from Allen in memory of
her contribution. What is also known, from Richard Lane's unpublished
memoirs, is that the three brothers discussed the project as they washed and
shaved. Publishers who were asked for the paperback rights on the first titles
ridiculed the venture. Jonathan Cape agreed hard terms to release a dozen
or so books; Stanley Unwin said Penguins couldn't possibly prosper at 6d.
per copy because the rising price of paper would quickly ruin the enterprise. Booksellers were against them because they didn't wish to give valuable space to such cheap items; George Orwell, as an author, objected to
them for the same reason but welcomed them as a reader. The board of
The Bodley Head agreed that the new series could bear its name as part of
the imprint and even use its premises but the Lanes must themselves fund

the venture, seen to be the latest preposterous idea of a reckless man. How could he propose a 6d. series of paperbacks on which the net profit would be one farthing per copy (24 farthings = 6d. 6d. = 2½p. today), a series moreover which would not break even until 17,000 copies of each title had been sold?

It sounded a wild scheme, though thirty-five years on, *The Times* obituarist of A.L. remarked stuffily, 'there was nothing original about the idea except that the books were to be well produced and printed'. Yet the manager of Martin's Bank, Cocks Biddulph Branch, was impressed and offered overdraft facilities. (It was a brave and wise decision: in 1968, A.L. said in an interview that Penguin had always been run on an overdraft.) The series appealed also to Clifford Prescott, the book buyer of Woolworths, the 3d. and 6d. chain store, to whom Allen had in an earlier attempt to find a new market successfully sold an edition of Disney's *The Three Little Pigs*. Encouraged by Blanche his wife, who saw advance copies of the books, Prescott gave an initial order greater than that received from the book trade as a whole and followed it within a few days with a larger repeat. Meanwhile, brother John Lane, who had cultivated the export market while at The Bodley Head, had taken the risk of supplying overseas booksellers he knew with orders they had not actually placed.

The Woolworth involvement with Penguin's initial success has been well aired. Selfridges, in Oxford Street, also backed them according to A.L., who stated they bought 100 of each title. On publication day he visited the store where the books were well displayed and already selling. He was asked to repeat the order. The gamble had come off. Little had been spent on promotion, there had been no market research. A pattern for exceptional success had been created by instinct.

A.L. told an apprentice, who like Mr Arnold had urged him to bring out cheaper books, that 'Penguins are not intended for the mass market; they are limited editions; editions limited to the size of the audience who can read them … ' (a nice piece of sophistry) '… .there are only two prices at which a book is commercial, 6d. and six guineas'. Curiously this argument was taken up by Stanley Unwin who initiated a controversy in the *Times Literary Supplement* based on the belief that the market was finite; if the public bought books at 6d. they would resist more expensive ones. (For once he was wrong. In the first three years seventeen million Penguins were sold and the market grew.)

Allen moved his office from The Bodley Head, whose name appeared on the cover of the first eighty Penguins, to Great Portland Street, close to Holy Trinity Church, Marylebone, where the company already rented storage space in the crypt. The Penguin warehouse was installed amongst the empty tombs, some of which were used to house the accounts books and petty cash. Female members of staff received sixpence a week to spend in the nearest public conveniences; the men used the graveyard. At times services were still conducted in the actual church while the warehouse was in use. The early employees, in the crypt or at the Great Portland Street offices, were expected to turn their hand to whatever needed to be done, a tradition which was maintained for well over a decade.

There was nothing revolutionary or avant-garde about the first ten titles published on 30 July 1935, nor was there anything, apart from an Agatha Christie whodunnit, with much appeal to down-market readers. The actual Penguin number 1 was a translation, *Ariel*, a biography of Shelley by André Maurois, a Bodley Head author. Among the other nine were novels by Ernest Hemingway, Eric Linklater, Mary Webb, Dorothy L. Sayers and Compton Mackenzie. Of these possibly only *A Farewell to Arms* was to stand the test of time. Twenty thousand copies of each were printed; *Ariel* went into a third impression in October that same year. At quarterly or two monthly intervals further batches of ten were issued. George Orwell in the *New English Weekly* was disparaging about the third, regretting the selection of P. G. Wodehouse's *My Man Jeeves*. In the first nine months there was a profit of £4,500 of which A.L. received £1,000. When Penguins Books Ltd. was formed, A.L. was still the chief shareholder in The Bodley Head which soon went into voluntary liquidation, a situation from which it was rescued primarily by Stanley Unwin.

It was when Lane turned to original non-fiction that he began to make sizeable profits. Members of the public writing in for books, lists, information, tended not to remember which bird had nested at Holy Trinity Church. Some, it was said, addressed their letters to 'Pelican Books'. Another version, also involving A.L. and a railway station, is that while at London's St Pancras, the publisher overheard someone asking at the bookstall, 'Do you have one of those Pelican books?' He realised that this was an imprint he should use before a competitor did. One had already come up with Jackdaw Books and there had already been two other small Penguin imprints, now known only to the historically curious. There is no copyright in titles but the use of brand names can be challenged, so A.L. moved fast. Bernard Shaw had written to him recommending *The Worst Journey in the World*. This classic of travel to Antarctica by Apsley Cherry-Garrard (who was GBS's neighbour at Ayot St Lawrence) was too long to be issued as a single volume at 6d. but Lane replied that he would attempt to buy it none the less; meanwhile would Shaw allow him to paperback *The Intelligent Woman's Guide to Socialism*? Shaw not only said yes, but offered to write two new chapters on Capitalism, Sovietism and Fascism. *The Intelligent Woman's Guide…* became the first original title, Pelicans A1 and A2, thus cageing the second bird. Later to follow were Puffins, Ptarmigans, Peregrines, Peacocks, King Penguins, Porpoisies; more immediately and significantly came Penguin Specials.

A.L. was fortunate in attracting the people he needed, and not only his brothers who had bonded naturally. From the earliest days, in addition to a well-disposed bank manager and the book buyer of Woolworths, he found academics willing to advise editorially. He had neither learned nor literary pretensions himself, he was not a writer or editor. Although he liked to be in overall control he was happy to delegate at the creative level, an attitude which led him to take risks that others might have resisted. There was little element of gambling about Pelicans, the early volumes of which named, as editor, Krishna Menon, an Indian barrister. He was a Labour councillor in St Pancras where Shaw had been a vestryman in earlier days and had edited a non-fiction series for The Bodley Head. He enlisted the help of H.L. ('Lance') Beales, an historian who taught at the London School of Economics (LSE), Peter Chalmers-Mitchell, a zoologist, and William Emrys ('Bill') Williams, a former official of the Workers' Education Association (WEA) who had become secretary of the British Institute of Adult Education (BIAE).

Menon conferred an immeasurable benefit when he introduced Williams, who stayed the course for three decades becoming not only A.L.'s closest colleague and friend but chief editor, adviser to and director of Penguin Books. W.E.W. received payments, or royalties, for titles he wrote or compiled but he was never on the payroll. Williams's salary was paid by the official body for which he worked – after BIAE came the Army Bureau of Current Affairs, the Council for the Encouragement of Music and the Arts (CEMA) and the Arts Council of Great Britain – yet Penguin was more than his spare-time job and editorial meetings, conducted informally, even hilariously, were often held at his offices.

Menon, an extreme ascetic, was not on the same wavelength as Lane and soon left the scene, returning to India where he subsequently became a member of the government. Beales, who was behind the commissioning of many Pelicans over a long period, was primarily concerned with his role at the LSE; similarly with Chalmers-Mitchell, whose first love was the London Zoological Society (he was the inspiration behind Whipsnade Park Zoo) while his second was Anglo-Soviet relations. So the effective editorial control of the entire Penguin list for the next few years passed to Williams, Eunice Frost, who had become Allen's secretary, A.L. Glover (from 1944), and the 'King Penguin' himself, although Richard Lane also claimed when not on war service to have been present at meetings.

The first Pelicans were published in May 1937. An introduction to them stated:

> Authoritative books, for people who want to keep abreast of the changes in the outlook of science and thought which are affecting our everyday life, have always been rather expensive. Publishers seem to have regarded them as appealing to a very small public of readers who are well-to-do . . .
>
> In publishing Pelicans we make it possible for everybody to own the best books of this kind which have been published in recent years ... dip into them in your bookshop to see what enthralling reading they make.

This announcement did not state that original work would be published in the series, nor that the first eight titles embraced history, archaeology and economics as well as science and philosophy. It was a modest plug for a list which was to range over the whole field of human endeavour. One of the first, transferred from the Penguin list, was H.G.Wells's *A Short History of the World*, which sold 350,000 copies.

For the publishers of Pelicans it was a small step to Penguin Specials, which were very much products of the dire state of European society in the late 1930s. The world was moving inexorably towards another major war. The Nazi regime was established in Germany, the Communists had control of Russia and vast areas of Asia, the Spanish Civil War was raging with help from both totalitarian powers, Japan had invaded China, Jews were being persecuted, and India was seething for independence from Britain. The Penguin Specials took the place of the pamphlets of previous centuries. They were written and published at speed, selling in huge quantities and complementing Victor Gollancz's Left Book Club. They were not so narrowly partisan as the latter, but there is no doubt that the editorial heads were all inclined to socialism – while A.L. was told by author and friend Ethel Mannin that some regarded him as a missionary of Communism. V.G. and A.L. were not always *en rapport*. Gollancz was much more of a political animal; both were great publishers.

Eunice Frost perfectly exemplifies the Penguin work ethos. Although officially A.L.'s secretary she became what she described as a 'literary midwife'. A.L. asked her one day if she liked reading, then pushed a pile of books across the desk. 'That's how I learned,' she recalled. 'You had to carry the baby home with you every night.' Large-scale editorial meetings were infrequent; much was decided by phone. 'Later things changed ... but we did inhabit a time of innocent awareness, dedications towards ideals and ideas ... and pursuit of the best ... and there was the constant support and enthusiasm of the press ... ' Also, there was lunch at the Barcelona, a restaurant off Regent Street. 'Work had to be got through but much wine had to be drunk too! A bit of a trial but also a time of regeneration.'

The success of the Penguin venture made new and larger premises essential. It also became necessary to vacate the crypt in the Marylebone Road before a health inspector, who had already turned a blind eye to it, officially condemned it as a place of work. Again Martin's Bank came to the rescue. The area in West London around what was to become Heathrow Airport was in urban terms under-used. A site on the Bath Road at Harmondsworth was found and there the offices and warehouse were erected. The purchase price was £2,112 + £200 for cabbages. (The site was a farm.) Allen instructed brother Dick to dispose of the vegetables; the foundation stone was laid by their father on 4 August 1937. A.L. moved into nearby Silverbeck, a seven-bedroomed, early-nineteenth-century house in nine acres of ground. This cost £2,250. (Around this time, for sentimental or whimsical reasons, he attempted to regain ownership of The Bodley Head but was repulsed by Stanley Unwin.)

In what remained of the pre-Second War years other series were added – Guides to the English Counties, Illustrated Classics (discontinued after the first ten), Poets, Shakespeare. It might have been supposed that during such exciting early years the founder, for all that he was willing to delegate editorial responsibility, would have stuck to his last for sixteen hours a day. Not so Allen Lane, and although he did his duty as he saw it by joining the Territorial Army, even to the extent of taking a commission, he indulged in world travel and holidays in Europe. In 1938, he was absent for months, accompanied by sister Nora, on an extended trip to Aden, India and the Far East.

The huge sales enjoyed by Specials and Pelicans had a vital effect on the expansion made by Penguin in the first ten years. Soon after war was declared in 1939, paper was rationed and publishers' quotas were based on the amount they had used in the two preceding years. Nothing could have been more beneficial to the young company. At one stage Allen also dabbled in the black market although warned by Bob Maynard, his production manager, that this might prejudice his entire allowance. A.L. replied, 'You'll get me out of it.' Until 1939, Penguins had stiff paper covers plus soft paper wrappers; the latter, dispensed with by Maynard as a wartime economy, were never reinstated.

Foreign holidays were not feasible for most people during the war. In November 1939 Nora and John Lane returned from America on the last passenger liner out of New York, whither they had been to set-up a Penguin branch, to be managed by Ian and Betty Ballantine. Even Allen's travels became restricted. Yet, despite the ban, during what was known as the phoney war of late 1939 to early 1940, when little fighting took place, Allen and John contrived to go winter sporting in Switzerland. *En route*, they toured the Maginot Line in France, that idiotic defence system which ended abruptly at the border with Belgium, through which country Germany made its main attack. A.L. also got permission, as a businessman, to visit the United States in 1941 where Kurt Enoch (founder of Albatross Books) had joined the Ballantines. Why this journey was permitted at a time when America was not yet in the war and there was an embargo on transferring funds abroad is not clear, but for A.L., who hoped to be allowed to print over there, rules were made to be broken. He was also in contact with Canada, whose government commissioned Penguin to produce books for their servicemen, paying for them partly in kind with desperately needed paper. He contrived too in December 1944 to fly to South America, possibly on British Council business. There in Montevideo, Uruguay, at one of their offices, a young woman employee took pity on him and invited him home for Christmas dinner. She, Tanya Kent, of Anglo-Russian parentage, sought his advice on how she could get to study at LSE once the war had ended. They were to meet again.

The Penguins earmarked for the armed services were the result of a scheme worked out by A.L. and W.E.W. who cheekily proposed to the War Office that titles for the Forces Book Club should be exclusively from their list and supplied by them at fivepence per copy. Their argument was that as they already held the paperback rights this would obviate the need to deal with many different publishers. They were printed on paper which was additional to Penguin's quota but A.L. withdrew from the scheme when sales fell far short of the expected 70,000 per title. Even so the arrangement was, understandably, resented by some established competitors who in retaliation formed the British Publishers Guild, mostly for fiction titles aimed at the armed-services market. The latter made-up a large proportion of the readership of *Penguin New Writing*, a monthly (later quarterly) magazine edited by John Lehmann, a publisher working with Leonard and

Virginia Woolf. The first number appeared in late 1940. It sold approaching 100,000 copies per issue and was widely read on all battlefronts by servicemen eager for intellectual stimulation. Much later its success led to *New Biology*, *Science News*, *Film Review* and *Music Magazine*, diversifications which were both time and paper consuming. Bill Williams in order to keep the main objective of Penguin Books on course had to dissuade A.L. from entering the journals market even more positively.

Penguins, and more particularly Pelicans, became popular educators partly thanks to the way in which the new, cheap series captured the public imagination. They were successful not only because they were cheap but because they appealed to a public which wished to better itself and to own books. Despite what he had told his apprentice, Lane did aim at a mass market and I belonged to it. I was one of millions to whom the Penguin – Pelican experience became a vital element of both secondary and tertiary education.

Like Mr Arnold in the thirties, I felt a compulsion to own books. As a schoolboy, on a shilling a week pocket money, this was just possible thanks to 6d. Penguins. In August 1940 I was thirteen. France had fallen. The Battle of Britain was raging over South-East England where I lived. Stanley Unwin and J.B. Priestley, supported by numerous publishers and authors, were fighting a threatened tax on books; my parents, with Drake-like phlegm, drove from our home near Tunbridge Wells for their annual fortnight's holiday at Bournemouth taking me, their youngest, with them (their eldest had recently returned from Dunkirk). The Germans were expected to invade at any moment. At Bournemouth I watched army engineers blowing out sections of the piers to make it more difficult for the enemy to land, but more of my attention was given to the *Penguin Political Dictionary* from which, along with another from the same stable, *Europe since Versailles* (cartoons by David Low), I learned much about contemporary affairs. Later, the threat of invasion having receded, my interests turned to the drama – Shaw's *Pygmalion*, illustrated by Feliks Topolski, a volume of Chekhov plays, then regarded as way-out and arty – and to Eric Linklater's *Poets' Pub*, with which I solaced myself while my parents slept through air raids. All were Penguins. There were also the Pelicans – *Lives of the Great Composers*, Roger Manvell's *Film*, Ronald Rubinstein's *John Citizen and the Law*, dedicated to all who read it in its entirety – I'm not sure I did.

The fame of Penguin spread as rapidly as the war. The best-selling titles during the early years of conflict were R.A. Savile-Sneath's books on aircraft recognition which, though hardly literary, were important as popular education. Many more series made their first appearance during the actual years of conflict – King Penguins, Editions Penguin, Handbooks, Modern Painters, Reference Books and both Puffin Story and Puffin Picture Books for children. The go-ahead for Picture Books, during one of the bleakest years of the war, surprised Noel Carrington, an editor at *Country Life*, who having devised them in 1938 supposed they would be shelved for the duration. A.L. was hugely enthusiastic about them, writing to him, '… evacuated children are going to need books more than ever, especially your kind on farming and natural history'. Eleanor Graham, former librarian and bookseller, received similar enouragement for the story books.

The Penguin Classics were still to come; in the blackout, on fire-watching duty, Dr E.V. Rieu, sometime managing director of Methuen, publishers, continued his self-imposed task of translating Homer. He it was who introduced Nikolaus Pevsner to Allen. Pevsner, a refugee from Hitler's Germany, and an authority on architecture and design, became editor of King Penguins after his predecessor had been killed in an air raid. A.L. took great pride in this series which was based on the German imprint Insel Books. They contributed a small area of excellence within the austerity of wartime production. Pevsner had a strong though benign influence on A.L. Their association was lasting and led indirectly, after the war, to Penguin employing Nikolaus's son Dieter.

Pelicans became the particular province of Alan Glover, who in the First World War, whilst imprisoned as a conscientious objector, had taught himself Latin, Greek, Russian and Sanskrit. On release he worked in a circus where he became heavily tattooed, made translations of medieval poetry and later became an editor at *Reader's Digest*. One colleague, Isabel Quigly, described him as wearing 'dark shirt, heavy tweed jacket, woolly tie, thick specs, and grey cotton mittens'. Another, Tanya Kent, said that for her he was 'the genius, the centre of Penguin Books … rather nice but awfully cynical … full of strange oriental beliefs [and] completely tattooed all over [though] he has had it scraped off his cheeks'. A third, Jack Morpurgo, called him 'an unsung hero of the Penguin story' whose scholarship was unbacked by a degree. His status was not clarified. He joined in 1944 at £650 p.a. A.L. invited him because he had been a persistent correspondent who, good-naturedly, pointed out errors in publications and who had 'a retentive and encyclopaedic memory'.

The Penguin organisation had been thrown into disarray when the Ministry of Aircraft Production requisitioned the new Harmondsworth premises, after which a warehouse was found at nearby West Drayton and the offices were moved into Silverbeck, Allen's home. In 1942, A.L. married Lettice Orr who had studied under Gertrude Williams (W.E.W's wife) at the LSE. Her presence was resented by his brothers when they were on leave from the navy. They were unused to sharing a home with a married brother and his pregnant wife who, according to A.L.'s second biographer, Jeremy Lewis, was maintaining an affaire with a Cambridge don.

At the start of this new era of his life, when the war was beginning to turn in favour of the Allies, Allen and John bought a farm, near Reading. John was not destined to enjoy it because, in November 1942, he went down with his torpedoed ship. His death had a profound effect on Allen whose relationship with Richard thereby suffered. John had borne a physical resemblance to Allen and usually shown the deference then demanded in a close-knit family from the youngest. J.E. Morpurgo, who was to become colleague, friend and biographer, wrote that John '… was a superb lieutenant, far better equipped than Allen to handle the minutiae of Penguin operations … had stamina, zeal for detail and overseas contacts … [and was] inclined to resent his subordinate role'. Following John's death, so Morpurgo surmised, the 'calm grief of Dick, who had shared the same risks, contrasted with the overt, almost hysterical show of Allen', who, as the brother permitted by law to remain a civilian and carry on the business, felt guilty. Morpurgo further suggested that A.L. felt that Dick's response to John's death was callous, thus opening a permanent breach between the surviving brothers. But it should be remembered that he knew none of them until after the war and expressed this view at a time when he had an axe to grind.

In the wake of Labour's sweeping majority at the 1945 election, the incoming head of government, Clement Attlee, was alleged to have commented that his 'road to Downing Street had been paved with Penguin Specials'. Those words do not go convincingly with one who was the dourest, least charismatic and possibly the most honest of all prime ministers and Morpurgo also notes that Bill Williams reported the same politician as giving similar credit to the Army Bureau of Current Affairs and the Workers' Education Association. Whatever the truth, the Second World War, notwithstanding the personal tragedy of John Lane's death, was a good thing for Penguin Books. The Specials had helped to provide almost adequate paper supplies until the quota was cut, and the actual war prevented effective competition in the UK and the Commonwealth for six crucial years of rapid growth.

The war ended in August 1945. Since September 1939, with a staff of just 40, Penguin had published 700 titles, half of them original. It had become a household name, synonymous with 'paperback'. Nor, by the end

of the century, had any other paperback imprint ranged as deeply and widely
into all realms of literature, from verse to cookery.

In January 1946 came the first of an enduring and commercially tri-
umphant series, Penguin Classics – Rieu's translation of *The Odyssey*. A.L.
was told he had blundered. There were numerous current editions of
Homer; who would want a new one? By the late 1970s it had sold more
than two million copies.

Also in 1946 there was a major promotion to honour Bernard Shaw on
his ninetieth birthday. One million copies of ten titles (two already on the
list) were printed. They sold out in six weeks. On publication morning
there were queues at London bookshops. One title, *The Black Girl in Search
of God*, raised a problem. It was banned in the Republic of Ireland. Every
parcel sent there had to be opened and reduced to nine titles only.

Two years later A.L. concluded a significant agreement with Chatto and
Windus, Faber & Faber, Hamish Hamilton, Michael Joseph and William
Heinemann to have first call on paperback rights in their books, and to issue
them under a joint imprint. He was conscious, years ahead of its actually
happening, that if these publishers inaugurated their own softback lists his
most important source of reprints would be threatened.

Financially less rewarding than Classics but immensely prestigious were
The Buildings of England and The Pelican History of Art and Architecture,
the brain children of Nikolaus Pevsner, who was given carte blanche to edit
them. Neither series made money. Pevsner, who received little payment for
them, was content, and said of A.L., 'I have never seen him put finance first
and the quality of a man or a book second.' Lane made Penguin afford
them because he had a philosophy of swings and roundabouts; Pevsner's
series were paid for out of the profits from bestsellers, one of which was the
same author's *An Outline of European Architecture* for Pelican. (In fact, in later
years, the Buildings of England was subsidised by grants from the
Leverhulme Trust and other foundations.)

Once the world was relatively at peace, Allen set about, in Morpurgo's
words, 'founding Penguin all over again'. Despite the high percentage of
exports, the Penguin base was still firmly in London and it was an essentially British company. Pan Books began in 1947; other successful series of
paperbacks would follow but Penguin always had the lead. To maintain this
it needed a more commanding, worldwide presentation than its rivals and
more senior staff in all departments. The quality of Penguin top people was
a matter to which A.L. paid much attention in his own haphazard style. He
did not believe in job descriptions and on the whole it was better not to
have had previous experience at whatever position was deemed suitable for

you. He looked for versatility before expertise, deftness and opportunism appealed to him more than a commonsensible, dogged capacity for planning, and he liked to find an element of friction among his subordinates, this being desirable because it 'struck off sparks', so he told a bookseller. He tended to engage superfluous staff because among them he hoped to find a few who would be his natural collaborators.

While still in uniform and working at the War Office, J. E .Morpurgo was recruited to be Penguin's first, and only (during the founder's reign), public relations officer. His terms of reference were typically vague. The climate under which all employees were required to turn their hands to whatever task needed to be done still prevailed; giving people titles might convey the wrong message and herald the formation of lines of demarcation. (The first person actually permitted to name himself sales manager was Harry Paroissien, in 1947.) Jack, who had been a contributor to *Penguin New Writing*, later joined the permanent staff. He found Allen had charm, flair, was intolerant of routine, loved book-trade gossip and was a benevolent dictator who was always approachable. All members of staff knew one another but there was a small, informal group, of which Morpurgo became a member, who met 'to discuss the most important and most interesting plans' at Silverbeck, in a bar or 'frequently at lunch in the Blue Diamond, the greasy spoon next to the Penguin building'.

The inner group included Tanya Kent, from Montevideo, whom Allen had contrived to have flown first to New York then to Halifax (in Canada). There she boarded a troop ship on which she met an army officer returning from years as a POW in Japan. This man had edited short stories for Penguin and must, I think, have been Alan Steele (see Postscript).

From the week of her arrival in Britain, in November 1945, Tanya Kent kept copies of letters sent regularly to her mother in Uruguay. Penguin was in process of reclaiming its premises at Harmondsworth from the RAF. A.L., after meeting her train, took her there, then on to Silverbeck where she was at first accommodated. '… If you want to have a picture of Allen Lane at home, as likely as not you would find him scrubbing out the larder or cleaning out the tool cupboard … ' She was taken to Priory Farm where she helped the brothers Lane cut ivy from trees with saw, axe and billhook. Mostly she worked in the Penguin office attempting to keep A.L.'s correspondence up to date. She was taken to a farewell, dress dinner for Woolworths' Clifford Prescott, she became a kind of chairwoman of the editorial board which produced *Penguin Science News*, lunched with authors and with the editor of *The Bookseller*, Edmond Segrave (ever a strong supporter of A.L.), attended Pelican meetings and ensured that writers signed copies of their books for her employer's unique collection of first-edition Penguins. At Silverbeck she read poetry and took dictation from her boss while he was having his hair cut; she was very much a maid of all work, earning £6.00 per week. The Uruguayan Embassy offered her an important and presumably better paid job as an attaché. She turned it down because she loved being at Harmondsworth. Her letters are an incomparable record of what it was like to be working with A.L. at that time, a time when, because he wished to attend the Nuremberg Trials of Nazi war criminals, he used his long-lapsed commission in the Territorial Army as the means of gaining admission, being made up to temporary brigadier for the purpose. They also reveal how she met and married Hans Schmoller, a future production director at Penguin. Her aspirations to study at the LSE lapsed. The Allen Lane she knew was always 'neat and spruce to the point of elegance', smartly, though quietly, dressed, clean-shaven and short-haired. He was of medium height, had blue eyes, a ready smile and a roundish face. All who knew him commented on his attentive response to other people. Williams wrote, 'He had a listening face – he never pretended'; Hans Schmoller agreed about the capacity for listening but added, 'though not for too long at a stretch'.

Most staff, Tanya remembered, addressed the King Penguin as 'A.L.'; he called her 'T.K.' (initials were in general use within the company). Eunice Frost called him 'Allen'. Editorial meetings, when held at Silverbeck, were quite unscheduled. Those attending them might suddenly be on a boat in the stream which ran through the grounds. Appointments already arranged at Harmondsworth were not kept. This made life tiresome for Eunice Frost who, says Tanya, 'practically ran the place'. For her part 'Frosty', as she was known to some staff, found Allen powerfully possessive, interested in everything down to the smallest detail and 'available to anyone from any department who wanted to see him'. He knew everyone by name. The only time she saw him uncalm and unconfident was when his brother John was drowned. 'I am convinced that much would have been different had he been able to remain Allen's shrewd collaborator.'

One editor in the late 1940s, David Herbert, observed that 'the Lanes did not distinguish between highbrow and lowbrow but between good and mediocre'. Margaret Clark, secretary and editor, described A.L. in his office in the early 1950s as 'working impulsively and restlessly, walking up and down, looking out of the window, biting his nails ... dictating in fits and starts, much of his negotiation being done on the telephone ... '

A.L. was reluctant to banish the element of individual authority which had allowed him to indulge Nikolaus Pevsner's wishes as well as his own.

He was always ready to innovate; new projects kept the adrenalin high. He was, after all, the man who, at the height of the blitz in 1940–1, had introduced Puffins and *Penguin New Writing* and who was to sanction Editions Penguin, a South American series, an Egyptian series, a West African series, an Italian series (only one title), music scores (though not for long), Penguin Modern Painters (a noble venture dropped when its editor, Sir Kenneth Clark, lost interest, though briefly revived in the late fifties), Penguin Prints, Handbooks on subjects such as cookery, and much else, while all the time the core lists of Penguins and Pelicans, each with many sub-divisions, grew. He was not yet fifty years old; the reins were still firmly in his hands but the list had grown so large and varied that some departmentalism became essential.

Morpurgo found that as PR man dealing with the press and the BBC, he also had to edit and write the occasional *Penguins Progress*, a publicity pamphlet, and to start what was virtually a book club for direct sales. He was rebuked by A.L. for making Penguin the generic word for paperback – '… because of you every sleazy production published by shoddy publishers in Warrington is called Penguin'. (Why Warrington?) None the less, he survived and when A.L. needed someone to go to Paris or Benelux Jack would be sent because he had a Dutch grandmother and was supposedly fluent in most European tongues. When he was invited to give lectures in the USA, Allen urged acceptance so that he could unload on him various duties necessary at Penguin in New York.

At an editorial meeting when A.L. showed dangerous signs of boredom Morpurgo was landed with Musical Scores, about which he knew nothing. He also related how he came to edit the Pelican histories. One day, he was unexpectedly informed by Bill Williams that it was thought he should move on and return to the company when he had gathered more experience; on the next day, A.L. came to his office, sat on the edge of the desk and said, 'You are always nagging about the lack of history titles. Go out and get us a History of England.' But, Lane insisted, each volume in the series must be written by a youngster who would become a GOM (Grand Old Man) in thirty years' time. That was the only briefing Jack received for the immensely successful sub-series which he edited for decades and which was frequently used by schools; invading the classroom (along with other titles), it made numerous old-fashioned textbooks redundant. 'The casual nature of Penguin planning,' wrote J.E.M., meant 'without question that the invasion was accidental.'

Boris Ford had a not dissimilar experience in becoming editor of The Pelican Guide to English Literature. He was invited by Bill Williams to outline a proposal. When it was handed over W.E.W. asked if Ford would let him submit it as his own idea. Ford demurred until he was informed that A.L. worked on the principle of accepting ideas from one person but commissioning the actual book or series from another. Ford was chosen and was paid £100–£150 per volume. It is interesting that Alan Glover does not seem to have played any part in the creation of these two important Pelican series. (I heard the Musical Scores story from Jack Morpurgo himself; Jeremy Lewis, in his life of Allen, says that Gordon Jacob, who came to edit them, claimed he suggested the series.)

Among those who returned to Harmondsworth after WWII was a former driver, Ronald Blass. He presented himself to the company secretary who told him that by law he was entitled to claim work and offered a wage of £4. 15s. 0d per week. Blass turned this down. As he was leaving the premises he met Allen Lane cycling in. (Petrol was still rationed; anyway he enjoyed cycling.) They exchanged greetings and Blass told him why he'd rejected re-employment. 'We'll see about that,' said Lane. Next morning Blass received a letter offering him £5.0.0 per week. The reason he accepted this meagre increase, he told me, was '… I thought dear Allen Lane was a sort of cheeky individual … and I might as well see what Penguins was all about now the war was over.' Nearly forty years later Ron died in office, as deputy managing director. One reason why his head didn't fall along with others is that he was less educated and literary than Lane, whom he didn't make feel culturally or intellectually inferior. Ron became a successful salesman and, unlike some of his senior colleagues, learned how not to tread on the wrong toes.

Even before wartime economy restrictions were relaxed, thanks to the work of designers Jan Tschichold and Hans Schmoller, Penguin production returned to its earlier simple elegance. In 1947, at all but twenty-four hours' notice, A.L. recruited Tshichold on the recommendation of the eminent typographer Oliver Simon. Despite the fact that Tshichold was German, though living in Switzerland, all the regulations regarding employment of aliens were waived and he soon arrived at Harmondsworth, at a salary greater than those of A.L. and his brother's put together. (Although presumably the Lanes had dividends and expenses.) He was introduced to a new warehouse which, against government advice, had been designed to ignore the austerity imposed through shortage of materials. It was 'both efficient and aesthetically satisfying', in keeping with Ralph Tubbs's original front-office building. Schmoller, who had not then joined the company, noted in his *DNB* tribute that 'Good design came high on his [A.L.'s] list of priorities in all things'; as did his appreciation of the visual arts generally.

This was instanced in his enthusiasm for Penguin Modern Painters. Some of those featured in that series – John Piper was one – had their work hung on the office walls at Harmondsworth. A visiting bookseller from South Africa expressed astonishment at seeing one in the typing pool. 'Where else should it be?' demanded the owner, implying that typists had as much right as anyone else to be exposed to fine art. Was he not, after all, a popular educator? (He was also a collector. Artists featured in the series were paid £100 but expected, so Lewis relates, to donate an original work to the King Penguin personally.)

The men and women at, or near the top of post-war Penguin were later portrayed in a painting commissioned from Rodrigo Moynihan. They are shown 'Leaving the meeting', posed in small groups or rapt in thought. In fact each person was painted separately wherever it was convenient for them or the artist to be. The setting is depicted as a room at the Royal College of Art, where meetings were never held. Jack Morpurgo makes amused comment on its phoniness, observing that A.L. wanted to be seen by posterity in the company of the distinguished colleagues he had gathered around him. (Was this a fault?) There was also a sentimental side to him which he indulged when choosing as Penguin 1000 Edward Young's *One of Our Submarines is Missing*. He disliked war books (Pan Books, astutely, saw a gap there and made them a speciality of their list), but because the author had drawn the first Penguin logos, and perhaps as a roundabout tribute to brother John, he gave this one honourable status. It illustrates a side of his character which helped sustain the affection in which he was held by most of those who worked for him.

From 1945 Lane was anxious to move ahead in Australia and the United States, although curiously tepid, on the whole, to 'colonising' Africa, possibly due to his dislike of apartheid in the Commonwealth parts of the south. Within ten years, according to W.E.W., half the total sales were in export, and A.L. had enthusiastically re-embarked on his travels, going annually to the States and, in most years, taking six to eight trips to Europe, often holidaying in Spain (where he bought property), Australia and elsewhere. He cycled too, going with Harry Paroissien to Normandy where they spent little on hotel accommodation and much more on wining and dining, which John Hitchin, another long-term employee, said reflected 'the Penguin approach to expenses for staff'. And he did actually visit South Africa where Philip Joseph, then a bookseller in Johannesburg, recalls him as being very dogmatic, uncaring and indifferent to his (Joseph's) staff. Penguin also had a brief flirtation with West Africa which attracted many

British publishers (see Alan Hill), but a series begun in 1953 soon fizzled out.

In the US, Penguin Books Inc (established in 1939 and dissolved in 1950) based in New York lost its key figures, Ian Ballantine, Kurt Enoch and Victor Weybright. The last named became known to A.L. during the war when he worked at the American Embassy in London. He was sent to New York to take over from Enoch, who resented the intrusion. Then, in the winter of 1945–6, A.L. dispatched his brother Richard to close down the American branch unless a way could be found to make Weybright conform to the Penguin image as Allen saw it. Weybright was asked not to inform Enoch of what was proposed, an admonition he rejected. Richard Lane would seem to have had little heart for his mission. He did not quarrel with Weybright and returned home leaving matters much as they were. Later Weybright and Enoch sank their differences and developed the New American Library, according to national requirements, becoming interested in mass-market titles with garish, full-colour covers such as Lane detested. There was a parting of the ways and a new Penguin subsidiary, managed by Harry Paroissien, was founded in Baltimore, in 1949. This satellite projected a quality image of books, staid by American standards. Paroissien, 'a loyal and unthreatening deputy', captured what Morpurgo named 'a sizeable if specialised segment of the paperback market'. He became as close to being autonomous as was possible with A.L. and referred to the benefits of 'the 3000 mile wide pond' which lay between them.

The problem with America and Australia, which he tended to think of as colonies, was that Allen wished for expansion in both but liked to ignore the fact that the company he had created could not be run by one man alone. He was reluctant to lose control of his empire and found it difficult to accept the fact that he couldn't be in three places thousands of miles apart on the same day.

Australia was at first looked after by R.W. Maynard, who had been an invoice clerk in the crypt at Holy Trinity Church before taking charge of wartime production. In 1946 Allen dispatched him down under with few resources. He hadn't even a car until one was sent out from England. This was a mixed blessing because he was based in Melbourne and Allen expected Maynard to meet him at Fremantle (thousands of miles west) to offer him a lift. Maynard successfully launched the subsidiary company in 1950 only to be cast out later in favour of Richard Lane when the brothers found it difficult to work on the same continent. Richard, although effectively removed from the centre of power, became reconciled to his new status when he met and married an Australian. Indigenous publishing, suited to a different environment from Britain's, began much later and led, as in America, to friction with Harmondsworth.

Although intent on remaining in charge of Penguin worldwide, A.L. devoted as much time as could be spared to farming. At the start he knew little about it but learned quickly and in a few years Priory Farm, near Reading, paid its way. It whetted his appetite; it made him confident. So he bought another farm in Hampshire. A basic need was being fulfilled; to be nationally recognised as a popular educator was not enough.

He seems to have been at least as attentive to his farm as to his family. A.L.'s enduring notion of a perfect daughter, so Morpurgo reported, was that she be decorative, perhaps a little flighty and, when he chose or had the time to gossip, ready to join him in a cheerful conspiracy against the world at large. His girls were not apparently seen by him as his natural successors (in his lifetime few women had top publishing jobs) but he toyed with the notion of having sons-in-law who might change their name to Lane. When Clare, the eldest daughter, was eight A.L. bought her a copy of *The Times* and told her she could never be expected to qualify for a significant career if she didn't read that newspaper. When she was eighteen he took her on a world tour. In Australia, she refused invitations to parties which, said A.L., she owed it to the firm to attend; later she criticised his treatment of senior Australian staff and was told it was none of her business.

When they were small, A.L. paid little attention to his children. Lettice took charge of their education. By the time Christine was at secondary level, the Lanes were at least semi-separated so A.L. reappeared on the scene and sent her to the North London Collegiate. Until he was knighted in 1952, Clare was said to have had no idea her father was a public personality. As they grew older, Morpurgo noted, Clare and Christine 'became his confidantes and cronies; with them he was as impulsive, mercurial and on/off as in his professional life ... warm, spontaneous, vivid in one mood; nonexistent or fugitive in another'. To their younger sister, Anna, who had been born with Down's syndrome, he showed 'tenderness, patience and protectiveness such as he seldom, if ever, revealed to any other'. The marriage lasted formally until his death but, although they never ceased keeping in close touch, after Anna's birth between A.L. and Lettice there wasn't any real chance they would find serenity in each other's company. There was a year when they went together to the Frankfurt Book Fair to meet a German book-trade couple, Ledwig Rowohlt and Susanne Lepsius, and swapped partners on leaving. Lettice had an affaire with Rowohlt; Allen installed Susanne at Whitehall Court, his Westminster apartment. Strangely, this extra-marital relationship did not give rise to much gossip even though, when answering invitations for two, A.L. did not always make it clear which lady he would be bringing with him. He was said to have consulted an astrologer and a graphologst before forming the relationship with Susanne. (According to Lewis the partner-swapping took place not at Frankfurt but after a weekend at Silverbeck.) At the end of Allen's life the Lanes were together again.

The 1950s brought more expansion, with Penguin staying comfortably ahead of its competitors except in fiction. Eunice Frost was becoming out of touch with current trends, especially those of American origin, and new paperback imprints were featuring titles which would once have been obvious orange-covered Penguin novels. Then, in non-fiction, Collins's Fontana list began to spread into philosophy, religion, adventure and other areas. The development foreseen by A.L. was imminent, with original publishers, once eager to sell rights, spawning their own paperbacks, Faber, strong in fiction and poetry and with a formidable backlist, prominent among them. American imprints, university presses mainly, introduced more erudite and expensive 'egg-head' softbacks at an academic level which were some threat to Pelicans, but in all categories there were still benefits for originating pub-lishers as well as authors when paperback rights were sold, with both the investment and the risk spread. What could have been a crisis for A.L.'s birds was no more than a market trend, but there was a lurking danger of Penguin resting on its laurels.

Although, since 1937, headquarters had been on or near the Great West Road, a presence had usually been maintained in Central London. Bill Williams provided a room, courtesy of his official employers, A.L. had an apartment in Westminster and, at various times, actual, editorial premises were rented for the convenience of authors, literary agents and other pub-lishers. Eunice Frost, although it hastened her own retirement, convinced A.L. that he must recruit a new generation of editors.

When I first encountered Allen, at a Society of Bookmen dinner in December 1958, it was my first meeting as a member. He was a guest. I was impressed by the attention he paid me. Whenever I mentioned a current book enthusiastically he noted its title on a scrap of paper. This would cer-tainly have appeared on an editor's desk next morning.

The desk might have been that of Tom Maschler, the whizz-kid editor (for another imprint) of *Declaration*, a controversial symposium mostly writ-ten by 'angry young men'. He came to Penguin with an instinctive under-standing of what was needed, and a genuine publisher's nose for trends in fiction and drama. Other newcomers of that era were John Curtis, Dieter Pevsner, Tony Richardson, Richard Newnham and Jill Norman. They were based in premises near Portman Square but were not totally detached from the main premises in Harmondsworth where Glover and some others remained because they were required, in the best Penguin tradition, to learn the whole job from picking orders on the floor of the warehouse to spending a spell in production and going out with reps. When Dieter started, in 1958, he was allocated to Glover to deal with history, psychology, architecture, social sciences, etc., and found himself working at both addresses. He learned on the job; Glover was a superb teacher.

In 1955 A.L. had appointed Bruce Hepburn, secretary of the Booksellers' Association, to become his sales director commanding an enlarged team of reps. This was a shrewd move because Hepburn was well known and liked on both sides of the trade. He lasted for several years, with a minimum of acrimony, before moving on to Longmans. John Hitchin, also recruited in the 1950s, survived for three decades. He was initially placed in charge of exhibitions and made mobile by being awarded A.L.'s second car, an ancient Morris convertible. To carry the necessary equipment he was forced to drive with the roof open in all weathers. Over the years the various roles within Penguin undertaken by John took him to 56 countries; one trip to West Germany was almost his undoing. Traditionally, A.L. had hosted his entire workforce on weekend breaks to Paris, Le Touquet or wherever his whim dictated. When, in the sixties, John (by then in publicity) helped to organise a large party of the sales force to convey booksellers at vast expense to Berlin to promote a Len Deighton novel, Allen took exception and threatened him with dismissal. This was averted by Chris Dolley, a new favourite, who pleaded for John's services in helping to launch Penguin Education. As educational marketing manager, Hitchin was invited to dinner at the Old Mill House, West Drayton, whither A.L. had moved from Silverbeck. There, beside the River Colne, they talked about the schools scene over shepherd's pie, Lane's favourite dish, and a bottle of claret. John, who once admitted to me that keeping a low profile had helped him to survive at Harmondsworth, was happier when catching only glimpses of A.L. at a distance, 'as a rather distinguished back view, in the queue for lunch at the Penguin canteen'. This reflects A.L.'s tendency to pit staff against staff. He confided in bookseller John Prime that 'one of the secrets of management is always to have a certain degree of tension at the top'.

This characteristic led to the writing of an undated and unsigned memo I saw in the Bristol Archive (see Sources). It was written, Morpurgo thought, by Glover but Dieter Pevsner believes this highly improbable. In it the attitude of senior staff to junior is analysed:

> We have three people in the front offices, I myself may be a fourth, who all in their respective ways, have unusually strong personalities; who all have an 'urge for power'; who none of them happen to be very tactful or psychologically penetrating in their methods of dealing with other people, particularly their subordinates, and who are all ... jealous of the people who work with them knowing too much or taking on too much responsibility.

That is devastating in itself as an analysis of top management. Then follows:

> You have got such an overwhelmingly definite personality yourself that they have set you up as a model, as it were without being at all like you.

There seems to have been no reply from A.L.

Following the Shaw ten and the H.G. Wells ten, in 1946, other authors had received similar promotions, D.H. Lawrence amongst them. Lawrence was given a further five when A.L. took the decision to issue the unexpurgated *Lady Chatterley's Lover* in 1960. The complete version had never been published in Britain. After the acquittal of publisher Fred Warburg in a prosecution under the Obscene Publications Act there was a strong feeling in the country that it was time for a rationalisation of the law. A.L. had behind him the record of publishing *Ulysses* before the war. *Lady Chatterley*, along with *The Memoirs of Fanny Hill*, was regarded as one of the most famous of 'dirty' books because of its scenes of explicit sex. The edition printed in Florence in the 1920s was a collector's item.

It was decided to include *Lady Chatterley* in the Lawrence batch but which edition was not specified. John Curtis related in an article nearly forty years on that he enquired at an editorial meeting which text they were to publish, knowing that the full version was currently on sale in the United States. This put A.L., who, Curtis says, had been unaware of this, on his mettle. Lane instantly decided Penguin must follow suit but rather than risk having a bookseller customer prosecuted for selling it he said, in announcing his intention, the onus should be on the publisher. So copies were delivered to the police – a task, according to Morpurgo, assigned to Hans Schmoller, placing him, at least theoretically, in the firing line rather than

A.L., who by then was holidaying in Spain. Subsequently the police called at Harmondsworth to deliver the summons and it became Ron Blass's turn to be temporary King Penguin.

It was at a party in my Hampstead bookshop that a North Country customer of mine confronted A.L. about *Lady Chatterley*, which he had already announced his intention of publishing. 'I wouldn't mind,' she told him, 'if it weren't for the boogery.'

'Is there buggery in it?'

'Oh yes.'

His eyes twinkled. 'I must read it again.'

In court the prosecution made great play with insinuations about sodomy without ever naming it; it also made itself ridiculous by asking the members of the jury if they would allow their maidservants to read the book. This led to a brief letter to the *Observer* enquiring, 'Would you let your gamekeeper read it?' Some believe the verdict would have gone against Penguin had the jury understood that sodomy was involved, a point mischievously raised after the trial by learned contributors to the magazine *Encounter*.

The case provoked wide publicity. The 'Book Trade Lawyers', Rubinstein, Nash & Co., were engaged by Penguin (Ronald Rubinstein had written the Pelican *John Citizen and the Law*; his nephew Michael handled the case). Authors, teachers, lecturers were marshalled to testify to the book's literary merits; the prosecution relied on vague moral assertions and was singularly inept. Penguin won a famous case.

The daily proceedings at the Old Bailey were transcribed for the defence. Dieter Pevsner then took them, of an evening, to a railway station in Surrey to meet the writer C.H. Rolph who absorbed them into a book (*The Trial of Lady Chatterley*) which Allen sent to his friends and customers for Christmas. (Pevsner recalled how this task fell to him because he happened to be the first person A.L. encountered in a corridor as the two left their offices. 'You be the control man,' said A.L., detailing him to consult Michael Rubinstein.)

Following the verdict, tens of thousands of copies of *Lady Chatterley's Lover* were swiftly produced by several printers to meet a huge demand coming partly from a public unaccustomed to dealing with booksellers. Lorry drivers left the engines of their vehicles running as they ran into shops, clutching three shillings and sixpence in coins. At mine, customers did not have to ask for what they wanted. The only words heard were from assistants, saying, 'Thank you,' as they took the cash. We set up an extra till to cope with the demand.

Soon after the Chatterley trial Penguin, easily absorbing the legal costs of the case which were not awarded to them, was floated as a public company. The shares were massively over-subscribed. Allen kept a controlling interest through the family and a Trust. Richard Lane, rather meanly dealt with considering it was his £100 which had floated the company in the first instance, took what was offered and retired. (Allen had written to his brother, off-handedly, in Februrary 1961, 'If you are going to cease to run the firm in Australia at the end of the year, I think it might be as well if you come off the board before the Issue is made … ') The Lane Trust of 1964 provided back-dated pensions for staff at the same time as commemorating brother John.

In 1962, A.L. was involved in an abortive bid for Jonathan Cape Ltd, the eponymous founder of the company having died. He offered to back a takeover by three directors of Michael Joseph which the now also deceased founder had sold to newspaper tycoon Roy Thompson. It failed partly because the other main shareholders in Cape – the Howards, father and son – felt it would make their new young editorial director, Tom Maschler, vulnerable. (Tom, who had created the Penguin Modern Dramatists and brought many contemporary novelists to Harmondsworth, was not basically a reprint publisher and had displeased Lane by moving to Cape.)

Penguin Books was a member of the Publishers' Association although Allen Lane did not personally take part in the voluntary work expected of leading members. He was never on the council or any sub-committee. The increasingly prominent Ron Blass was deputed to play a role and Dieter Pevsner served on the PA's paperback sub-committee. Occasionally A.L. attended the annual Booksellers' Association Conference and for a while he was in the Society of Bookmen, until asked to resign for not attending sufficient meetings. (This happened to several distinguished publishers.) Yet he enjoyed a social life at the Garrick and threw parties at the slightest excuse at Whitehall Court, at the Arts Council headquarters in St James's Square and elsewhere. On these occasions he was liable, when he became bored, to leave while guests were still arriving. He visited bookshops a great deal during the celebratory years around 1960, when Penguin became twenty-five years old. He performed the opening ceremony at new bookshops or at those, such as mine, which found new premises. He was very consciously friendly to booksellers. When John Prime, master bookseller, bought his shop in King's Lynn in 1968 and asked for a Penguin opening he found himself dealing directly with A.L. who 'discussed even such details as shelves, flooring, lighting, with the knowledge and enthusiasm of one who understood how a bookshop really worked'. Prime added that, although ill, A.L. drove two hundred miles to proclaim the shop officially open.

A.L. had constantly troubled relations with his Australian subsidiary. He did not identify with the sub-continent as Alan Hill and Paul Hamlyn did. There was an occasion when he flew there with Bruce Hepburn to sort out problems. Nothing had been decided by the time they were due to fly home. Then, at the actual airport, to which they were accompanied by the three most senior local employees, all determined on a solution, A.L. allegedly said to the second-in-command, 'You're in,' to his superior and the other man, 'You're out ... and *I'm* off.' It's a good story and I certainly heard Bruce refer to 'the time we went to Australia and sacked everyone', but a variation on this episode was given me by Trevor Glover, one of Richard Lane's successors in the Antipodes. He maintains it was Ron Blass, not Hepburn, who on this occasion flew with Allen. After A.L. had made the much quoted comment they went on to New Zealand. *En route* Blass remonstrated with him: 'You can't leave things like that.' 'All right,' said A.L., 'you go back and sort it out.' Morpurgo's version does not feature either Hepburn or Blass at the airport. Dieter Pevsner believes there were two not dissimilar incidents; Penguin-Australia, it seems, always seethed with revolt and seemed to bring out the worst in Allen. Lewis does not commit himself but relates how Lane and Blass, returning on one occasion from down under, stopped off in East Africa to go on safari, driving intrepidly into jungle from which they were lucky to escape.

Another trip, in 1961, shows A.L. in a better light. Writing from Shiraz to the Schmollers about the extremes of poverty and wealth in Iran, he records that his hotel room cost him £2.50 a night, teachers were paid only £15 per month and 'workers' £6 per week. Penguin books were much in evidence but lecturers he met complained of supply difficulties. The comments were handwritten to Hans and Tanya as friends rather than colleagues.

One instance of competition which displeased A.L. was when New English Library (an offshoot of Victor Weybright's New American Library) brought out a rival Four Square Classics list claiming that this was an important cultural innovation. Allen was proud of Penguin Classics but felt it would savour of sour grapes if the company publicly responded to this inaccurate and unfair assertion. Instead Hans Schmoller, by then on the board, asked me to write a letter to *The Bookseller* making the point. I was happy to do so. Penguin was perfect to deal with at all levels, and in my thirty-two years trading in Hampstead it was always the largest single account, just as, for nearly twenty of those years, we were the leading Penguin stockist in North and North-West London. And among our huge-selling titles were not only the classics and literary novels but cookery manuals such as *Plat-du-Jour* and a Pelican entitled *Group Psychotherapy* which spoke directly to Hampstead. I was invited to address the Penguin sales force, with a car sent to convey me to and from Harmondsworth. It was driven by the head van-man who lamented that the firm had got too big; he yearned for the days when A.L. knew everyone and everyone knew him. He told me how A.L. had once sought to solve the problem of providing parking space for an ever increasing number of cars belonging to employees. When consulted, he promised to give it thought. Next morning he was seen riding into the drive on his beloved bicycle.

Things had not always been sweetness and light between myself and Penguin. In 1954, when I was the director in charge of a wholesale book-selling company which also had a retail shop in Bloomsbury I received a fiercely worded letter from Mr H. Paroissien in Baltimore complaining that we were supplying Penguins on which the American rights had been sold to shops in New York. If we continued to do so he would ensure that Harmondsworth ceased supplying our retail outlet. I submitted and, in con-sequence, lost my job. There were subsequent altercations in which I was involved, over my counter, with customers who used airports and who could not understand why a Penguin title available at, say, Heathrow, was not in our stock. This was because when United States Rights were sold the European and many other markets were open to all and it was legitimate for both UK and US editions to compete in them; Heathrow Bookstall was deemed to be outside our 'territorial waters' and therefore in Europe.

Less than ten years after my exchange with Paroissien, such had my status changed, that I was offered a job at Harmondsworth. A.L. rang one day to enquire if I would be attending a party they were giving that evening to mark the opening of a Penguin Bookshop, in Charing Cross Road. I scarcely had time to grab a glass of wine before he led me to a recess and invited me to join his sales department in what I took to be Bruce Hepburn's job. He didn't actually specify the position but told me Bruce was leaving and I knew that Paul Scherer, who went on to a most distinguished career else-where, wasn't in line for the sales directorship because Ron Blass already had his eye on it. I was flattered but rejected the job on the spot because I knew it wasn't for me. I would not have lasted three months. A.L. took the refusal without any argument.

It was surprising that I had the strength of mind to turn down A.L.'s offer because at the time I idolised him. Hero-worship is not good for the object of it and it can unbalance the person it afflicts. For me it came to a head in the early sixties when I invited Allen to lunch at Kettner's in Soho. We had a long, convivial meal, both of us seasoned topers and fluent conversationalists. I told him I would like to write his life. He took it on the chin, with an appreciative smile, and did not dismiss my proposal with the promptness I had his.

'I don't know what Bill Williams would say. I think he wants to do it.' Then, as though he had already come round to favour the idea, he remarked, 'You'd have to get in touch with Krishna Menon. I've heard he's ill. He was important at the start of Pelicans.' (By this time he was India's Defence Minister.) For the rest of the meal we talked round the subject and gossiped generally about Penguin and the book trade, agreeing how awful it was to be Stanley Unwin, not a favourite of A.L.'s. 'He never has a drink,' he exclaimed. No decision was made about 'the life' but I felt optimistic. Weeks, then months, went by and I heard nothing. In fact in the meetings I had with him after that, usually at parties, he never referred to it. I received my answer in a curious way through one of his farming friends. I met Ross Pearson, an official of, I think, the National Farm Workers' Union, in a Hampstead pub. Ross had encountered Allen while doing his duty by his members and calling on them at Priory Farm. This led to invitations to himself and his wife to stay at A.L.'s villa at Carjaval, near Malaga. Ross had Allen's ear so not wishing to write myself I asked him to sound out on the biography. He came back with the answer I expected but no reasons were given. (W.E.W. wrote that A.L. was in favour of 'a definitive history of Penguin' but not of a life. 'He realised that he was not the stuff of which biographies are made.' A strange judgement.)

In 1967, at another party in a Charing Cross Road bookshop, I told A.L. that Mavis and I were planning a holiday in the Dordogne. He gave me the address of his friend and author Philip Oyler, a farmer who had written a deeply felt account of tilling the soil of another country. 'It's a bad book,' said Allen, 'but he's a lovely person.' I don't know whether he had actually read it (John Hitchin thinks he had), but I found it an understanding, warm-hearted account of living and working in France, in no way a bad book. He meant it hadn't sold well. In fact most of the edition was subsequently pulped.

In 1958, Allen had been one of a consortium of publishers who bought the prestigious but ailing Oxford Street booksellers, J.&E. Bumpus, to save it from liquidation. They engaged, as managing director, the brightest book retailer in London, Tony Godwin, a man who claimed not to have passed any school exams, had been a field officer fighting in Germany in WWII and who had borrowed £5,000 to buy a small bookshop just down from Foyles in Charing Cross Road, renaming it Better Books. Tony dealt ruthlessly with Bumpus, moving it (disastrously, as it transpired) to Baker Street, then accepted Allen's invitation – some say on Tom Maschler's recommendation – to join the editorial staff at Harmondsworth. (Williams officially/unofficially retired in 1960.)

Tony had had no experience as a publisher, an author or a journalist. He was a typical Allen Lane appointment. At first he was an adviser, then he became fiction editor, finally chief editor, always, so he claimed, at the same salary he had been paid at Bumpus.

Godwin, surrounded by brilliant young editors eager for change, gave Penguin a face lift, a task which A.L. knew was essential but which he partly opposed. Tony brought in Kaye Webb as successor to Eleanor Graham at Puffins. He started Penguin Modern Classics (which some thought a misnomer) and Peregrines (egg-head volumes to compete with those produced by university presses on both sides of the Atlantic) and he took chances with young novelists such as David Storey and Robert Shaw. In temperament he was as difficult as A.L. He could be abrupt, surly, downright rude; he had no tact. His team worshipped him. In a jointly signed *Bookseller* obituary, Oliver Caldecott, Charles Clark and Dieter Pevsner, wrote, 'He drove us, with his enthusiasm and his daunting demands, to surpass our own expectations of ourselves ... insisting on standards, standards, and still higher standards ... nothing could be good enough but the very best.'

Under Godwin, Penguin Specials, so integral a feature of the company's early success, had a renaissance lasting almost a decade. The Cold War was at its height, so were negotiations for Britain's admission to the European Union; thirteen years of Tory rule were about to end. Tony and most of his editors leaned politically to the left, as did the King Penguin. Social consciences were worn high and proudly. In July 1962, Godwin wrote to Dieter Pevsner:

> What's happened to the *Common Sense about Smoking*? Do you realise that the longer you delay, the more people are going to die of cancer? I want it for January. Please.

(Correspondence about Specials and all aspects of Penguin publishing makes Steve Hare's *Penguin Portrait: Allen Lane and the Penguin Editors, 1935–1970*, one of the most compulsive reads in book-trade literature. It also provides evidence of how large a part A.L. played in dealing with authors without becoming an editor.)

One of Godwin's early achievements was to persuade Allen to accept partly illustrated covers. The decorous, tasteful appearance of the first Penguins and Pelicans had lasted until the fifties, despite tactful innovations from Hans Schmoller and John Curtis, and they were looking outmoded. A.L. remained against what he called 'bosoms and bottoms'; he didn't wish his books to resemble those of his rivals, but the pressure was on him.

Iain Brown, in the *Penguin Collector*, wrote that '... Lane enticed T.G. to work with him in revitalising the company ... Godwin resembled a whirl-wind, sweeping the company into a frenzy of excitement and creativity. Almost overnight the character of Penguin altered. He changed the face of the books, literally ... to A.L.'s dismay. In seven years he trebled the Penguin list, doubled the sales figures, nearly trebled the profits ... encouraged other outlets, exploited TV and film tie-ins ... was extravagant but discriminating about bold, aggressive advertising ... ' One facet of his brilliance, Brown noted, was helping authors hone and polish their work.

In my *Bookseller* obituary of Tony I asked how it was that the man who was a monument of tactlessness in bookselling circles, who for all his inventiveness and modernisation alienated so many of his fellow booksellers, and who did not even like serving customers on the floor of his shop, became a highly regarded publishing editor? Yet it was so, as verified to me by Margaret Drabble and other authors when Godwin had moved to Weidenfeld. David Farrer, of Secker & Warburg, who wrote a biography of his fellow publisher confirmed this – 'He was emphatically a great editor.'

Godwin was also involved with the setting-up of Allen Lane, The Penguin Press, an imprint devised for the purpose of publishing new hard-backs, thus attracting authors on whose books the parent company would have automatic first call for paperback rights. This was a shrewd move for the time. Its first offices were at 8 Vigo Street, where John Lane had started The Bodley Head. (Lady Lane unveiled a plaque to this effect in September 1985.)

It was Tony Godwin's policy to publish as much contemporary work as possible. He took on *Massacre*, a volume of cartoons by the French artist Sine. This was to be his downfall. A.L. thought the cartoons were obscene but appeared to accept the decision of the board, on which Godwin sat, to publish. Shortly after distribution of the book had already commenced, at dead of night, by arrangement with the chief warehouseman, Lane visited Harmondsworth and had the entire stock of Sine loaded onto a lorry and driven to Priory Farm. There it was destroyed.

Writing over thirty years later, it seems extraordinary to me that this incident was not more widely known or commented upon. The first ref-

erence I heard was in Robert Lusty's address at A.L.'s memorial service and
then the actual title was not mentioned. I don't recall stocking the book or
discussing it with my colleagues or anyone else. Una Dillon, of London's
eponymously named university bookshop, wrote regretfully to A.L. saying
that, although deeply opposed to censorship in principal, she was, for the
first time ever, not proposing to stock a Penguin title because she found it
blasphemous; Blackwells and other booksellers also objected, but Arthur
Crook, editor of the *TLS*, supported the Penguin board's decision.
Booksellers when asked to return copies apparently did so. They were then
on Harry Paroissien's instructions placed under lock and key and counted
daily. What subsequently happened to them, who knows? What is even
more singular is that Tony Godwin, about 1972, after he had left
Harmondsworth for good, in a long memo headed Allen Lane but sent to
Ron Blass, wrote that although the board had given the book its approval,
A.L. had dined with him for the purpose of getting his agreement to
destroy all copies of *Massacre*. In the same document he relates even more
bizarre incidents. A.L. had summoned Dieter Pevsner to his West Drayton
flat to say he had decided Tony must go. He then dined with Tony in Soho
and confirmed this decision, airily referring to 'in the next few months', but
not implementing it. Meanwhile he talked to friends at the Garrick about
'that shit Godwin', as a result of which there were rumours in the press.
Tony in the meantime went on working from Albany and Vigo Street on
the Penguin Press, until there was a further meeting, with Charles Clark,
director in charge of Penguin Education, present. (It was Clark who told
Jeremy Lewis that Godwin had 'the best uneducated mind' of anyone with
whom he had worked.) After lengthy arguments over compensation, a
press release was drafted and redrafted several times. It noted, wrote
Godwin, the 'incompatibilty between A.L. and myself'. After it had been
signed the three men sat quietly over a bottle of white wine for a quarter
of an hour.

Godwin had survived for nearly seven years. His colleagues (including
Charles Clark) signed a letter to *The Bookseller* proclaiming their faith in
Tony but Allen stood firm.

It was inevitable that the two should fall out but the irony was that
Godwin had precisely those qualities which had made Penguin. He was
innovative, demanding, impatient; he had vision. But he was not flippant
and complained that A.L. '... preferred mischievous jokes, anecdotes, gossip
... to serious, exploratory discussion ... ' Tony had no small talk and little
by way of social grace, except when he deliberately set-out to charm. He
was uninhibitedly direct, without guile or hypocrisy, carrying his editors and

authors with him. In his long memo to Blass he deplores A.L.'s 'ruthless public denigration of Harry (Paroissien) on both personal and professional levels'. He records dining one night with A.L. who '... became steadily drunker and drunker ... [and] began to talk about Harry and others ... [showing] ... terrifying rancorous contempt ... ' for his cronies. 'I never saw that tremendously disciplined public persona and iron control slip again except for his moments of panic over cash flow during my last year.'

Tony, thought by Morpurgo to be '... the right editor for the time ... volatile, charismatic, buccaneer ... ', made at the end of his sojourn an elementary mistake in trying to enlist the support of Ron Blass, who had no reason, or motive, for anything but total loyalty to Allen. Godwin left, went to Weidenfeld and ended his careeer with Harcourt Brace, in New York. There, he regularly lunched with John Hitchin, then in charge of Penguin, US, who regarded him as 'beside A.L. himself ... the most extraordinarily exciting person I've ever been lucky enough to work for ... infuriating but inspiring'. In the same city, Godwin met Paroissien who told him, 'Allen Lane: I truly loved that man.' Tony died in March 1976. (His notes to Blass, quoted above, are amongst the most fascinating documents in the Penguin Archive at Bristol University.)

Dieter Pevsner, one of those who signed the letter to *The Bookseller*, recalled that Tony cautioned them against sending it but no purge followed. Dieter had taken over Pelicans in the sixties when Glover retired and worked closely with both Lane and Godwin. When reviewing Morpurgo's book in *The Author*, he commented that although their relationship had ended in tears there had been a bonus side to it as well, although 'after the decline of the fifties' he thought Morpurgo had not recognised the achievements of the 1960s team which had given '... Penguin another renaissance which was at least as fruitful as its earlier peaks'. Few who helped to create it had been interviewed by him. D.P. maintained that all those who rejoiced in having been involved, including Godwin, looked directly to Lane. A.L. was inspired more by people than by ideas and could be totally supportive – 'once he decided it was a good trench to be in he stayed in it'. In the same review, Pevsner maintained that there were great editors and/or teams at all times, apart from a fallow period for contemporary fiction when Eunice Frost's star was waning.

Kaye Webb had first met A.L. on a health farm where she interviewed him for a magazine. She was a journalist, broadcaster and, with her estranged third husband, the cartoonist Ronald Searle, a publisher (Perpetua Books). She was also the daughter of journalists, and had as a girl sometimes written her mother's film criticisms for her. At twenty-one she found herself editor of *Caravan World* and *Sportscar*, then moved on to *Lilliput* and *Picture Post*. She was a professional who had had experience relevant to Puffin by once editing a magazine for children, the *Young Elizabethan*.

She was a jolly, large (she said, 'fat') earth mother of a woman, with a twin son and daughter. She cared passionately about children's literature. 'I choose,' she said, 'stories with pace and a strong moral sense though I try not to be prim. I don't think a little violence in a story does anyone any harm. Also I don't care a hoot if they (the children) don't understand all the words. Words give colour.'

When she took over Puffins, A.L. took immense interest suggesting, among others, the Professor Branestawm books. 'He used to beam with pleasure,' Kaye recalled, 'when there were parties on and everyone was looking happy ... it was marvellous going through the warehouse with him ... he'd know the names of the people ... and know about their families.' She also said that '... He was not devious or dishonest but if something unpleasant had to be done he avoided it ... ' She was a colleague with whom A.L. never quarrelled. He called her 'a great publisher', made her a director ('Frostie' having retired, she was the only woman at that time on the board) and obviously felt quite unthreatened personally by her presence in the firm. She embraced the entire readership of Puffins not only giving them exciting new authors but also befriending them through the Puffin Club with its incomparable, exuberant, informative and partly do-it-yourself magazine *Puffin Post*, which was sent free to all members. (In my household the children and adults fought to have first read of it.) The club enrolled one hundred thousand members in under ten years. When Kaye took a party of them on a trip to Lundy Island, A.L. said it was too far to go in one day and invited the kids to stop off and stay at Priory Farm where he gave them a barbecue.

Kaye brought many talented new writers into paperback – Joan Aiken, Clive King, Philippa Pearce, among them. I tried to persuade her to buy the rights in Richmal Crompton's William Brown stories, which three generations of my family had adored, but they didn't fit with her vision of Puffin. For her they were perhaps too class conscious, but millions found them funny, and still do. She supported authors and booksellers at promotional evenings in schools. I was fortunate in winning her friendship through devoting more space than was strictly economic to children's books. They occupied nearly one third of our floor and shelf space but contributed less than one sixth of turnover, not through any lack of volume sold but due to their relatively low prices. I shared Kaye's view that children were the readers and customers of the future so it was worth rejecting the 'sales-per-square-metre syndrome' in their favour.

While I was chairman of the Society of Bookmen, Kaye came out of a spell in hospital (she suffered from acute arthritis) to speak at one of the dinners. During the course of the evening she realised that we were a male-only institution. 'I wouldn't have come if I'd known,' she told me. I promised her that if during my term of office I didn't get the rules changed to admit women members I would resign. I didn't have to. The following year we admitted the first seven women members, including Kaye, who remained with us until her death in 1996. Dieter Pevsner or I would escort her home to Maida Vale after a dinner until she found it necessary to attend by taxi and in a wheel chair. She could by then eat little and was forbidden wine but she retained her interest in books and the trade and also something of the looks which had made her a strikingly handsome woman. Kaye and Tony Godwin contributed so much to Penguin; she also signed the letter to *The Bookseller* defending him.

During his last decade, A.L. was rightly concerned about the succession. One of those earliest tipped to take over was Jack Morpurgo who had left Penguin to become director of the National Book League, a body dedicated to spreading the reading habit particularly amongst the young, but always chronically short of funds. Morpurgo supposed himself to be a serious candidate but once when agreement seemed to him to be close there was a dispute on the trivial issue of whether or not he should have a company car. (A.L. was mean about cars; long before, Eunice Frost had resented the fact that one was not allocated to her.) The larger issue was resolved unhappily when Clare, Allen's eldest daughter, married Michael Morpurgo, Jack's stepson. Jack thought the marriage would wreck Michael's army career. The King Penguin and his supposed crown prince fell out about this and from that time never spoke to each other again. Christine Lane married David Teale, a member of staff not at odds with A.L., who was dispatched to André Deutsch to gain experience before returning to Penguin. Thereafter both sons-in-law distinguished themselves in the world of children's literature.

Other contenders for the throne were the Tory politicians Monty Woodhouse and Edward Boyle (Penguin vice-chairman for a short while), the Labour MP Jenny Lee, 'mother of the Open University' (on W.E.W.'s recommendation), Harry Paroissien, (back from Baltimore to become deputy MD) and, some thought, Tony Godwin – but we know what happened to him. In fact the one who became crown prince was Chris Dolley, who, having succeeded Paroissien in Baltimore and edited a bestselling *Penguin Book of Short Stories*, was appointed managing director.

In the very late sixties when he wasn't in hospital, Allen, who was suffering from cancer of the bowel, spent four days a week at Priory Farm. He was made Companion of Honour in 1969 and accorded many other awards, mostly from universities. In the same year he published *Ulysses*, for the second time, as Penguin number 3000, and paid Max Reinhardt, then owner of The Bodley Head, £75,000 for the rights, but he was no longer an active presence at Harmondsworth. Bill Williams, himself recovering from a serious illness, visited him and recalled that 'sometimes he was back in bed again after a fresh attack; but often we spent hours in the garden drinking wine and talking over the innumerable experiences we had enjoyed or endured together. He was frequently in great pain, sometimes submerged in depression. But I never remember a time when he failed to produce a good measure of gossip and gaiety. I often felt he was cheering me up, and not the other way round.'

In the early summer of 1968, A.L. appeared far from finished. At the Torquay Booksellers' Conference that year a large party of delegates was invited to dine with him at a country pub in Devonshire, where he was entertaining two cousins, or maybe nieces. He dispensed with all formality, didn't enquire what anyone might prefer to drink but walked among us clutching bottles of white wine and pouring it liberally into our waiting glasses. Dolley was in genial mood, as well he might be, his shrieking laugh too often dominating the occasion while the friendly Blass, secure in his sales role and close to the founder, looked on.

A.L., according to Morpurgo, was meanwhile consulting astrologers and soothsayers and ignoring the advice of his mistress who told him Dolley was 'not the man for the job'. He continued to dither about the succession, rejecting an offer from McGraw Hill, the American giant, which many believed would have alienated authors. Long before this, Penguin had contracted with Longman, when it was the oldest independent publisher, to co-publish for the Nuffield Foundation. By 1969, Mark Longman, the last member of the family to head the firm, was also terminally ill and his company had become part of the Pearson-Longman conglomerate, owned by the Financial Times.

A.L. is said to have entertained the possibility of Paul Hamlyn buying Penguin (see p.224) but on 8 July 1970, the day after Allen's death, the sale of Penguin to Pearson-Longman, who paid £15m for the privilege, was announced.

Lane left £1,216,474, gross, but a cash gift of £500,000 made to a charity was not allowable against death duties because he died less than a year after donating it. Had he put his affairs in order in time much inheritance tax could have been avoided. He was survived by Lettice and his three daughters.

Allen Lane was cremated and his ashes sent to St Nectan's Church at Hartland in North Devon. In London, a memorial service was held on 18 August at the church of St Martin-in-the Fields. Appropriately it was filled to capacity. I daresay that most of us who attended felt a genuine need to celebrate his achievements and to identify with one who had influenced our lives. Prayers were said and there was a blessing. St Martin's is a church with an active secular arm, extending care unconditionally to the deprived, but not unreasonably it expects those who rent it for memorial services to offer some tribute to the religion it upholds. Allen was as ambiguous in this respect as in most others. Two years earlier he had told an interviewer that 'he was a humanist, not an agnostic, and believed in a supreme being'. So we were treated to a concert of viols, with choral accompaniment, a pavan by John Jenkins, and a wind octet by Mozart performed in an unoppressive Christian setting where the priestly presence was overshadowed by publishers and an author. The sermons were addresses spoken by colleague Harry Paroissien, friend Robert Lusty and academic Richard Hoggart, each of whom climbed the snaky, vertiginous steps to the high pulpit. The service exemplified a lot of the best and some of the worst of an obsequial occasion. We had all respected, liked, even loved, the departed, but the orators were not over-reverential. Hoggart, whose *The Uses of Literacy* had been a successful Pelican, struck a note of social realism when he referred to the 'openness' and 'classlessness' of Penguins; Paroissien spoke briefly and discreetly of one with whom he had worked; only Robert Lusty dared to hint at something less than perfection. Having mentioned A.L.'s 'quiet smile, the sparkle in the blue eyes', and his complete honesty and absolute loyalty to his friends, 'who were legion', he went on to say, 'There was a kind of Allen language it was wise to comprehend. The storm signals might not involve oneself but it was sometimes kindly to send a message down the line … some name, some project might strike a certain chord and on the instant … cold little shutters would close upon the light of his eyes. Someone, something, somewhere, had had it.' Lusty then returned to the more familiar language of the eulogy. 'Those who watched [his death] were witness to an unconquerable spirit. Belief became conviction that Allen Lane was no ordinary man. In very truth a companion of honour.'

Hans Schmoller, in the *DNB, 1961–70*, wrote, 'Many business associates testified that they would agree to requests from him they would never have granted anyone else.' Hoggart, writing much later, told of how, when he had a chair at Birmingham and wished to start a post-graduate centre for Contemporary Cultural Studies, he asked A.L. for a seven-year covenant. Bill Williams was consulted and advised, 'Give him the money, Allen. You've made a fortune out of contemporary cultural change.'

Every writer about A.L. recorded facets of his complicated character. Richard Hoggart, reviewing Morpurgo's biography, listed around fifty 'contrasting epithets' used about Allen in that book, ranging from loveable and spontaneously benevolent to bland, bold, callous, devious and perverse. Many of those who knew Allen were eager to depict him as at best semi-literate. In my presence Jack Morpurgo more than once referred to him as never having been a reader of books, yet in mellower mood he cites *The Uses of Literacy* as 'one of the few modern sociological books that Allen had read'. Williams, more generously, stated that his favourite book was Mark Twain's *Tom Sawyer* – but why shouldn't it have been? The scholarly Ian Parsons was another who rated it highly. Lane himself claimed that he read two books a week 'for pleasure', while Dieter Pevsner thought that he read much more than legend allowed and maintained that 'he knew publishing and the world of books from every angle'. The latter is indisputable and I believe that fact should not be allied to an image of some kind of noble sav-age from the West Country who led the world to a new level of literacy whilst deriving no benefit himself from reading. Williams seems on surer ground when he states that A.L. was not a good administrator, played no part in public life, had no interest in politics – though he voted Labour – and was equally indifferent to religion (was he?), never watched or played games and 'lacked even a nodding acquaintance with music of any kind (did he?), but sums him up as 'an infuriatingly mercurial comrade who was dearer to me than any other man in my life. Nothing,' he wrote to him, 'has been as rewarding and exhilarating, or as worthwhile, as my place – at your side and two paces to the rear.' Gertrude Williams observed, 'I think each loved the other better than any other man.'

Dolley, in practice, was the successor during A.L.'s last months but he never enjoyed the founder's financial dominance because Penguin was soon to become owned by another, larger company. He resigned in 1973, by which time Charles Clark (whose influential role in Penguin Education I have only hinted at) had gone to Hutchinson to succeed Robert Lusty as man-aging director, and Dieter Pevsner and Oliver Caldecott had departed to found Wildwood House. After Dolley came Peter Calvocoressi, via the Royal Institute of International Affairs and Chatto and Windus. Jim Rose, placed in authority by Pearson's, ordered retrenchment. Penguin Education was ditched and, much later, the venerable Pelican list. Viking, America, became part of the group. Then, in 1975, a new messiah, Hampstead-born Peter Mayer, was brought over from New York and he, assisted by Ron Blass, worked the next renaissance by concentrating on massively-selling lead titles and ignoring, at first, the backlist. Viking Penguin, a conglomerate including some of those imprints from which early paperback rights had been purchased – Michael Joseph and Hamish Hamilton, for instance – became a vital part of Pearson's while the founder's name was perpetuated into the twenty-first century, in the imprint Allen Lane.

Sir Allen Williams Lane, born Redland, Bristol, 21 September 1902, son of Allen and Camilla Williams. Married Lettice Orr, 1941. Died, Mount Vernon Hospital, Northwood, 7 July 1970. (Lettice Lane died in 2003.)

Four

JOHN GREY ('JOCK') MURRAY

Had there been publishers in the Middle Ages, and a Murray among them, Jock of that ilk would have been a prince with his authors members of a medieval court. In the 1930s as heir to the Albemarle Street throne he was already gathering 'his' writers around him, writers destined to remain loyal to the list and he to them for decades to come. They included the poet John Betjeman, the intrepid woman traveller Freya Stark and the cartoonist and architectural historian Osbert Lancaster; others, equally distinguished, were to follow.

When Jock, born John Arnaud Robin Grey, nephew to John Murray V, joined the partnership in 1930 he, like Allen Lane changed his name by deed poll. His mother was a Murray, sister of his childless uncle. He was familiar with the hallowed ambience of 50 Albemarle Street, Piccadilly, where Byron's dangerously overt – so it was supposed – memoirs had been burned in the first-floor drawing-room fireplace, because he had spent much of his childhood there.

Until 1929 the house doubled as family residence and publishing offices. Jock had sat at breakfast while his grandfather (Murray IV) opened the post, he had slid down the bannisters, played with the Corunna pistols which had belonged to Sir John Moore, inspected what a future friend and author called 'an Aladdin's cave of relics and mementoes' where 'there was hardly a stick of furniture without an anecdote ... ' and been confronted since infancy by a Thorvaldsen bust of Byron. The building was already an integral part of his life, with its vivid boyhood memories of Barnes the butler who became his hero, instructing him in the mysteries of laying tables, opening bottles and cleaning silver in return for being permitted to play in the nursery with Jock's toy train set.

The first John Murray, a retired lieutenant in the marines, had moved to London from Edinburgh in 1768 to set up his shop in Fleet Street. His son's and grandson's lists, in the nineteenth century, were graced not only by Byron, but by Jane Austen, Walter Scott, the missionary David Livingstone, Erasmus Darwin, whose seminal work disturbed the very roots of Christianity, and Samuel Smiles, upholder of Victorian morality. The house was also to publish the *Letters of Queen Victoria*, which brought the family into the realms of knighthood.

'Jock' was educated at Eton and Magdalen, Oxford, from which he graduated with a degree in Modern History. At Eton he was flogged by Ian Fleming for committing the crime of reading alleged pornography; at university he entered upon a lifelong friendship with John Betjeman. (The book which led to his beating was *La Vie Parisienne* which Jock thought merely 'saucy'. Fleming took sadistic delight in administering the punishment so the victim was not surprised, when he came to read them, by the descriptions of torture in the James Bond novels.)

There never seems to have been any doubt that he would join the family firm – for which his father, Thomas Robinson Grey, known as 'Robin', also worked – although it was said that 'he had a youthful fancy to be an architect' and, again like Allen Lane, had a deep interest in design. Architecture may have been a mere passing attraction because he recalled more than once a meeting with Arthur Conan Doyle who was delivering a new manuscript to Albemarle Street. 'During one of my holidays from school, when my grandfather was ill … he treated me with such courtesy as though I was a grown-up … that I fell under his spell. If this is an author, I said to myself, what fun to be a publisher.' There are other versions of this incident, which Jock related to various interviewers, but that is the essence of it.

In 1917 many of the office staff moved to Clerkenwell Road, the former warehouse of Smith, Elder, the venerable nineteenth-century imprint purchased that year by Murray's. This was to be the warehouse, accounts department and trade counter for much of the century. The family home remained at Albemarle Street for another twelve years but even after that Jock kept a bedsit there.

In the school holidays the young Grey was employed, in his own words, as 'slave and bottlewasher' to Robert Gibbings of the Golden Cockerel Press, where he claimed to be the only publisher who had 'typeset in the nude'. The hirsute Gibbings had adopted a naturist phase and his assistants had to follow his whim. Jock felt it was unfair because 'when he [Gibbings] had nothing on he appeared to be wearing a fur coat'. One of his early tasks on behalf of Murray's was to look after their venerable author, the whimsical Swede Axel Munthe who, when in London, required a flat where he could see trees and hear birdsong. Jock also had to escort him home to the Villa San Michele at Anacapri, protecting him *en route* from hordes of female admirers . 'Yock, Yock,' lamented the author, 'you must get rid of these ladies.' Munthe's *The Story of San Michele*, a bestseller over several decades, had just been published but he was not, as stated in a *Times* obituary, one of Jock's personal authors; he belonged to the era of an earlier Murray.

Jock's more formal duties began when, as a slightly stammering, hugely enthusiastic young man bursting with ideas, he joined his uncle, soon endearing himself to colleagues, authors and the trade as a whole. He became assistant editor of the *Cornhill Magazine* (founded by Thackeray but, until 1917, published by Smith, Elder), and of the *Quarterly Review*, both now owned by Murray. He was elected to the Society of Bookmen in 1933 and attended at least one of the Ripon Hall Conferences (see p.19). He also did a stint with a printer and visited booksellers, going through the customary stages of acquainting himself with all parts of the industry. From the start he was fascinated by typography which became one of his many hobbies. They were listed minimally in *Who's Who*, as 'Forestry and Music'.

Betjeman's first verses were privately published by one Edward James. The young poet's initial London publisher was the Architectural Press, for whom he wrote the first of the Shell Guides to the counties of Britain. These later passed to Faber where his sometime prep-school teacher, T.S. Eliot, was a director. It is thought that Eliot made overtures to him about his verse and certainly Betjeman flirted with other publishers before Jock signed him for the Murray list, on which he remained until his death. Initially, the costs of publication were underwritten personally by Jock in the face of objections from Sir John (as his uncle had become). Jock risked his shares in Bovril, a popular beverage, to back his judgement, but he did not have to sell them; Betjeman went on to become, over and above Eliot, the bestselling English poet of the century. Jock described him as 'one of the most inspiring people in my life'.

Murray V was knighted in 1932. He seems to have been a scholarly but cautious publisher and there has never been 'a good time' for publishing poetry. At that stage he was very much in charge of the imprint which was one of the oldest and most renowned in British publishing. Jock was well aware of being a sixth-generation entrant into a partnership so he trod softly. At the same time, being young and eager, his approach was certain to be different from his uncle's. Betjeman remained on the list, joined by Freya Stark with *Baghdad Sketches* (1933) and *Valley of the Assassins* (1934) and Osbert Lancaster with *Progress fom Pelvis Bay* (1936). Two others of those who became his inner-circle authors, were Kenneth Clark, director of the National Gallery, then published by Cambridge and Constable, and Patrick Leigh Fermor, an expelled schoolboy who was making the leisurely, learned journey from the Hook of Holland to the Black Sea which would lead to books with far-distant publication dates. Another lifelong friend and associate, introduced by Betjeman, was John Piper, who illustrated some of the poet's books and became godfather to one of Jock's children.

It was in the early 1930s that Jock met Diana James, 'at a rat hunt', so that lady recorded on her tape for the NLSC. Jock later said of the occasion, 'I didn't catch a rat but caught a wife.' Diana, although primarily interested in music – she played the cello and was a singer – also read for publishers. They married in 1939 and thereafter she took an increasingly active role at Murray's both editorially and socially; she also bore Jock two sons and two daughters.

The Second World War deferred Fermor's literary career and interrupted Jock's publishing. The writer's audacious military career in Crete featured in memoirs by other hands; he was later, in contrast, to record monastic life and travels in Greece. Jock had a quieter war with the Royal Artillery which he joined in 1940, later becoming commissioned. By 1945, when he was awarded an MBE for his part in planning transport for the battle of Arnhem, he had been promoted to major. He and Diana bought Cannon Lodge, Cannon Place, Hampstead, in 1944 and moved in the following year to remain there for almost half a century. A near neighbour was Kenneth Clark whose *The Gothic Revival* Jock admired and reissued. It established him as Clark's publisher and friend, bringing him, in 1956, *The Nude*, a handsome volume produced to the highest standards by the printer Clark (not related) of Edinburgh and highly priced, for the time, at three guineas. *The Nude* was a great coup for Jock who was not seen as a publisher of art books, and it became a bestseller both for Murray's, and later, Penguin.

It was in the immediate post-WWII decades that Jock gradually assumed the leading role at Murray's, although Sir John remained active into the 1960s. There was no breach between them; mutual respect was maintained but the younger man set the pace, becoming within the trade and in literary circles something of a legend in his own lifetime.

The appointment of Kenneth Pinnock as education manager, in 1953, was significant and allowed Jock to concentrate more on his personal style of publishing. He had realised how precarious fiction and general literature had become for small and medium-sized publishers in an era fast moving towards mergers and conglomerates. Large advances, favoured for obvious reasons by literary agents, were more than ever before the means of securing new talents and of luring established authors from their familiar imprints. The educational market, especially in the former colonial territories of Africa and the Far East, but also at home, needed new, contemporary textbooks. Murray's had long had a finger in this market with its Latin and

Greek primers and other somewhat outdated text books; it now wanted a larger stake to contribute to overheads and profits. Pinnock, whose previous experience had been with Christopher's, was engaged and soon landed a very large fish indeed – Mackean's *Introduction to Biology*, destined to sell over seven million copies. Later came the involvement with the Nuffield projects on mathematics and manuals for the Association for Science Education. Some believed that it was only the success of the educational list which kept Murray's afloat for the rest of Jock's lifetime. Certainly Pinnock's contribution to the health and comparative wealth of the list was significant and welcome to the Murrays, allowing Jock to switch to Byron-mode, in order to concentrate on the general list, which produced some big bestsellers in the sixties to eighties, and to maintain 'his court'.

Osbert Lancaster was wont to look in to No. 50 in the early evening for a tipple after dispatching his daily cartoon for the *Express*, 'Betj' was often around, Paddy Leigh Fermor and 'K. Clark', as Jock always referred to him, were in evidence, 'Freya' less frequently because she was so regularly 'in the field', and there were other newcomers – C. Northcote Parkinson, whose *Law* became fashionable for several years, former colonial governor Arthur Grimble (*Pattern of Islands*), Lesley Blanch with her haunting *The Wilder Shores of Love*, Iris Origo and Doris Langley Moore, another Byron expert, plus new entrants to the inner circle, the eccentric Irish-born traveller Dervla Murphy and the youthful journalist Bevis Hillier, who was to become official biographer of Betjeman. Also on to the list to the surprise of some had come the 'daring' French novelist Francoise Sagan, (*Bonjour Tristesse*, etc.) and the Booker-winner, Ruth Jhabvala, whose elegant style had more than a hint of Jane Austen. The latter arrived through an editor, Osyth Leeston, but her writing was much admired by Jock. She was often a guest at Cannon Lodge, where many years later some location shots were taken when her novel *Heat and Dust* was filmed.

The description of Jock at the start of Kenneth Pinnock's obituary in *The Bookseller* quotes Peter Phelan, of the Publishers'Association, who observed that of all publishers he had encountered 'Jock Murray was the one who most looked the part'. Pinnock himself refers to 'his habitual gesture, at lavish lunches, of sweeping the air to fend off hovering waiters' while 'clawing back locks unfashionably long and little greyed or thinned by age'. At work, expansive gestures would 'reveal red braces flanking his invariable bow-tie', and he was likened 'to some great crow' stooping 'among precariously heaped papers covering every inch of flat surface and much of the floor of his office'. The obituarist notes him, 'embarking with delight on a long railway journey (second class, of course) with a book-bulged army knapsack slung on his shoulders.' He was 'far too large, untidy and exuberant to be labelled "executive", "company director", or by any other terms appropriate to the briefcase brigade. Everything about him announced his identity in a single word – Publisher'. (By 'large' Pinnock surely is referring to his personality rather than his frame?) He goes on to recall Jock 'literally dancing with excitement' in the Albemarle Street drawing-room, 'bursting to tell his audience about the latest new book' on which he was working. Paddy Leigh Fermor's was '*maaaav'lous*', Dervla Murphy's latest exploits were '*extraooooordinary*' and he could not resist revealing some of what they had written ahead of publication, such was his enthusiasm. Pinnock also relates the story told to his wife by Diana Murray revealing another facet of Jock. With midnight approaching and her husband supposedly still out at a dinner, Diana on her way to bed came across him, in full evening dress, seated in his study so engrossed in a typescript that he had overlooked his engagement.

Kenneth Pinnock recalled Jock's behaviour towards those authors who did not join the court, the ones whose work he felt obliged to reject. He did so with the softest of touches which led Sir John, at a staff party, to say that sometimes the spurned author found it difficult to decide whether or not he had been accepted. Against this, Jock advised colleagues to be wary of writers. 'In our editorial meetings,' he recorded, 'if someone suggests a book I ask if the proposer has met the author. If not, I always say, "I would advise you not to put forward an agreement until you've seen him, better still, till you've eaten with him!"'

Of all who are profiled in this collection Jock was the one I saw most frequently over a period of forty years. He did not become an intimate friend but was always a figure in my landscape, one who was often in close-up. In four decades we probably lunched or dined together less than a dozen times but, as a Hampstead resident and the most attentive of 'local' publishers, he visited my bookshop most weekends and came to all of our parties.

In 1956, as related in Chapter Six I became a bookseller in Hampstead, managing a shop which was in the hands of the receiver. Jock was deeply concerned that it should not close. It was unthinkable to him that NW3 should lose its High Street bookshop. It didn't and, in due course, I became the proprietor with Jock playing a multi-purpose role as supplier, resident, customer, mentor and friend. From the outset he had established himself in the role of delivery man. One of our 1956 bestsellers was the Kenneth Clark book mentioned earlier. My staff took innocent pleasure, when instructed to reorder, in phoning the trade counter and requesting, 'Could

Mr Murray please put six *Nudes* in his car to deliver to us when he drives home?'

When I think of Jock two powerful images come to mind. The first belongs to the 1970s when he was guest of honour at the annual dinner of the London branch of the BA at the Strand Palace Hotel. We had an indifferent meal but the evening took wing when Jock rose to speak, instantly hitting the right notes for the occasion. I forget the content of his address but, at one moment, after a great burst of laughter from every table, he flexed his shoulders several times, beamed at us all, and declared, 'I say! I am enjoying myself.' David Holloway, literary editor of the *Daily Telegraph*, was to record on Jock's eightieth birthday that '... no one can get more variation of meaning into those two simple words, "I say".' David's further description of him might well have applied to this occasion; 'the loosely-knotted bow-tie, the slow, slightly percussive diction, the expansive gestures and a wonderfully expressive pair of eyebrows raised in benevolent surprise'. (The same literary editor once complained to me of the paltry sum he received from Murray's for advising on a book, but as a Fleet Street journalist David was accustomed to significantly higher rates of pay than pertained in book publishing.)

The other memory cannot be pinpointed to a particular day or even year; it happened often, usually on a Saturday. I would be at the front desk of what we called 'the main shop'. Jock would walk briskly in, arms swinging, dressed in a fairly 'loud'-patterned sports jacket with leather elbow patches, weekend slacks, tie askew (or sometimes tieless). He was never without a shoulder bag, bulging ominously with copies of the current Murray bestseller, or the most recently issued volume of *Byron's Letters*.

After greeting me and asking if I could oblige by cashing a cheque (it took almost fifteen years to persuade him to accept ten-pound notes which he thought vulgar) he would enquire, 'How are you off for Dervla?' (or Betj, or Osbert, or Paddy – but never for K. Clark whose books were too large for his valise). What I needed he would supply on the spot. If I required something he hadn't got with him, he would say, 'I think there's one at home.' Later he might return bearing it. Often he would ask, 'Do you have the new *Cornhill*?' Always I would answer, 'Yes.' 'Need any more?' 'No, thank you.' *Cornhill* was a blind spot of his; he so wanted people to love it as once they had. Jock gave much time to the magazine which he relaunched in the late 1940s, and at first co-edited with Peter Quennell before going it alone until its final number, doggedly believing that although its circulation was small it brought authors to the list. His son John disputed this but, according to Janet Adam Smith, it was through

Cornhill that Jock first met Freya Stark who had submitted an article to it. Publication continued until the 1970s; the *Quarterly*, edited by Sir John, died with him, in 1967.

It was Jock who inaugurated the practice – greatly to my benefit – of buying books at the published price although he could have ordered them through his publishing house and received trade terms. Hampstead was blessed by many resident publishers who were my regular customers. It seemed to me to be exceeding the rules of eccentricity for Jock to attempt to purchase, at full price, one of his own publications which he needed urgently, lacking a copy at Cannon Lodge. He argued the point vigorously but I eventually persuaded him that all he need do was to send me a replacement. (Probably, he would have sent two.)

Business done, we would then gossip. Between us we had almost a computer store of knowledge of what was happening in the book trade. I would break off to serve customers; he would disengage to greet neighbours, authors, celebrities. Jock knew everyone – Jonathan Miller, Michael Foot, Peggy Ashcroft, and many others, some of whom I could not identify. In his encounters with them there would be moments of serious head-nodding, bursts of laughter, expansive gestures, expressions of goodwill. He had an especially jovial relationship with George Malcolm Thomson, author and senior Beaverbrook journalist. Whenever a new volume of Lancaster cartoons was imminent, if they met in my shop, Jock would call out, 'George, how many copies of Osbert's new book have you ordered from Ian?' George then, good-humouredly, would reserve two or three.

On those Saturdays when Jock did not materialise to cash a cheque, bring goods or to make a purchase, we missed him. My colleagues loved his visits. He got to know all those who stayed with us for years; he collected people and valued them.

I don't know that he ever actually commissioned a book on the floor of my shop but the possibility of his doing so was always there at the back – or even the front – of his mind. He was, like a policeman, on duty for twenty-four hours a day. He knew how Stanley Unwin had mixed business with marriage in 1914 at a chapel down the road (see p.35). When 'Uncle Stan', a resident for more than half a century, died in 1968 Jock became the doyen of publishers on the NW3 hillside.

Unwin and Murray could hardly have been less alike, physically or in personality. Jock was outgoing, hospitable, eccentric, literary, his house often alive with visiting authors; Unwin was seldom seen on the High Street and did not entertain authors on his estate. His personal Daimler was occasionally directed to deliver goods to my shop whilst taking Sir Stanley home but only once did he himself bound in off the pavement; Jock, self-driven, frequently arrived, not only laden with parcels but to take a stock order too if necessary. It is unlikely that the two men and their wives met socially although they lived within walking distance; it was not the Unwin style nor, despite his essentially gregarious and sociable nature, was it Jock's, who did not particularly seek the company of other publishers. This was why he was not a member of the Garrick but belonged to Pratt's, the Beefsteak and Brooks where he might eat lunch always supposing he remembered that a meal was due.

Pinnock, in his obituary, related also how Jock became a scholar when co-editing, with Leslie Marchand, the multi-volume edition of Byron's *Letters and Diaries*. He became so conversant with the poet's handwriting – often illegible to others – that he could spot a forgery on sight. Marchand was one of many Murray authors who stayed at Cannon Lodge (Diana said it was 'like an annexe to Albemarle Street'). During one visit Jock called in at the bookshop and told me of how he was working at home and had come out for a breather. 'Diana insists that we can talk Byron at lunch, or Byron at dinner, but not at both meals.' Pinnock relates that the lady 'used at times to complain, though never bitterly, that she felt she was married to Byron'. Her role went far beyond occasional editing and being supportive to a husband who overworked; she became hostess to his authors and staff, organising luncheons, dinners, outings on the Thames and an annual get-together of the Clerkenwell Road and Albemarle Street employees, who did not mix easily. When staff were invited to Hampstead, Jock always advised that the evening should end by nine-thirty to give the guests time to go on to a local pub where they could let their hair down and 'complain about the Murrays'.

Freya Stark was a regular Christmas guest at Cannon Lodge. A friend recalled her arrival one year bearing a cardboard box containing two live hamsters. 'It will teach the children about sex,' she explained. In the event, her gifts quickly mated and produced more hamsters, after which the female killed the male and ate their offspring. (John R. – Murray VII – believes this alleged happening became embellished through the memory of a famous Roald Dahl story but something like it did occur.) Jock advised the great traveller on other than editorial matters; she had to be restrained from attempting to sell him her copyrights because she wished to buy a fur coat. He also had to help choose her hats.

Jock would break off a visit to the shop if he remembered Freya Stark's arrival was imminent, but he didn't bring her to High Hill. Dervla Murphy sometimes accompanied him, hailing me in her deep contralto voice. She would also come in alone, or with Rachel, her tough young daughter, a child who had endured travelling some of the world's bleakest terrains. In her appraisal of Jock in *The Oldie* in 1993, Dervla wrote vividly of how she came to be on the Murray list. Thirty years earlier she had cycled into India where, in a bazaar, she encountered Penelope Chetwode (Mrs John Betjeman), another intrepid traveller. They became instant companions, Penelope immediately enthusiastic about Dervla's as yet mostly unwritten book which she insisted must be sent to Jock Murray.

'"To whom?"' remembered Dervla, 'I yelled above the blare of rickshaw horns.'

'"To Jock Murray in Albemarle Street. You'll *adore* Jock. Everybody adores Jock."'

Back home in Ireland, her book completed, Dervla Murphy sent copies of the typescript simultaneously to three separate publishers all of whom swiftly offered contracts. Her immediate reaction for a then totally unknown author was odd. Instead of registering euphoric delight at capturing a choice of publishers she was suspicious. She was a county librarian's daughter and knew something of the wily ways of 'heavy editorial hands all poised to turn *my* little book into *their* little book'. So she sent a further carbon copy of her typescript to Jock who, one week later, summoned her to Albemarle Street by telegram. There she 'ascended the hallowed staircase, quite unwomanned by suspense and awe' to Jock's 'cramped, chaotic' office, where 'in a corner sat "young John", as he was then known, experiencing his first week as a publisher and looking almost as nervous as I felt.'

Few authors are as fortunate in finding their ideal publisher with their first book. Dervla and Jock deserved each other. A literary agent might wryly say that Dervla deserved more material benefits; she would have disagreed. On advances, she wrote, 'He rightly expected a book to prove its worth before its publisher disbursed.' She noted his frugality over such matters as switching off lights in unused rooms but also his generosity in providing open house for his closest authors, adding that those 'who enjoyed the hospitality of Cannon Lodge will remember Jock's disingenuous habit of suggesting that "early beds" would be a good idea'. This was not for the purpose of giving them time to discuss their hosts but because he wished to spend a few late hours editing a typescript. On that subject she reveals that Jock and Diana were a team, 'inspired and inspiring', each producing a different batch of notes on what they had read.

Bevis Hillier, who was actually John R.'s author, having been at university with him, was invited to both home and office. He thought Jock 'one of the best raconteurs I have ever known'. At Cannon Lodge at dinner he twice met Peggy Ashcroft, a particular friend of Diana, and a Hampstead neighbour. Bevis recorded, 'In the calm light of her eyes and character [she] somehow reminded me of Jock', an interesting observation somewhat puzzling to me because I did not associate either of these wonderful people with 'calmness'.

John R. claimed that neither he nor Jock ever poached authors from other lists, that agents were seldom used and that books just came to them. If they liked them, believed they had potential, they contracted for them. Some came by chance, some through old friendships. 'We were Murrays; we were not publishers' – a comment capable of several interpretations, but there was absolutely no doubt that Jock was a publisher in his bones and a professional. It was he who passed on to his elder son a pride in not filching his competitors' writers. He resented Billy Collins's efforts to lure Murray authors with large advances. Collins, scion of a younger but more powerful publishing dynasty than Murray's, had a passion the equal of Jock's for authors, though he was not always so gentlemanly in pursuing it. 'I hate to poach,' he told him, adding disingenuously, '… Give me a list of your favourite authors and I promise not to make them offers.' Jock, ever courteous but with antennae alerted, gave him a copy of his current list. Allegedly, Billy Collins wrote to every author on it but all refused his blandishments.

Once Jock had a fight to retain 'K. Clark', who without consulting his publisher signed a contract for a major television series which included the publishing rights. He told Jock he had done so 'in a sort of panic'; Jock, supported by him, persuaded the BBC that by the terms of Murray's agreement with the author, they were entitled to be joint publishers of *Civilisation*, which in 1969 was screened at a peak viewing time on Sunday evenings for thirteen weeks. The published versions, in hardback and paperback, sold one and a half million copies. Alan Clark, the notorious Tory MP and diarist, who was 'K.'s' son, dared to suggest that Murray's had been stingy with royalties, an argument he pursued until Jock forced him to concede that the original BBC agreement had allowed for a 7½% rate which Jock made them increase to 10%. (In fact many successful authors had been earning 15% and more for much of the century but 10% remained a notional, median figure possibly because agents were thought of generally as 'ten per centers'. In the 1980s and 1990s traditional terms for retailers rose sharply when emerging, powerful, nationwide groups of booksellers demanded and sometimes received 60%. Between them literary agents and booksellers could be said to have pushed traditional publishers, such as Murray – and Billy Collins – out of kilter.)

Late in life Jock confessed to an interviewer that he had a terrible vice – envy of other people's literary skill. He had attempted to rationalise this as admiration but knew it was actually envy. The revelation raises a certain doubt. Was he saying this to make the interview more interesting? Was it a passing fancy? If he really experienced this so-called deadly sin it was not apparent in his dealings with authors who ranked among his closest friends. There was no limit to what they might expect from him. Iris Origo sent him a page of scrawled notes with the message, 'Dearest Jock, I can't read what I've written. Please type it out and send a copy to me.' Joanna Richardson, a Hampstead neighbour, published one book with him, a study of Enid Starkie. While walking her home after dinner at Cannon Lodge, he asked, 'When are you going to *like* Enid? In a fortnight perhaps?' The writer later made objections when he suggested removing a phrase from her typescript. 'But if you take it out,' said Jock, 'the echo will remain.' She replied admiringly, 'I thought only authors thought like that'. (He had his way which may surprise anyone who knows how difficult Miss Richardson could be.) When Lesley Blanch visited Albemarle Street to correct proofs she had to be provided with a pair of Turkish slippers to wear; Jock always insisted that 'K. Clark's' massive royalty cheque should be tucked into his Christmas stocking.

Sometimes, it was said, Diana Murray would travel from Hampstead to Albemarle Street of an evening to drag Jock from his desk. She was only too aware that he overworked and probably associated this with the periods of depression which both he and his elder son endured.

One of the evenings when she remained in Hampstead the following incident happened. (I had this from printer and mutual friend Alan Steele; both he and Jock enjoyed good stories.) Jock had been working particularly late. Immediately before the pubs were due to close (eleven p.m. in those days) he slipped out to buy a sandwich and a drink. Returning to the office, still fatigued, he thought he saw the figure of a woman in a long white dress disappearing through his inner sanctum and up the back stairs. 'My God!' he thought. 'It's the ghost of Lady Caroline Lamb!' and took this as a warning that it was time to cease work and go home. Next morning, he encountered the Albemarle Street housekeeper and noticed she was limping. When he expressed concern she was evasive. Later he learned that she, about to retire to bed, had heard noises and descended from her attic flat to investigate. There were steps on the stairs to the first floor. She realised it was her employer, so she fled not wishing to confront Mr Murray while wearing her nightdress. In her haste she had knocked her hip against Jock's desk and was badly bruised.

There are other versions in one of which it was *Mr* Stafford the caretaker who saw the figure in white which he took to be Jock's mistress. In another, *Mrs* Stafford is described as a former Irish nun who occasionally accommodated in the basement others who had 'leapt over the wall'. These tales add to the potent ambience of 50 Albemarle Street, the childhood home Jock never left although he complained to Kenneth Pinnock at their first meeting it could be like living in a museum. When the caretaker was away, he said, some American would probably ring the bell 'wishing to see Byron's boot'. This involved a guided tour of the house. But, he added, 'the nice ones give me a tip'.

Despite a slight but usually overcome stammer, Jock was, as Hillier commented, an excellent raconteur, telling stories about and against himself, authors and other publishers. Once, at a Society of Bookmen dinner, he related how he, Diana and their daughter Freydis lunched with John and Marghanita Howard, Hampstead neighbours. John owned the Cresset Press; his wife was better known as the outspoken writer and broadcaster Marghanita Laski. After lunch Freydis withdrew with Lydia Howard to play while the adults chatted over coffee. On returning home Diana asked Freydis how she and Lydia had passed the time. Freydis said they had hidden in a cupboard to read a book.

'Why did you have to hide?'

'It's a book that Lydia's mother wouldn't like her to read.'

The Murrays were disconcerted, knowing that Marghanita took a principled stand against all censorship. Whatever book could it have been? They slept on their worry and at breakfast next day casually enquired the title of this book which had to be read in a cupboard because its nature offended even Marghanita.

'Oh,' replied Freydis, 'it was by Enid Blyton.'

(Bevis Hillier sought to use this in a book about Blyton but Marghanita objected.)

In 1972, Jock took time off from Byron to become absorbed in Derek Hudson's life of a Victorian gentleman named Munby who made it his mission to befriend working-class women, especially those engaged in menial, manual tasks. Munby's researches were supposedly undertaken in the same spirit in which Gladstone investigated prostitutes, but who can tell? Certainly he married one of those whom he studied. When Mavis had a minor illness, Jock sent her a copy of Hudson's biography inscribed, 'Don't let Ian get hold of it. It's not a book for husbands.'

Jock's idiosyncrasies were, in my experience, endearing, never irritating.

At the end of the 1950s when Mavis and I had two infant daughters, in age only thirteen months apart, he invited us to supper, or maybe lunch, at Cannon Lodge. I had to decline, explaining that Mavis was housebound and needed my help. At least a decade later he said to me one day, 'It's no use inviting you and Mavis to lunch is it, because of your children?' I told him they were now much older and that we were able to enjoy a social life with or without them. So we went to Cannon Lodge for Sunday lunch. During the course of it, Diana, seated at one end of the table, apologised sotto voce to me for being inactive, saying, 'Jock insists that because I pre-pare and cook the meal I should not serve it or clear away.' Afterwards Jock walked us along heavily parked Cannon Place. He was carrying a contrap-tion used by keepers on the Heath for picking up rubbish. With it he cap-tured a discarded beer can, which he thrust triumphantly aloft, then let it go by mistake. It landed on the bonnet of a neighbour's vehicle. 'Osbert,' he observed, 'won't walk with me in Piccadilly when I carry this thing.'

Mavis and I took less than fifteen years to return the Murray hospitality. They came to lunch on a fine day at our house in Hadley Wood on the extreme northern edge of Greater London. Jock swept into the garden and leaped on to the permanent picnic table to get a better view, observing this shrub and that tree with approval, uttering several 'I say's'. I was surprised he did not know another publisher (Gordon Graham) who was present. That was soon remedied when Gordon and his wife were invited to Cannon Lodge, a fact which rightly questions the generalisation I have made about Jock's relationship with others of his profession.

At a Booksellers' Association conference at Torquay in – I think – 1969, I dined one evening with Jock and John R. The food was far from excit-ing. At the end of the main course Jock beckoned the maître d'hôtel, who came quickly to the table, eager to please. Jock, in the hesitant voice employed when he thought he might stammer, said, 'Will you give my compliments to the chef … ' The waiter beamed expectantly. '… And tell him that … the lamb-ah-chops … ' 'Yes sir?' The waiter looked delighted. 'The chops … were absolutely … STONE … COLD. Ah … thank you.' I never heard him speak rudely to anyone but he was not one to tolerate the second-rate.

Ronald Church, long-term rep for Central London, previously employed in the accounts office, had a regular, weekly, half-hour appoint-ment, over a glass of sherry, with Jock to keep him abreast of trade gossip. Once Jock offered him, instead of wine, the caretaker's special cabbage water said to have curative properties. Church, in the Murray archive, records this incident as 'my only unenjoyable memory of him'. Jock inspired devotion and loyalty from staff at many levels, not least from John Gibbins, for many years the affable and tubby publicity manager. If anyone, in Gibbins's presence offered any kind of criticism of the way Murray's was administered, daring to suggest there could be shortcomings concerning pay, pensions, working conditions, he would say, with an implacable look, 'I'm a Jock man.' Similar devotion was expressed by a former stock-keeper at Clerkenwell Road who recalled how Jock would make him feel an essential part of the publishing process by introducing him to an author he had in tow, saying to 'Betj', or it might be 'Paddy', 'You know our Michael Holman, don't you?'

Jock gave the presidential address to the English Association in 1976, apologising in advance for a speech which must have lasted all of an hour. 'I have to keep you waiting for lunch,' he began. 'This is surely the kind of torture which Amnesty International was set up to prevent.' Inevitably his subject was Byron – *A Poet and his Publisher*. It was a talk brimming with erudition and humour. 'I have known Byron all my life,' he told his audience. He spoke of his editorial involvement with the complete letters and the complete poetry as an ongoing experience. 'Byron is therefore a little on my mind. Moreover, as my wife forbids me to talk about him at meals, the opportunity to do so *before* lunch is irresistible.' (Diana, presumably, had now imposed a total ban.) He went on to describe publishers as 'inconspicuous characters … properly obscured by the figures of creative authors', but thought they might be 'of a peripheral, pre-prandial interest, bearing in mind … that in our day the magic of a Prime Minister's wand can turn publishers into Peers' – a reference to Harold Wilson's ennoblement of George Weidenfeld. The printed text of Jock's address runs to over seven thousand words. One must hope the meal was kept hot.

Jock was the longest serving council member of the Royal Geographical Society. As publishers during the nineteenth century of the Murray Handbooks to various countries and subcontinents the family imprint had long been strong in what the trade categorises as Travel and Adventure. In 2004, it received the Society's Award for 'The Greatest Contribution over 200 Years to Exploration and Travel Writing'. Jock travelled more for business than pleasure; Diana recorded that he thought of 'abroad' as 'dangerous' and was happiest at home. He was not much of a linguist – his French being likened, by his elder son, to Churchill's – and when in Tuscany visiting Alan Moorehead, a highly successful author friend whom he did not attempt to poach, he made do with Italianate endings to English words. Late in life he went to India carrying with him the reissued relevant Murray

Handbook. He made regular trips by QEII or QM to New York; he and Diana also went several times to Greece to visit Paddy Leigh Fermor, an author who might have tried any publisher's patience by taking literally decades to write two of his best books. Jock was totally understanding and revealed another side to Fermor who regarded him as 'an accomplished tree surgeon; one glance at an ailing growth would send him shinning up into the branches and putting things most knowledgeably to rights with saw, twine, bast and tar'. (Addressing the Society of Bookmen in 1979, Jock commented, 'Publishers naturally take to forestry because they can cut and chop to their heart's content without authors complaining.')

Jock never became president of the PA although he served on its council intermittently during four decades. He felt he could not take sufficient time from looking after Murray's to go through the six-year course involved in taking office. He was an ardent upholder of the Net Book Agreement, he believed that some censorship was justified, he was an irregular delegate to the annual BA conference and resigned from the Society of Bookmen through failing the minimum attendance commitment.

Outside the trade Jock was also on a committee named Nobody's Friends, comprised of clergy and lay people who met at Lambeth Palace to further the cause of Christianity; yet, despite being a believer who attended Christ Church in Hampstead, he told an interviewer in 1992, 'I have become a little less religious. Though I read the lesson in church when I'm asked, I feel ashamed that I attend church less often. I try to analyse this but I can't … But I firmly believe that churchgoing is important for unifying a community.' According to his elder son, the cardinal virtues appealed to Jock rather more than the seven deadly sins. This was not, perhaps, reflected in his work for the Archbishop of Canterbury's copyright committee when it was dealing with the revision of the Prayer Book. On Jock's insistence the words 'the devil and all his works' were retained. John R. notes he enjoyed using emblems on title pages and endpapers illustrating the sins.

Throughout my thirty-two years at Hampstead Jock was a wonderful support, a good friend and a constant entertainer. The last party I held at the shop was for Michael Foot's book about Byron which bore the Collins imprint. 'I should like to have published that,' Jock told me. It was hard for him to accept that others had the right to issue works about 'his' poet. He and Michael, much of whose book was actually about Hazlitt, spent most of the party engaged in deep, passionate discussion.

At the end of my time on the Northern Heights of London I felt I had failed Jock by deciding to sell the property. He came to my office wishing to know the reasons. They were that two leases were coming up for renewal with the prospect of more than 100% rent rises, Camden Council had run out of money which lost us about 7% of turnover overnight, Waterstone's had opened on a better site in the High Street and neither my deputy managing director, Trisha Nunn, nor my daughter Amanda wished to succeed me, whereas I was ready for early retirement. Our chief asset was an increasingly valuable freehold. He didn't actually say so but, from his look, I knew Jock thought I was opting out of a commitment to Hampstead. I sensed that, in similar circumstances, he would have felt it imperative to carry on. I knew I had let him down. Despite this he agreed to speak at my farewell lunch which Diana also attended. She chatted to me about Tim Waterstone, saying appreciatively that his shop, unlike mine, had a good stock of Bibles. I didn't stock them, not because I was anti-religion, though I am, but due to the infinite variety of bindings and editions available (people always wanted the one we didn't have) and also because the Oxford Press rep confirmed my view that 'Hampstead was the worst Bible territory in Britain'. The Murrays were practising Christians. Neither of them held my agnosticism against me but I think Tim Waterstone, also a believer, scored a hit with Diana.

Jock never gave up but he became one of an endangered species. The publishing world he had entered between the wars had inherited a sense of wellbeing and continuity dating back, in his case, more than one hundred and sixty years. Until the 1950s it was not uncommon for family firms to be partnerships; Murray's did not become a limited company until 1951. It was in a different league from William Collins which, though also a dynasty, had gone public; Murray's was relatively small but prestigious in worldwide literary and book-trade circles, a name with which to conjure. By the 1980s it had acquired the status of a gallant, independent small nation threatened by super states. There were rumours that its hallowed premises had been remortgaged, there were years when it made a loss. Funds were not available to bid vast sums to gain authors whose sales might run into millions of copies, nor was the inclination to raise them. Jock's particular court of writers was ageing beside him. Some even had died. Only Dervla Murphy among them was still young. Along with Stanley Unwin, Billy Collins and others, Jock hung on too long: he could not bear to do otherwise.

It was not entirely all gloom. The late seventies had brought a newcomer to the list, a jolly, irreverent artist named Beryl Cook who specialised in paintings of fat, sexy, improbable people usually in urban environments. This was an indication that the House of Murray was not in a rut. Then

Paddy Leigh Fermor at last completed two of the three volumes recording his 1930s trips across Europe (by 2005 the third had still not appeared) and Bevis Hillier had written the first volume of his life of John Betjeman. Jock suggested that perhaps the typescript was too long, to which Bevis tartly replied, 'I have created a castle; I cannot have it turned into a semi-detached'. Subsequently the author apologised. The publisher responded graciously, remarking, 'One tries only to remember the *good* things.' 'That,' Hillier observed, 'could almost have been his epitaph.'

Jock was less pleased by the proposal from Cape's Graham C. Greene of a joint edition of Conan Doyle stories, but was forced to agree because the copyright owner of the time insisted. In fact, it made sense because Cape with superior sales and distribution methods found an untapped market for Sherlock Holmes. Graham maintains Jock admitted ruefully that Murray's half-share in the enterprise had brought in greater revenue than they had enjoyed from Doyle for some years.

In an interview in 1992 with Naim Attallah, then owner of *The Oldie*, a monthly magazine which published interviews with prominent people of Attallah's choice, and replying to a request to describe his own character, Jock said he had 'no greed, no wish to have yachts or a second home'. He also had incorrigible curiosity and an ability to help people on with their coats which embarrassed American publishers – and also fellow old Etonian and publisher Ben Glazebrook – 'since I always put my hand under the coat to pull the jacket down'. This action caused them to 'look around at me with the gravest suspicion.'

Attallah asked Jock about Bernard Shaw who was responsible for Murray's publishing a book about his friend Dame Laurentia, a Benedictine abbess. Jock related that his intermediary was Dame Felicity and that he could only ever talk to her through a double grille. On his first visit, the idea petrified him but the lay sister who conducted him to her cell said, 'You needn't worry. It's not like them Carmelites what have spikes on their grilles.' He told Attallah that he adored Shaw even though he could be more heartlessly rude than anyone other than Evelyn Waugh. 'I was never at ease with Evelyn,' he said, 'I was always afraid he would do something unpleasant to somebody I was with.' He did not publish either man.

Remarking that his elder son was set to be John Murray VII, Attallah enquired 'Did that come about easily?' Jock replied, 'I put no pressure on him … Every Murray but one had one son and none revolted.' His younger son, Hallam, apart from a spell in the warehouse, did not join the family firm but had experience with other publishers when he was not identifying with certain Murray authors by riding his bike on distant con-

tinents. Daughters Freydis and Joanna were not conscripted, although the
former founded a medical publishing house, PassTest, in Manchester, while
the latter became a designer and printer of limited editions.

Jock was a hard act to follow and it would be wrong to suppose that the
succession came easily to John VII who inherited at an exceptionally difficult time when recession was looming. Relatively few independent general
publishing houses had survived into the eighties, let alone the nineties. John
R. took advice and appointed a non-family managing director, Nick Perren,
with whom he formed an effective relationship. Turnover and profit
increased, many books in the Murray tradition were published and while
Perren steered the company back to economic viability John R. (for
Richmond) turned his attention to editing, marketing and compiling a
wholly delightful volume from the scribbled, pencilled notes in Jock's commonplace book. All his life Jock had made entries, wherever he happened
to be, of sayings, notices, proverbs, sentences, paragraphs in books and
newspapers of any written offering which appealed to him. The sources
extended across the entire world of literature and graffiti. His son's selection contains gems of wisdom and wit, some with attributions, others without because either Jock had not written one down or the author's name had
become illegible. On every page there are entries which are touching, relevant, thought-provoking and, above all, funny. The anthology was a huge
success drawing critical acclaim and big sales. The slender, beautifully illustrated, immaculately produced volume – 120 pages – is a fitting tribute from
son to father; its title, *A Gentleman Publisher's Commonplace Book*, derives
from the quotation, 'When *Childe Harold* was published Byron woke up to
find himself famous and his publisher, John Murray, woke up a gentleman.'
The volume – which by 2004 had sold 33,000 copies – celebrates Jock's joy
in reading, illustration, typography. Each of his particular authors is represented – Osbert Lancaster in words and drawings, and there is a frontispiece
of Jock, in braces and bow-tie, standing beneath Byron's portrait in the
first-floor front of No 50. The entire book is quotable. I must limit myself
to one extract only. It was supplied by Dervla Murphy who saw this notice
in a jeweller's window in Cork – 'Ears pierced while you wait.'

The inevitable takeover of Murray's occurred in 2002 when Hodder
Headline (then owned by W H Smith) bought the 234-year-old company,
eventually moving it to the Euston Road. There was a subsequent sale to
Hachette in 2004. The Albemarle Street premises were retained as the
property of a family trust established by Sir John Murray in 1951. There is
talk, as I write, of the archive held there being moved to the National

Library of Scotland but the trust will maintain the house. I hope it may never become a shrine. The early-nineteenth-century terrace house has rung to the laughter of the Murrays, their authors, their friends and family. What Jock saw as the ghost of Lady Caroline Lamb was actually a real person in distress; his blithe spirit (wrong poet) will surely always haunt it.

Publishing was Jock's raison d'être; it also provided his bread and butter. He was not an innovator. He did not, like Hamlyn, Hill and Lane, alter the face of the book trade; he was the essence of conservatism, a traditionalist, C. of E., loyal servant of The Queen, a pillar of the establishment. His distinction lay in his editorial flair, his deep love of literature and people and his exuberant celebration of life.

John Grey Murray, MBE (1945), CBE , FSA, FRSL, born (John Arnaud Robin Grey), Wargrave, 22 September 1909, son of Thomas Robinson and Dorothy Evelyn Grey. Married Diana Mary James, 1939. Died Hampstead, 22 July 1993.

Five

IAN PARSONS

You could say that he had all the advantages. He was born into a comfortably off middle-class family, with father 'something in the City', living in Pont Street, Knightsbridge, and he missed the First World War. He was educated at Winchester and gained a place at Trinity College, where he took a first in English, edited the *Cambridge Review* and became acquainted with academics, some of whom he was later to publish at Chatto & Windus. Little is known of his father. His mother was of Scottish ancestry and there was a strong sense of thrift in his upbringing which led to his being sent off to prep school wearing his older sister's outgrown underclothes. In student and adult life he was protected from financial worries, but although generous by nature when officially retired, far from impoverished, he wrote to a former colleague to remind her that he had not received the first part of an advance due on a book of which he was joint author. He was a tall, handsome youth who sailed a bit and was proficient at golf; he played rugby for Blackheath and was a member of MCC; he had a light tenor voice and was an elegant ballroom dancer. He came down from university in 1928 to become an assistant in the design and production department of the publishing firm with which he was to spend almost his entire career, reflecting a way of life not unusual for one of his generation.

The partnership of Chatto & Windus, long since lacking anyone descended from either, belonged to Harold Raymond, a former teacher, and Charles Prentice, who had sent the young Parsons (hereafter often referred to as I.M.P.) a novel by T.F. Powys for a notice in the *Cambridge Review*. It was an imprint, not untypical of its time, smallish, economically run, with middle-to-highbrow authors such as Lytton Strachey, Aldous Huxley, Sylvia Townsend Warner, Daisy Ashford, the Scott Moncrieff translation of Marcel Proust and Constant Garnett's of Anton Chekhov. It had been founded in 1855 by John Camden Hotten and had long-established links with Ameri can writers – Mark Twain (*Huck Finn* was one of I.M.P.'s favourite books), Bret Harte, etc. It exemplified the best of literary publishing combined with financial viability. Huxley and Strachey came into both categories; Daisy Ashford's *The Young Visiters* and Helen Bannerman's *Little Black Sambo*, were both bread-and-butter and the best of pancake; there were whole series of books besides which added to the basic prosperity and allowed room for experiment.

Before joining the partnership I.M.P. worked for a while with Hunter & Foulis, the Edinburgh bookbinders; from the very beginning of his career he was imbued with high standards of production, which he maintained all his life, though it very quickly became clear to the partners at Chatto & Windus that he had an editorial role to play.

Harold Raymond has a special place in twentieth-century book-trade history for having invented book tokens; a kindly man, a perceptive editor, one who famously declared this verdict on a certain manuscript about which no one could be quite sure – 'Let's take a risk and turn it down.' Parsons' subsequent career illustrated how H. R. was his mentor. He taught him that although it is legitimate to publish a book of literary merit which might make a loss, overall a healthy list must operate on ample margins. I.M.P. swiftly learned about the trade, visiting booksellers and printers, becoming acquainted, as was relatively easy in a smallish firm, with everything from typography to packing.

But I.M.P.'s first love was poetry. In addition to the influence this had on the Chatto list it led him to suggest to Janet Adam Smith, who worked on *The Listener*, original poems for the feature she had introduced into that magazine. Some of these were frowned upon by BBC director, Sir John Reith. Ian defended her choice and subsequently published a selection of them as *Poems of Tomorrow*. His second love was what is unsatisfactorily known as literary criticism, or lit crit. At its highest level this implies appraisal of literature as an art form; at its lowest, a hastily penned, probably ephemeral, book review. Parsons' credentials were impeccable. At Cambridge he had attended lectures given by F. R. Leavis whose standards were so rigorous they excluded almost all writers, and whose views were shared by his wife, Queenie (Q. D. Leavis). Some said she actually wrote his books. Certainly Chatto, thanks to Ian, came to publish them both, along with works by less censorious luminaries such as William Empson, E.M. Tillyard, Basil Willey and L.C. Knights.

I.M.P. himself wrote criticism, mostly of poetry, for highbrow journals and was well regarded in Bloomsbury and other 'groups'. He founded poetry magazines, published by Chatto, and one modelled on *The New Yorker* named *Night and Day*. This was prosecuted for libelling the child Hollywood star Shirley Temple in a film review by Graham Greene. *Night and Day* folded after five months. Another journal, *The Geographical Magazine*, founded in 1936, did not. I.M.P. had a hand in that too.

In addition to being a serious young publisher Ian was a naturally social creature, amusing, well breeched, smartly dressed and usually engaging company. He played the ukelele and knew how to put over a number, having, according to colleague Peter Cochrane, 'a rich repertoire of ballads, folk songs and old music-hall ditties'. He was the wittiest of speakers, one who polished and worried about his usually brief addresses. He could be as nervous as an actor on a first night. As a listener he had a habit of repeating softly any phrase which appealed to him, nodding his head simultaneously to show appreciation. Sometimes he would add an editorial comment – 'beautifully phrased' or 'perfect syntax'. It could be disconcerting until you, as the speaker, realised that he was on your side. Politically, he was inclined to the left and this led to his lecturing on literature at the Working Men's College.

In 1934 Ian married the painter Marjorie Tulip Ritchie (known as Trekkie), who was a divorcee and ardent feminist. One of her sisters had a decade earlier become a rep selling Hogarth Press books for the Woolfs, which was an uncommon occupation for a woman at that time and for many decades to come. In 1937 Norah Smallwood joined Chatto as a secretary. Trekkie and Norah were to become the most influential women in Ian's life although he enjoyed the friendship of many others.

By the time of his marriage I.M.P. was already a partner and had published with John Lane, under its then managing director Allen Lane, a facetious fantasy illustrated by George Watts, *Shades of Albany*. He was compiling an anthology of verse from Hardy onwards to be published by Chatto in 1936. He had become a member of the Garrick and of the Society of Bookmen, and was interesting himself in the affairs of the Publishers' Association. In 1935 he and Trekkie attended a private performance in Vanessa Bell's studio in Fitzroy Street of Virginia Woolf's play *Freshwater*. It is probable that they met Leonard Woolf on the same occasion but Ian may have known him earlier. Leonard was later to become a fellow publisher under the Chatto umbrella and possibly, even probably, Trekkie's lover. I.M.P.'s offer to include novels by Virginia in the Chatto Phoenix Library was declined; all of V.W.'s novels, after she left Duckworth, had been published by the Hogarth Press.

By the mid-1930s, still aged only twenty-nine, I.M.P. had made firm and good impressions on the book trade, despite his carelessness one morning in leaving a manuscript on the back seat of his open sports car outside the Chatto offices. It was *Ultramarine* by Malcolm Lowry, and it was stolen. Worse than that, the author had not made a copy of it. (No doubt Ian had learned to believe in those words used by every publisher: 'We can take no responsibility for loss or damage to your typescript.') When Lowry had rewritten the book he generously excused Chatto from publishing it when they forecast a sale of only 1,500 copies. So it went to Cape who sold almost precisely that number.

When WWII began in September 1939, Ian joined the Auxiliary Fire Service and applied for aircrew duties in the RAF. He might have been thought tailor-made for the Battle of Britain but his age was against his becoming 'one of the few'; instead he was commissioned in the RAFVR in 1940, served in France briefly – becoming involved in the crashing of an aircraft there during the phoney war – then returned to England to spend much of the duration working in the basement of the Air Ministry study-ing aerial maps of Europe for RAF Intelligence. By 1945 he was a wing commander and partly resident in Victoria Square, Westminster, partly at Iford Grange near Rodmell in Sussex, where Virginia Woolf had commit-ted suicide in 1941. When the Hogarth Press was bombed at Mecklenburgh Square, Leonard Woolf moved in next to the Parsons' in Victoria Square where Norah Smallwood eventually also had a flat (her husband Peter was killed on active service in 1943). Woolf lived in London during the week and at Rodmell at weekends, accompanied by one or both of the Parsons'. He wished Trekkie to divorce Ian but she, who basically disliked the insti-tution of marriage, loved both men. The sharing of Trekkie's affections seemed not to cause a rift between Leonard and Ian, nor did the later alliance of Ian and Norah end the Parsons' marriage. In a sense these rela-tionships were a reflection of the lifestyle of the Bloomsbury Group, most 'members' of which were published by either Chatto or Hogarth, but, as I shall relate, Ian was more hurt by them than he usually disclosed.

In 1946 Leonard Woolf sold his press to Chatto, retaining total editorial independence during his lifetime; details of the deal may be found in a file in the Chatto Archive at Reading University, penned on a small, lined sheet of exercise-book paper. It does not mention either company and is unsigned. The scrap of paper reads:

Half share price £7,376
Whole share price £14,752
⅓ paid £4,917 6s. 8d.
⅔ paid £9,834 13s. 4d.
Paid £7,376
Balance £2,458 13s. 4d.

A further piece of paper records payment of the balance, one-sixth, on 29.10. 46. The arithmetic is puzzling, suggesting a total payment of two-thirds more than the whole share price. (On Leonard's death in 1968, most of his estate was left to Trekkie. By then Chatto/Hogarth had merged with Cape.)

The Woolfs had, in the thirties, engaged John Lehmann – brother of the novelist Rosamond and the actress Beatrix – to manage Hogarth. The relationship was always tense and during the war he was mainly concerned with editing *Penguin New Writing* . He agreed to sell his interest in Hogarth when Chatto bought its holding and later founded his own imprint which failed, quite simply, by being uncompromisingly highbrow. (Subsequently he founded *London Magazine*, with Chatto as its first distributor, and wrote a disgruntled memoir, *Thrown to the Woolfs*.)

In 1945 Harold Raymond, being the only working partner in Chatto, petitioned for I.M.P.'s early release from the RAF. J.W. McDougal, the third partner, had gone off to work for Chapman & Hall but Norah Smallwood, by now production manager, was waiting in the wings and was brought into partnership in that year. Harold's son Piers also joined the company to take charge of sales; he took a particular interest in the increasingly strong children's list but was treated very much as 'the boy' by Ian and Norah whose intellectual equal he was not. Another new editor recently demobbed was Peter Cochrane who had been recommended by Jamie Hamilton. He was paid £4 per week to be a reader, was sent to a printer's to learn something of that craft and, for one year, to an evening class at the London School of Printing, much as I.M.P. had been twenty years before.

Cochrane has left a personal account of I.M.P. on his NLSC tape at the British Library. Parsons, he recorded, was a perfectionist, a good book designer and a very good editor, able to spot potential in a writer. He could be impatient of books he personally found uninteresting and didn't have an eye for presentable, reputable, middlebrow novels, although he was quick to spot a first-rate – or even a second-rate highbrow one. Jeremy Lewis disputed this view, maintaining that Lynne Reid Banks was one of I.M.P.'s authors. Another middlebrow and close friend was Compton Mackenzie whose memoirs of WWI, censored in 1922, were published by Chatto twenty years on, and whose post WWII comic novel, *Whisky Galore*, was a popular success for the list. Mackenzie, who had been publishing fiction since the late Edwardian era, remained to contribute volumes of diaries, *Octaves 1–8* … at least.

Peter Cochrane remembered Ian Parsons' application, as creative editor, to an immensely long typescript of a historical novel by Hope Muntz. Its subject was King Harold, its title *The Golden Warrior*. He reduced it to more readable length and high saleability with the approval of the author who wisely accepted his suggestions. When interviewed for his job, Peter found Ian 'a very open, amiable, forthcoming person who asked sensible questions. He was tall, very handsome, very well-built, striking looking with a half-smile most of the time. He seemed to care; he took things seriously but was also jovial. He was a good instructor, impulsive, exceedingly intelligent, with a first-class brain, but he had a habit of switching off in mid converse when some important thought occurred to him, then returning moments later to the matter in hand and giving it his full attention.'

The Parsons', who were childless, were outstandingly hospitable to their friends' offspring. The Davids (Dick and Nora, of Cambridge University Press) and the Cochranes, who had two daughters, valued this. All were invited to the house to which Ian and Trekkie had moved – Juggs Corner, at Kingston, near Lewes in Sussex, three miles from Rodmell where Leonard still dwelt at Monk's House. There the children were shown suitable books from the Chatto list and Peter Cochrane was quizzed about typefaces and fonts in volumes selected at random from the shelves.

Both Piers and Peter became partners (Harold Raymond lending Cochrane £1,000 interest free on condition that his assistance remained secret) but the financial arrangements of Chatto were not easy for men with young families. The senior partners all had private incomes; at the end of the financial year dividends were paid, but although these could be appreciable sums it was the policy to plough profits back into the firm and twelve months was a long while to wait for a large portion of your income. Peter says that Piers drew attention to this problem by smoking a foul-smelling tobacco in his pipe, explaining that it was the only brand he could afford. Eventually, with reluctance, Cochrane left to become a printer at Butler & Tanner, thus earning the salary he required although he remained connected to Chatto as an occasional reader and, in 1977, as author of a war memoir – *Charlie Company*. Piers left too, some years after the partnership had become a limited company in 1953, when his father was ready to retire. H.R. wished to hand over a large number of his shares to his son, thus giving him a greater holding than Norah Smallwood, which did not please that lady. The matter was resolved when Piers resigned and went first to Methuen, then to Dent, as sales director. Relations were strained for a while between the various parties, but, subsequently, as letters in the archive at Reading indicate, they became cordial again.

I.M.P.'s standing as a literary publisher during roughly the middle fifty years of the century was due to his sensitive response to creative writing in prose

and poetry. He was an optimist who believed there was a public for high /
upper-middle brow authors and he became a positive salesman in helping to
promote those he admired. He and Norah wrote countless letters to individual booksellers expressing their enthusiasm and eliciting support. Those
of us who esteemed their judgement usually responded positively by agreeing to stock and display the books which they were championing. Often
they were right. Sometimes – as with Quentin Bell's biography of Virginia
Woolf – they were so right that their initial print order proved inadequate.

Ian did not inherit, as did Jock Murray an established and much revered
family imprint; he did not, like Allen Lane and Paul Hamlyn, discover a
whole new market for books, nor, like Jonathan Cape, Hamish ('Jamie')
Hamilton and Victor Gollancz, did he found his own list. He joined an
existing one of quiet distinction and enhanced its status at the same time as
playing a leading part in trade affairs both administratively and socially. He,
belonging to a generation and a culture which held that mankind was open
to enlightenment through the arts, believed in excellence. He went on
believing this despite living through two world wars. So did many others.
What was the particular quality in him that earned such praise from his contemporaries and justified Alan Hill's assessment of him as 'the most professional publisher of his time'? I believe it was to do with his instinctive
recognition of the best coupled with a desire to make it available, without
dumbing down, to anyone capable of appreciating it. It was a distillation,
in practical terms, of what he had learned at Cambridge from Leavis. For
him, the Chatto & Windus office (for most of his time in William IV Street,
close to Trafalgar Square) was an appropriate environment from which to
operate. He did not need luxurious accommodation. He was a publisher for
the working day, an essential portion of which was usually spent in the elegant ambience of the nearby Garrick Club .

Ian's pre-war poetry anthology *The Progress of Poetry* included six poems
by Isaac Rosenberg whom he was very proud to have 'discovered'.
Rosenberg, the impoverished son of a Lithuanian refugee, was both painter
(he studied at the Slade) and poet. He was killed on the Western Front in
1918. Little that he wrote was published in his lifetime and he was not
included in the *DNB* until the *Missing Persons* volume appeared in the
1990s. I.M.P. published him eight years before his work featured in the
Faber Book of Modern Poetry; he also contributed a 750-word appraisal of
Rosenberg as introduction to the *Collected Poems* (1979). For this he endeavoured to obtain an Arts Council subsidy, writing to Charles Osborne, then
its literature secretary, 'He [Rosenberg] is now widely recognised as one of
the outstanding poetic talents, along with Wilfred Owen, that the great war

destroyed; [he was] also a remarkable painter and draughtsman … with self-portraits in the National Portrait Gallery and the Tate.'

The Second World War interrupted I.M.P.'s hobby as an anthologist, but in the fifties he relished the opportunity provided by the educational publisher, Ginn, to edit *Poetry for Pleasure* in eight volumes, a selection from which was brought out twenty years later by Chatto and, in the USA, by Norton. This had a trade rather than a school market but it may well have been the association with Ginn which led Chatto to purchase, in 1954, the small educational list of Christophers.

Another compilation which met with wide approval in both trade and school editions was Ian's anthology of First War poets, *Men Who March Away*. The publishing history here is misty, the archive at Reading leading the researcher to suppose that the original was a Chatto book for the general market, but Alan Hill's autobiography gives a different impression. Hill, head of Heinemann Educational Books (HEB), states that at a dinner he was seated next to Ian and referred to the Chatto edition of Wilfred Owen's poems, saying he would like to publish a collection of First War verse. Parsons replied, 'And I would like to edit it.' In his 70th birthday tribute to Ian, Alan affirms, '… The title came from Hardy. I invited him to compile and edit it.' The book, he added, was published jointly in 1965; a note at Reading, in October 1977, gives stock of a hardback edition as 500, of a paperback edition as 4,000, and records a sale of 10,000 to Book Club Associates. Two years later stock of the hardback was 351 and of the paperback 480, and there is a comment from Norah Smallwood that Heinemann had sufficient stock for two years. An edition I have, published by Chatto in 1993, gives no publishing data beyond 'First Edition, 1965' and in neither the acknowledgements nor in I.M.P.'s sixteen-page introduction is there any reference to HEB or Alan Hill. Ian's introduction is a gem of self-disciplined editing. From it there gleams a passion for poetry, scholarship lightly worn, mastery of his subject and spare use of words.

Chatto was by no means the only important publisher of poetry. It was not even the market leader, a distinction which lay with Faber & Faber who had T. S. Eliot (a working director of the company), W. H. Auden, Stephen Spender, Louis MacNeice, Ezra Pound and, later, Philip Larkin, Ted Hughes, Seamus Heaney and Andrew Motion among others. I.M.P. certainly knew Geoffrey Faber, through the PA and the Society of Bookmen, and was probably acquainted with Eliot but, in the spirit of idle speculation, recalling that the Woolfs were the original publishers of *The Waste Land*, supposing the great man had remained with Hogarth? What a heritage might then have come Chatto's way, twenty or so years on!

Certainly Chatto became richer than Faber in literary criticism, a part of
the list being dominated by the mighty Leavis with whom there survives
much correspondence, some of it acrimonious. Frank Leavis had disputes
with the Cambridge hierarchy and with I.M.P. over a long period, but he
remained loyal to both, his major works bearing the Chatto imprint throughout his life. Richard Hoggart's seminal – and bestselling – work, *The Uses of
Literacy* (1957), is in the tradition – 'great', if you like – of the Leavises's
explorations into reading and the popular press. Would it have come to
Chatto but for the reputation for so-called 'lit crit' which Ian had established?
I.M.P. and F. R. Leavis published together for nearly half a century; each had
the measure of the other. Their correspondence – handwritten on Leavis's
side – was often on the verge of provoking a rift. It came close to it in 1974
when I.M.P., exasperated by what he saw as niggling complaints from an
albeit distinguished author and old friend, wrote to him concerning a book
scheduled for imminent publication. His royalty would be 15% and, 'You
will receive 48.75p per copy whereas C&W – after three or four years – will
have made 23p per copy.' This was the publisher speaking from the heart; it
was also one first-class mind telling another that the publishing of lit crit, even
at its most hallowed, must not ignore financial commonsense.

Although he gave time and thought to verse, as publisher and anthologist, I.M.P. did not neglect the adult prose adorning the list. Once, at the
annual National Book League cricket match, played on the Westminster
School ground at Vincent Square, a social occasion when aged publishers
put on whites and played an Authors' XI (comprised largely of test-match
players who had not actually written the books bearing their names), Ian
and Norah distracted my eye from the ball by haranguing me about a forthcoming title. The book was *Now I Remember: A Holiday History of Britain*
by Ronald Hamilton, 'Which Mr Cortie [their rep] will be showing you.'

'He was my housemaster at Winchester,' said Ian, as I tried to concentrate on watching, for the only time in my life, the fine, veteran West Indies
all-rounder, Learie Constantine. 'It's a marvellous book going reign by
reign from the Conqueror to the present Queen. It tells you briefly all the
most important events, has a thumbnail appraisal of each monarch, plus
illustrations. You'll sell it very well.' He and Norah pushed books at me far
more aggressively than Ronald Cortie, or any other rep who knew me,
would have dared. Constantine was soon out so I attended to them. They
were right. It sold well in Hampstead; it filled a gap, that elusive niche
which every publisher needs to find.

There was no question of Ian being a bore – he could never have been
that – but he saw this sporting occasion as extra-curricular in the book-trade

calendar which meant we were both *officially at work*. He would never have behaved in that way at Lord's, during a test match, where I met him more than once. Then we would have talked about cricket, although we were both truanting from work, or, as once happened, he would have tried to foist on me some sandwiches – 'I bought them for my spastic friend and I've lost him' – because he was scheduled to give lunch to Peggy Ashcroft who was somewhere on the ground awaiting his company

When an opportunity arose, I.M.P. would have no hesitation in beating the Chatto drum. Although there was nothing on his list to compare with the depth and breadth of Dent's Everyman Library, or even with Collins' Classics and Oxford's World Classics in numbers of titles, Chatto had several long running and newly instituted series. After he was dragooned by Graham C. Greene, of Cape, with which company his had become linked, to give editorial advice to me on my revision of *Mumby's History of Publishing and Bookselling*, I.M.P. was extremely helpful, but he couldn't resist commenting that I had not, perhaps, done justice to Chatto. He enlarged on this assertion in his clear, thin-nibbed handwriting:

Saturday 11.11.72

... The first is The Phoenix Library, started in 1927–8 and still going strong at the outbreak of war. Along with Secker's Adelphi Library and Cape's Travellers Library, I think it was reckoned among the leaders, if not THE leader, of the fashion for cheap cloth-bound, pocket-sized books. After the war it was re-started as the New Phoenix Library, and survived until the late fifties, when it was finally killed by the paperback revolution. It was infinitely more important than Cape's Florin Books, which you mention.

The second is our Zodiac Press series of reprints of classic novels. Started in 1946, immediately after the war, it was planned to provide the public – and the public libraries – with exceptional, well-designed and -produced books, at modest prices. That it succeeded in doing so is proved by the fact that a quarter of a century later it is still moving along very nicely, and has over 30 titles consistently reprinting. Frankly, it would be absurd to mention Hamilton's Novel Library (brilliantly designed by Oliver Simon as they were) which sank without trace in a few years, if you don't also mention the ZP series.

Last and certainly least important except that it exemplifies another specific (and more recent) trend – that of reprinting out-of-print titles that were once in great demand – our Landmark

Library perhaps deserves a passing glance. Started as recently as 1968, it will probably have clocked up the better part of 50 titles by the time your book appears.

It is, of course, only one of many such reprint series, and indeed reprint IMPRINTS that have started up in the last 7 to 8 years, but the trend is unmistakable and should perhaps be recorded.

Forgive these ill-written and seemingly self-congratulatory notes. They are written against time, at home where I have no secretary, and can only be excused by the well-known fact that if one doesn't blow one's own trumpet (by which I mean C&W's not IMP's) nobody else will.

It is interesting that he didn't mention the Phoenix Living Poets, a series which had grown to at least thirty volumes by 1968, was published jointly with Hogarth and was edited at one time by C. Day Lewis. The series survived into the seventies and eighties under Denis Enright and Andrew Motion.

When I.M.P. became an editor 'unofficially' on *Mumby* because of the Chatto/Cape merger, Graham C. Greene derived enormous pleasure from getting his services free, chortling to me one day, as he said, 'Now we're under the same umbrella we can ask Ian to comment on your typescript and we won't have to pay him.' Publishers who were personally generous enjoyed these little meannesses. I was deeply grateful. Ian put me right on so many points and persuaded me to drop ill-judged blasts against certain people and companies. (In the Reading archive there is an excellent example of Ian's editing in a two-page comment on a book about Isaac Rosenberg by one Richard Anderson. Every observation and correction reveals a mind brimming with knowledge. He tells the author that 'gibbous' is not an uncommon word 'as you state. It has been used for centuries as the almost cliché adjective for the waxing moon.' He also takes him to task for a far-fetched interpretation of the line, 'And jewels at his nose.' This, he tells Anderson, 'has nothing to do with the jewel worn by adult Indian women in the nostril, which is not worn by boys, and is not a caste mark. It simply means that the boy had drops at the end of his nose!')

I.M.P. and N.S. were right about *Now I Remember* and also about Laurie Lee's charming memoir of childhood and youth, *Cider with Rosie*, and even about the same author's impertinent few pages recording his delight in fatherhood, *The First Born*, at the then outrageous price of six shillings. Ron Cortie had a hard time urging that one on me in large quantities but, to my disgust, it sold. And Ian was the champion of William Humphreys, an American novelist who became a close friend of his. In addition to a block-buster which didn't do as well as they had hoped, there was a short book about fishing, rather in the Steinbeck vein, called *A Spawning Run*. We moved a great many copies at my shop partly because Ian had sung its merits to Peggy Ashcroft. She bought numerous copies, as was her way, when a book took her fancy. There was, for me, an unforgettable Saturday morning in the seventies when I looked up from the counter to see Dame Peggy and Ian, radiating goodwill, entering the shop. He had, I suppose, been staying at her Hampstead home; they had come down the High Street to say 'Hello' and remained while he became slightly admonitory.

He regaled me with the tale of how when Harold Nicolson's *Some People* was published (1927), J.G. Wilson, of Bumpus, had stood at his Oxford Street door beside a great pile of the book in which he believed so fervently and handed a copy to each customer as they left the shop, saying, 'We shall charge it to your account. You won't regret it.' I.M.P. was possibly reminded of this because I had a stack of Iris Murdoch's latest novel on display. I defended the fact that I was not acting like J.G. by telling him that in the sixties, when Tony Godwin became managing director of Bumpus, many customers' accounts had not been settled for decades. But it was typical of Ian that he admired Wilson's zest for promoting a book about which he cared. He had been at my shop on another occasion for a party we gave for Robert Shaw's first novel, *The Hiding Place*, which Chatto did not have to exert pressure on me to stock because Bob was a customer and I had played cricket with him. (Not everything in those days related to market forces.)

Shaw was an actor, and later a famous film star married to Mary Ure, but he was more talented, in my opinion, as a writer and wrote several succesful novels for Chatto before his hectic lifestyle ended early in a heart seizure. Another actor who featured even larger on the Chatto list was Dirk Bogarde, whom Norah Smallwood heard one day talking on the radio. She sensed a book in him and was right; she pipped Alan Hill or maybe his colleague Edward Thompson at the post. Luck is a necessary part of publishing but it was not personally Ian's in this case although he backed her judgement. Or was it, as some in Chatto said, John Charlton's? In all publishing houses when a book succeeds there are many who claim that they first spotted it.

After 1946 when the Hogarth Press joined Chatto the two imprints merged, certainly in the minds of booksellers, although Leonard Woolf was always the one associated with psychoanalysis and Sigmund Freud. And Virginia Woolf became an industry. After her suicide in 1941 there were no undiscovered novels, but in 1951 came her *Writer's Diary* which was a huge success, followed over the years by volumes of letters and memorabilia to such an extent that it became a popular belief in the trade that Virginia Woolf's laundry lists would be the big Chatto/Hogarth book for the following Christmas. It was not only Virginia Woolf but the entire Bloomsbury Group who were associated with the imprints. Lytton Strachey had been with Chatto in the first place but most of the group were Hogarth and remained so; the five superb volumes of autobiography from Leonard Woolf and the two-volume life of Virginia by Quentin Bell were all Hogarth titles. Laurence van der Post was also a Hogarth author and he featured large on the post-WWII list. To the trade and the reps the two lists were really one and equally distinguished; following Leonard's death in 1969 it became a matter of historical association which decided the imprint to be used on new books.

The reps at Chatto were self-employed, working on commission with a low guaranteed annual income. They owned their cars and were allowed generous expenses. The two whom I knew in London, from the fifties until the merger with Cape, were more affluent than most of their opposite numbers in other publishing firms. Chatto always had highly saleable new titles and a good backlist; unlike the former partners the reps did not have to wait for an annual settlement. I.M.P. and N.S., and even Piers Raymond, could be incredibly naïve about the activities of the two convivial characters who travelled their books to Central and Outer London and, in one case, also to towns and cities as far away as Nottingham and Brighton. Neither was a formally educated man; one of them, Gilbert Hart, I would bet had rarely read a book in his life. The other Ronald Cortie, who became my close friend, was self-educated, had a genuine love of literature and music and could be as enthusiastic as his directors in promoting a book. Gilbert had the Central London territory, which he increasingly neglected; Ron devised a system, approved by Piers, of calling only on booksellers who could be relied upon to place reasonably large orders. He was not dilatory about making these calls, often bonded with his customers and enjoyed lunchtimes with them. He also used his country visits to pursue to some extent his own interests, for instance, taking his charming wife with him to the South Coast for a short break. Occasionally a sales manager was appointed. One was Geoffrey Barry, who, for his opposition to apartheid, had been forced to leave South Africa in a hurry, but Ron had little truck with him. He dealt through Piers, Norah and Ian, as he referred to them, although formality was required when he actually addressed them. Gilbert increasingly spent his time in pubs more than in bookshops. He had good friends –

not only Ron and Tommy Thompson, the trade manager (the three of them had been with the British Expeditionary Force in France in 1940), but booksellers too who frequently helped him out. On one occasion Una Dillon, of the London University Bookshop named after her, phoned me at home to ask if I would advise her to ring Mrs Smallwood. 'You see, their rep, Mr Hart, never calls to see me and I'm sure we are missing important books.'

'Una,' I said, 'leave it with me.' I rang Ron and said, 'Get Gilbert round to Dillon's.' It worked. Gilbert, in haste, took his bag to Torrington Place where he charmed Una, who was a forgiving, tolerant woman. The visit saved his face and, perhaps, his job.

There was another occasion when Gilbert had actually made a call – at Selfridges' book department. One of the titles he subscribed was an item of lit crit by a distinguished Cambridge don with a low saleability rating. At the reception before a Society of Bookmen dinner, Ian and Norah cornered me in the bar. Ian was indignant. 'Mr Hart,' he exclaimed, 'went to Selfridges with the new Tillyard (or whatever) and came back with an order for only one copy. Now that is not good enough.' I looked Ian straight in the eyes and said, 'I think he was lucky to get one. It's not their book.'

Gilbert, who survived this momentary focus on his salesmanship, did not deserve to be blamed for failing to sell quantities of lit crit to an Oxford Street store. What astonished me was that none of the intelligentsia within Chatto had rumbled that he was just not up to his job. It didn't matter that he was only semi-literate. Booksellers didn't wish to hear his opinion of Huxley, Leavis or anyone else, but it was his job to get Chatto books on display in the shops and he was on commission. 'Mr Hart', as he was known by the hierarchy, was allowed a generous rein. Ron Cortie's approach was different; he tended, until he learned to read his buyer, to push for too large an order, but often he had read the book, really loved it and, usually, for practical reasons, as well as the loyalty he felt to the company, he did well by Chatto. (He had a genuine admiration for Piers, Norah, and I.M.P. and he revered Harold Raymond who had engaged him and who, at his interview, treated him, a cockney boy from South London, like a gentleman.) Ronald even, so he claimed, dared to speak at sales meetings, giving his opinion about books; he was forever in trouble with Norah with whom he had a long love/hate relationship. Ron's comeuppance at her hands is recorded in Jeremy Lewis's *Kindred Spirits*. Many of the Chatto staff had gathered for Christmas Eve drinks at the Marquis of Granby close to the offices; Norah had graciously consented to join them. There came a moment when Ron felt it was his turn to stand a round and asked, 'What will you have, Norah?'

All merriment ceased. There was a hush. '*Mrs Smallwood*, to you, Ron,' She replied. (This story is sympathetically embellished by Jeremy who wasn't actually present when it occurred.)

A few years later N. S., I.M.P. and other directors of Chatto, Cape, Bodley Head attended the retirement lunch I organised for Ron at a hotel in Bloomsbury. Their manner to him could not have been more genial. I recall I.M.P. calling along the top table to me, when the proceedings were well into the late afternoon, 'Any more plonk, Ian?', and Norah's alarm, for she was always anxious about his health, when he was served it. There was also a mock trial one December at the Bookmen, when Ian was the judge and appeared, to Norah, to be knocking back brandy after brandy; it was actually, in the best theatrical tradition, cold tea. By then he had had, in 1965, a serious coronary attack.

In addition to his work as an active publisher and anthologist, I.M.P. gave much time to trade affairs. His work for the PA involved him intimately with the defence of the NBA, the price-fixing mechanism imposed by publishers on the sale of net books which, at the time, most publishers and booksellers believed gave stability to the trade. They spent large sums of money defending it before the Registrar of Restrictive Practices in 1962. Ian had been president of the PA from 1957–9 and became part of the case for the defence. In a tribute at his memorial service, R .W. (Dick) David, who succeeded him as president, said his evidence was 'wonderfully lucid, concise' and provided 'a comprehensive statement of how the publishing trade then essentially operated … His ability, under cross-examination, to parry the lunges of opposing counsel with quick, humorous and effective replies was remarkable.' Asked about the economics of publishing he made it clear that his company did not expect to make profit from much of the poetry it published.

I.M.P. was briefly on the PA council before WWII, again in 1949 and from 1951–61. He also became chairman of the sub-committee on copyright and of the Book Production Training Committee. At the Society of Bookmen he was chairman from 1950–3 and became its second only president on the death of Stanley Unwin in 1968. Chairing the Bookmen – thirty meetings over a period of three years – was an exacting task as I knew when the honour fell to me. After two years I hinted to Ian that perhaps I might be allowed to hand over. He became headmasterly and said, 'Basil [Blackwell] did three years, Rupert [Hart-Davis] did three years, Bob [Lusty] did three years, YOU'LL do three years.' That was that.

I.M.P.'s lectures on literature at the Working Men's College, Camden Town, were probably his nearest approach to political activity, although his closeness to Leonard Woolf and, later, Norman Mackenzie, both of whom were leftish activists, may have involved him sometimes with the Labour Party. Certainly, he claimed to be a socialist. An institution which played a more potent role in his life was the Garrick Club where, only a few minutes walk from Chatto's, he regularly lunched and often dined. In his mature years going to the club was much like joining a session of the council of the PA and, although discussion of business was officially frowned upon, it was a topic which cropped-up at 'the publishers' table' frequented by Hamish Hamilton, Wren Howard (partner of Jonathan Cape), Robert Lusty, John Boon, Jack Newth and others in the book world. Most directors of Chatto became members. Ian was an immensely convivial and clubbable person (he also belonged to the Beefsteak and the RAC) and he served on the committee at the Garrick where his interests extended to supplying the chef with the recipe for his own egg mousse. At home, in Sussex, he was active in the garden and the kitchen as well as on the golf course. At Jugg's Corner, the writer and critic Janet Adam Smith, remembered him:

> ...From the first welcoming hug at the front door one's spirits start-
> ed to shoot up ... I can see him in the garden – did ever man grow
> beans with such passion! ... or in the sitting-room after dark
> watching the badgers play on the lawn – then later himself playing
> the ukelele and singing ... Next morning he would look eagerly to
> see how many Morning Glories were out in the conservatory. He
> enjoyed such a variety of things and made one enjoy with him.

Given this wide-ranging activity it is unsurprising that Ian suffered a severe heart attack in 1965 and was prevented from working for many weeks. By then there had been several additions to the Chatto board. When Hogarth became linked in 1946, Leonard Woolf had automatically joined. Others appointed over the next quarter of a century were Peter Calvocoressi (later to become MD at Penguin), Hugo Brunner, sometime sales director, John Charlton, Christopher Maclehose, D. J. (Denis) Enright – editors in the true Raymond/Parsons tradition – and the poet laureate, Cecil Day-Lewis.

The severity of the 1965 illness probably played some part in determining the future of Chatto and Hogarth. Mergers and takeovers had already become the norm. Three years earlier, Jonathan Cape had been restructured after the death of its eponymous founder. Two talented young men, Tom Maschler and Graham C. Greene (nephew of the novelist), became major shareholders and when Wren Howard too died, they and Michael, his son, looked around for likely imprints with which to merge, particularly for administration and distribution reasons. Also, as Graham put it to me at the time, 'to protect us against American takeover'. (No comment.)

The brief story of the merger, which was first mulled over as early as 1962, is well told by Eric de Bellaigue, a City financier interested in the book trade who, in his retirement, became an analyst and historian of its business dealings. He has related the almost cloak-and-dagger nature of the discussions between Ian Parsons, Michael Howard and Graham C. Greene which often took place at the last-named's apartment in Albany, close to the Royal Academy. The 'plotters', in the interests of secrecy, used the tradesmen's entrance to this exclusive enclave, built in 1804 to provide pieds-à-terre for the affluent. (Albany, it is worth remembering, was the subject and setting for I.M.P.'s youthful book described on its 1930 jacket as 'A Facetious Fantasy'.) The talks proceeded in a leisurely, gentlemanly way from 1967 until 1969,when Chatto, Cape Ltd became a reality. At that time Cape's turnover was near to £800,000 p.a, Chatto's slightly less than £600,000. This gave shareholders a 60%–40% holding in the new company but, by what could be called creative accounting, this became 50%–50%, with editorial independence preserved on both sides. (Ian made an eleventh-hour proposal that the two companies should share Cape's offices but this was strictly against the spirit of the merger and was rejected.)

Over the next decade, once he was declared fit from his coronary, I.M.P. engaged again in Chatto and book-trade affairs for about three days a week but also took holidays. He was not in the class of Unwin, Collins or Hill, combining commerce with pleasure in pursuit of export markets; his journeys were undertaken mostly for the delights of travel, although he made regular trips to New York to visit his friends, Donald Brace, the Knopfs, other American publishers and author Bill Humphries. He particularly loved driving in France and once gave me a detailed, authoritative itinerary to follow on my first visit to the Loire, informing me which chateaux were 'musts' and which could be, as it were, 'turned down'. He went to Egypt with Trekkie late in life but did not accompany her to Ceylon whither she journeyed with Leonard Woolf to visit the scenes of his pre-1914 colonial service. Norah Smallwood also travelled in France and seemingly engineered encounters with the Parsons' which drew acid comments from Trekkie such as, 'She is like dry rot in a house. She seeps into everything.' Trekkie repented flying into a rage with Ian when Norah infuriated her; Ian broke off a platonic relationship with a younger woman publisher when, after hearing him express his distress at having to share Trekkie with Leonard, she queried, 'But what about you and Norah?'

• • •

In 1971 the Society of Bookmen celebrated its golden jubilee. I was in the chair, the theme of the meeting was 'Now Let us Praise Famous Men'. Four former chairmen spoke – Gaffer Blackwell, Ian Parsons, Robert Lusty and Philip Unwin. It was an occasion which brought out the best and the worst in Ian. The dinner was held at Stationers' Hall, where he arrived in a great flap.

'My dear boy,' he exclaimed, 'I'm sorry I'm late, but I'm very unwell. I took off my sling because I thought it would attract attention.'

'Yes,' I replied, without enquiring why he should have had a sling since both arms seemed to be performing extravagantly well. I bought him a double whisky.

Throughout dinner he was polite but distracted. We talked about Leonard Woolf who had willed most of his estate to Trekkie and caused outrage among his blood relations, who were contesting it. It was not the most soothing of subjects to have introduced. He said that Trekkie would win. 'My wife is a formidable woman, you know.' When I called on him to speak to the meeting I could all but hear his relief. He rose, his hands shaking. Then the actor in him took over. He was dazzling. There was laugh after laugh. He sang a mildly racy song about a soldier who 'when he was up at the front always had his trousers hanging out at the back'. To cap his performance he produced a dummy rabbit from his shirt front. After dinner, utterly relaxed, he bounded off to catch the night train to Edinburgh – 'to see my binders'.

That evening went superbly but conviviality did not always bring out the best in Ian.

In 1973 The Bodley Head, in which Allen Lane had made his entry into publishing long before, joined Chatto, Cape, to make a formidable although still small group of literary publishers. I.M.P., already sharing the chairmanship with Graham C. Greene, then became part of a triumvirate including Max Reinhardt who had owned most of The Bodley Head. The three met at the Garrick where Ian, the host, offered to propose Graham for membership in the presence of Reinhardt to whom he did not make a similar suggestion. On another occasion, at the same venue, Edward Young attempted to introduce Ian to his chairman, saying, 'Would you like to meet George Rainbird?' Ian replied, 'No,' and stalked away.

Piers Raymond once related how Ian, on returning to Chatto from the club, met a young office girl running out of the building. 'Where are you going, my dear?' he enquired. 'To get some cakes for tea, Mr Parsons.' 'Do you usually do this, etc., etc.?' He catechised her until she burst into tears, ran back into the office, handed in her notice and went home. Piers commented ruefully that she was one of the best of Chatto's accounts clerks. And it was at a time of full employment.

Everyone has their bad moments and Dick David's expressed view that Ian 'really *liked* people … warm friendliness radiated from [him]' is not invalidated by these incidents.

For a while the separate imprints of Chatto, Bodley Head & Cape behaved as intended. Editorial independence was hallowed. A distribution centre at Grantham, in Lincolnshire, was established but at Cape the management team was at least a generation younger than that at Chatto. Ian was due for retirement in 1974, Norah was to succeed him but she too was elderly and seriously afflicted by arthritis so could not expect to reign for long. In 1982 Carmen Callil, whose Virago imprint had joined the group, succeeded her. A few years later Graham C. Greene and Tom Maschler, with the indignant disapproval of Max Reinhardt (he complained to me that he made only £1.7m from the deal), sold to Random House of New York for more than fifteen million pounds.

In retirement I.M.P. indulged numerous activities. In addition to editing the Rosenberg *Collected Poems*, he was co-author, with George Spater, of *A Marriage of Two Minds*, a study of Leonard and Virginia Woolf. He was already involved with the Scottish Academic Press and Sussex University Press. He was awarded, in 1975, an Hon. D.Litt. from the University of St Andrews. The involvement with Sussex went deeper. The University at Falmer was close to his home and he was friendly with the author and journalist Norman Mackenzie, who was one of the founder faculty members, and with the vice chancellor, historian Asa Briggs. The existence of these new presses stimulated I.M.P., whose professional advice was welcomed by them. They did not ultimately flourish, partly because the resident dons who were already authors saw no advantage in moving from established imprints.

In 1976, at his seventieth-birthday celebratory dinner at Kettner's in Soho sponsored by the Society of Bookmen, Ian was slightly more reflective, speaking for rather longer than usual though the wit still prevailed. He was presented with a Festschrift – one privately printed copy only – comprising tributes ordered alphabetically, starting with lines of affectionate doggerel by Peggy Ashcroft and ranging through thirty-six contributors, including the Gaffer, John Boon, William Empson, Alan Hill, V. S. Pritchett, Norah Smallwood, Sylvia Townsend-Warner and Basil Willey, one of 'his' lit crit dons. I treasure one of the few cyclostyled copies, given to me by chairman Gordon Graham. After the speeches Ian was prevailed upon, at Piers Raymond's suggestion, to play the ukelele. He performed impeccably. There was nothing undignified about an elderly man reverting to a youthful role. He had style.

The seventieth-birthday tributes came in prose and verse, handwritten, typewritten, elegantly calligraphed within decorated borders, some with small drawings, at least one by telegram, one partly in Greek, another in Latin, one as original sheet music – all emphasising I.M.P.'s wit, scholarship, companionship. Norah Smallwood, parodying Shelley, exclaimed, 'Dull thou never wert'; Ivan Chambers, eccentric, endearing, independent bookseller of Museum Street, Bloomsbury, referred to 'the unaffected eighteenth-century elegance in everything you do'; John Boon hailed him as 'companion at Twickenham' and 'one ... who shared trade gossip and politics ... also dry Martinis ...' Bruno (Sir John Brown of OUP) thanked him 'for instructing me by precept and example, for making me laugh so much ... you are like one of your marvellous speeches ... a mixture of the hilarious and the serious ... '; Alan Hill remembered his description 'of a well-known Sussex bookseller as "the man who put the F into Uckfield",' and also recalled a meeting with him at Chatto's trade counter 'when an old lady came in asking for a book ...which Ian told her had been published in 1886.' The lady agreed it was an old book but said, 'I thought you publishers kept a copy of every book you published.'

'"Madam," replied I.M.P., "in some cases we keep thousands." '

Four years later Ian died, after dinner with Trekkie at Jugg's Corner, from a heart attack, having that day passed a check-up at a hospital in Brighton. It was a good way for him to go. At his secular crematorium funeral service, Thomas Hardy's poem *Regret Not Me* was read to mourners who crowded the aisle and lobby or squeezed into pews, but how could we not lament? At a subsequent memorial meeting at Stationers' Hall, Janet Adam Smith and Dick David addressed another large gathering and Dame Peggy read poetry. It would have been appropriate if someone had quoted former colleague Peter Cochrane's eulogy of Ian from the 70th birthday book where he describes him as 'the scholar who is never a pedant ... the wit who is never otiose ... the man with as discriminating a palate for claret as for literature (whether Chatto-bottled or not) ... the bookman who has always brought the vital ingredient of sagacity to what Johnson called "the mercantile ruggedness of publishing".' In fact, I. M. P.'s best obituaries are embedded in this rarest of volumes.

Trekkie wrote of her husband, in a letter, 'Nothing can ever mitigate the loss and one wouldn't want it to' – but she continued to cherish old friends until her death in 1995. These words were quoted by the recipient, Janet

Adam Smith, in her tribute in the *Independent* and afterwards published in a pamphlet by Roly Atterbury of the Westerham Press. Atterbury, a long-standing friend of Ian and Trekkie, had printed books for Chatto and his work was highly esteemed by them.

Ian Macnaghten Parsons, OBE (1944), CBE, born Pont Street, London, 21 May 1906, son of Edward Percival and Mabel Margaret Parsons. Married Marjorie Tulip Ritchie 1934. Died Kingston, Lewes, 29 October 1980.

Six

CHRISTINA FOYLE &

THE FOUNDING BROTHERS

Although her father and uncle were formidable businessmen and book-lovers who gave their name to what they claimed was the World's Greatest Bookshop it was Christina Foyle who became the best-known member of the family. She was liked and admired by some for her literary luncheons, deplored and loathed by others as a notoriously harsh employer and capricious manager.

Christina Agnes Lilian Foyle was the younger daughter of William Alfred Foyle, co-founder, in 1903, with his brother Gilbert, of the bookshop which still bears their name. William and Gilbert were the youngest of eight children born to William Henry and his first wife, Deborah, over a period of ten years. William Henry was one of nine. According to the *Dictionary of National Biography, 1961–70*, William Alfred was 'the seventh child of a seventh child of a seventh child' … 'It was to this that he attributed his remarkable visionary and intuitive gifts.' (The Foyle Family Tree shows his grandfather to have been a *third* child. Christina Foyle signed the *DNB* entry.)

On the Foyle side, Christina was descended from a great-grandfather who successively earned a living as a butler, commercial traveller, cleaning-powder manufacturer, dry salter and general merchant, and a grandfather who was a wholesale grocer in Shoreditch, East London; on her mother's side, she came from seafaring folk in the Shetland Isles, the Tullochs. Mother was also named Christina and according to Norris McWhirter, a family friend, 'she spoke with the soft precision of a Lerwegian'. After her parents' early deaths this Christina became the legal ward of Admiral Sir Richard Webb, a cousin of George Bernard Shaw's, and moved to London where she became a bookseller in Oxford Street.

The brothers William and Gilbert (born 1885 and 1886) were first educated at St John's Higher Grade School, Shoreditch, from which they won scholarships to Alice Owen's School, Islington, before studying briefly at King's College, which was part of the University of London. In 1900 both boys took and failed the entrance exam for the Civil Service. Gilbert opted for clerical work with Shoreditch Borough Council while William's first job was as a clerk to the lawyer and politician Sir E. Marshall Hall, who sent him to salerooms to bid for silver. There he found himself more interested in the books which were auctioned and this led him and his brother, in 1903, to advertise and sell their by then unwanted textbooks. The amount received impressed them, so they bought more books and in the evenings improvised a shop in the kitchen of the family home, now in Hoxton. Next they rented, first a warehouse in Islington (turnover in the first year was £10); then, shop premises in Peckham. They sent out handwritten catalogues and asked customers to return them for recycling. It is not clear which of the brothers became a full-time bookseller first. The early accounts state it was William; the latest (in 2003) gives Gilbert. All agree that by 1904 they had moved to Cecil Court – a wide, pavemented passage running between Charing Cross Road and St Martin's Lane, lined almost exclusively with small bookshops – and both were engaged in the business. In the following year they took on an assistant, Tom Gale, who was still with the educational department fifty years later. The first address in Charing Cross Road proper was at number 135, which they took on a fourteen-year lease in 1906. From there a printed circular was issued and handed to people sheltering from the rain beneath their shop blind encouraging them to;

> Walk downstairs and inspect one of the finest second-hand book saloons in London where you will notice how small are our charges for the cream of knowledge, the choicest wisdom, and the most fascinating fiction.

The Cecil Court premises were retained for a time, according to Penny Mountain's account (see Sources), while branches were opened in at least four London suburbs. The brothers bought stock from other booksellers, one of whom, in Oxford Street, was Christina Tulloch. William married her in 1907. She gave birth to a son and two daughters over four years – Winifred (1909), Christina Agnes Lilian (1911) and Richard (1912) – but was said to dislike children. In her brief *Who's Who* entry Christina Agnes did not record her own year of birth or mention her mother. In the year that she was born in Hampstead, Gilbert Foyle married Ethel Ellen Cook at, probably, St Michael's in neighbouring Highgate; they had two sons, Gilbert Eric (1915) and John Ernest (1920).

From 1912, when it commenced to sell newly published as well as second-hand books, Foyles settled at 121 Charing Cross Road, on the corner of

Manette Street, and gradually expanded northwards to 125. (The number-ing of this part of the Road is, to this day, vague.) Some indication of the rapidity with which the business had grown comes from a photograph, taken in the following year, on a staff outing to Epping Forest. Almost fifty people, a few of them children, posed for it.

In 1907, the year in which he also walked from London to Brighton, Gilbert, the only member of staff who could drive the bookshop van, took out his first car licence. In World War One he joined the Army Service Corps, was at the front in the Battle of the Somme and remained in uni-form until 1918; William was not called-up but became a special constable; he was partially deaf.

William's family moved from Hampstead to Ilfra Lodge, a house on the A1, at the Finchley end of Highgate. Christina recalled that she saw little of either parent during the war when they were busy running the shop. She was brought up in a middle-class home, with servants; she was not required to help in the house and never learned to cook, a fact of which she still boasted at the end of her life. In childhood she contracted tuberculosis and was admit-ted to a hospital in Margate where she remembered being in a ward adjoin-ing another catering for shell-shocked soldiers. She was too far from home to be visited by her parents and the experience was thought, by some of her family, to have soured her nature. After the war, to recuperate and finish her education, she was sent to Aux Villas Unspunnen, Wilderswil, in Switzerland. She claimed not to have passed any exam or taken part in sport but she danced, played the piano and was 'quite interested in Geography'.

On his return from the war, Gilbert rejoined a business over which his brother had exercised total control for four years. Adjustment to shared ownership and management must have been difficult for both men. Gilbert, the brother who could drive, wisely concentrated on travelling about Britain, not only to buy up libraries for the shop to resell, but more signif-icantly to solicit business from schools and educational authorities. This could have accounted for his absence from a 65-strong party comprising, according to a *Bookseller* report of September 1920, 'most of the staff of Messrs W.&G. Foyle who enjoyed a day's outing by steamer to Southend on Thursday 12 August', although he may have been minding the shop for William and his wife.

Certainly, by the following year Gilbert was primarily concerned with the affairs of Foyles' Educational Ltd (FEL), which had become a subsidiary company, while William, who often worked twelve to eighteen hours a day, expanded the shop and inaugurated, in 1926, Foyle's Welsh Co., fol-

lowed one year later by Foyle's Welsh Press which published in the ver-
nacular. Not that the older man was all work and no play. According to
Christina, her father joined 'clubs … of the Bohemian variety', and
explored 'the estuaries of the Blackwater and the Crouch, in Essex, with
sailing friends'.

Christina's first task at Foyles, in school holidays, had been helping to
wrap catalogues, for which she was rewarded with 30s a week, fifty per cent
more than junior assistants were paid a decade later. She joined the firm full
time, in 1928, when 75% of the stock was second-hand; she accompanied
her father to sales and was permitted to bid. She also spent time on the shop
floor. Always an avid reader she enjoyed her meetings with authors,
encountering Arnold Bennett who showed her a five-pound note which,
he said, he carried with him to give to the first person in a bookshop whom
he saw reading one of his books; he never had to part with it. She also met
Harpo Marx who told her he liked thrillers. 'I was proud of persuading him
to buy a bulky and expensive volume entitled *Who Moved the Stone?*' Only
later, she recorded, did she discover it was a scholarly, theological work.

By this time the company was about to embark on its biggest expansion
to date. On a site said once to have housed Goldbeater's House, across
Manette Street from the existing shop, Trefoile House was built on five
floors, its main entrance on the minor road though eventually there was also
access from Charing Cross Road. (Manette Street never featured on letter
headings which, for decades, placed Foyles firmly at 119–125 Charing Cross
Road.)

The fine new premises were officially opened by the Lord Mayor of
London on the afternoon of Monday, 7 October, 1929. The Lord Mayor
was welcomed by the Mayor of Westminster, publishers were represented
by Sir Godfrey Collins, booksellers by W. J. Magenis, secretary of the trade
association, and authors by the prolific but now forgotten W. B. Maxwell.
All three gave addresses; William Foyle replied. (Gilbert seconded the vote
of thanks to the Lord Mayor.) The brothers had well and truly arrived, with
Christina already hovering not so far from the foreground. There is no
mention of what if any role was taken by her mother, her elder sister or her
brother. In fact, Winifred was employed in the music department and
brother Dick (christened William Richard) may well have been still at
school. The deckle-edged programme for the opening of Trefoile House
stated that 'A Topical Film "The Magic of Books" will be shown at frequent intervals before and after the ceremony'.

A bound volume, *The Romance of a Bookshop 1904–1929*, was privately
printed for the occasion. The author, Gilbert H. Fabes, was manager of the

rare books department. His is one of seventeen photographed (mostly head and shoulders) employees illustrating the book. All are formally attired, some with starched, winged collars, apart from Fabes himself who wears an open-necked shirt and has a pipe hanging from his lower lip. Mr B.M. Goldberg, manager of the foreign book department, looks ready to embark on Arctic travels, Mr J.M. Kelsey, music company manager, is in evening dress. Dr Duncan, manager of the theological department, captioned as 'convincing a customer', resembles an amateur thespian in the act of converting the heathen, while Tom Gale, almost the first employee, seems to be prematurely embalmed. Yet these camera studies, and the text, celebrate a very human enterprise far removed from the image of Foyles in the latter part of the twentieth century.

Author Fabes traces the family back to the thirteenth century when Winchester's mayor was Robert de Froyle; he notes that the sign adopted for the new shop is the trefoil, or clover *Trifolium*, a plant which 'sends out trailing stems from the root stock … known in France as "*Treflepuant*", and in England as "The Right Trefoile" – fittingly symbolic of the activities and prestige of the Two Brothers'. In the conclusion to his book, Fabes writes, '… one broad distinction is possessed by both of these men; their strong sense of duty to each other'. (Penny Mountain, writing much later, was to take the family back only to 1374, in Fontmell Magna, Dorset, but her co-author Christopher Foyle in a separate publication of his own notes one Robert Foil in the same town in 1332. Christopher described Fabes's researches as 'fanciful'.)

The opening of the new premises coincided with the Great Depression. The shop, plus increased educational contracting by FEL, presumably generated some of the capital needed to build Trefoile House, but it was a bold step to take at this time. It more than doubled the sales area as well as providing a commercial picture gallery – motto, 'Art for All', which opened in January 1930, and a private film theatre. This was used to promote another innovation, Foyle's Educational Films, which aimed to assist film making at every level 'outside mainstream entertainment'. The firm's silver jubilee, celebrated, according to twenty-first-century in-house research, one year late, also emphasised that the bookshop was no longer primarily dealing in second-hand books. It had become a potential major outlet for newly published titles in all categories.

There is no reference in Fabes's book to Christina, who was destined to innovate and dominate for much of the next seven decades, with the blessing of her father but with less approval from other members of the family. She had a significant encounter with John Galsworthy on the floor of the newly opened premises but was not aware of the identity of the elderly man asking for something to read on a train journey. She enthusiastically recommended *The Forsyte Saga*. The man bought it and left the shop, only to return soon after and present it to her, inscribed by himself, the author. Later, on 15 October, 1929, Galsworthy gave one of the fortnightly evening literary lectures which William had inaugurated earlier in the decade. Christina's meeting with him led to her suggestion that Foyles should hold a series of literary luncheons to promote both themselves and authors. The first took place, in October 1930 at the Holborn Restaurant in Kingsway, when the chief speaker was the Lord Chief Justice, Lord Darling, who had recently brought out a volume of verse. One of the guests was Lord Alfred Douglas whom, Christina said in a 1981 broadcast, had been sent to prison by Darling. (She was presumably confusing him with Oscar Wilde.) The matinée-idol actor, Gerald du Maurier, took the chair, which was certainly a coup for the young organiser. 250 tickets were sold at 4s. 6d. each.

The series, from this modest beginning, lasted throughout the twentieth century – including during WWII – and beyond. Very soon a Park Lane hotel became the venue, either the Dorchester or the Grosvenor House, with the majority of the clientele attracted to the luncheons being ladies resident in Belgravia, Kensington and Knightsbridge. In their heyday the lunches received wide publicity in the national press and on the media. Credit for much of this lay with Ben Perrick, who joined the publicity department in 1934 and was permitted to return after defecting for a brief spell to work for the magazine *The Studio*. This is the only known instance of Christina *re*-employing anyone at Charing Cross Road.

Another in-house diversification which had for long appealed to 'Miss Foyle', as she was always known in the business, was the music department selling 78 rpm gramophone records and sheet music. This was allied to the Piena Music Company, dealing in 'musical instruments and accessories', and Foyle's Music Company, which organised concerts. Christina played the piano and shared musical evenings with the publisher Robert Lusty. In his memoirs (1975), he mentions being conducted around the London book trade by the senior Hutchinson rep who introduced him to 'the stalwarts of that time ... Willy Foyle in the Charing Cross Road, and Christina, whom I lived and laughed with then and love and laugh with still'. (That is what Bob wrote, make of it what you will.)

An extra-curricular duty of Christina's in her early years with the firm was to travel. Foyles' trade was already worldwide, with customers even in the Soviet Union where her father sent her partly in an attempt to collect bad debts. She failed. Nor did Hitler react as hoped to her suggestion that

Basil Blackwell ('The Gaffer')

William Foyle

Gilbert Foyle

Stanley Unwin

Allan Lane

John Grey ('Jock') Murray

Trekkie & Ian Parsons

Christina Foyle

Jock Murray & Alan Hill

'Kip' & Elsie Bertram in front of the famous chicken shed.

André Deutsch

Paul Hamlyn

William Foyle

Elsie Bertram

Alan Steele

Rayner Unwin

Philip Unwin

instead of burning books he should sell them to Foyles. (She did not actually visit Germany to make this request.) She wrote newspaper articles
about her travels and gave lectures for a company which Foyles subsequently bought. The Pope also comes into the saga during the 'thirties.
Willie, it is alleged, sued him for failing to pay a subscription to Foyles'
Catholic Book Club.

The company sponsored several book clubs (including, as a rejoinder to
Victor Gollancz's famous enterprise aimed at the political left, one for right
wingers). It also published under its own name a vast series of Foyle
Handbooks, while FEL's souvenir publication to mark the coronation of
George VI sold close to one million copies, many of them purchased by
municipal councils to present to children in their boroughs. (I was given
one. Reading it failed to shake my innate republicanism.) The company also
supplied a nationwide chain of lending libraries, opened a literary agency
and retained several shops in the London suburbs, Ireland and South Africa.

A history of Mills & Boon records that 'Foyles' Libraries … supplied 747
libraries with an average of over 200 books each per week, in 1934.' Foyles',
it stated, bought in bulk and rented volumes to 'retailers, newsagents, clubs
and institutions at a rate of 10 shillings a week for 250'. That number of
books cost Foyles' £30, so if the figures are correct the margin of profit
must have been infinitesimal. (Penny Mountain's centenary volume states
there was 'a chain of three thousand two-penny libraries' which extended
over several continents.)

The handbooks were sold around Britain by freelance reps; John Gifford,
another imprint, was established in 1937 at 111 Charing Cross Road with
directors named F.L. Powys and F. Adams. They were replaced, in 1939,
by Christina Foyle and Ronald Batty, whom she had married the previous
year. Batty contributed a title to the Gifford list, *How to run a 2d Library*,
priced at 2s.6d., for which a market as wide as that mentioned in Mountain
must have been anticipated.

Foyles' rapid expansion, undertaken at a time of acute economic turbu-
lence which would have stretched the resources of most companies,
brought it close to bankruptcy. In old age Christina said that Barclays Bank
had been marvellous and that publishers were understanding. She was especially grateful to John Dettmer, of Heinemann, and Sydney Goldsack, of
Collins, who long after their assistance became unnecessary were rewarded
by regular invitations to literary luncheons.

In 1936 Christina contributed an article to the *Manchester Evening News* in
a series called 'Your Children's Career'. About bookselling she wrote:

...to spend from nine to six every weekday in a book shop is not
work but one long round of pleasure ... A girl considering a bookshop career must have a secondary education. Knowledge of typing is helpful. A degree is unnecessary. Our girls start at £1 per
week and for the first six months work in the shop library ...

There they acquired a knowledge of titles, authors and publishers, becoming shop assistants at £3. 10s .0d a week, departmental managers at £5 a
week, and later, buyers at £10 a week. They would be expected to attend
lectures about the trade and to read all the reviews in the chief Sunday
papers. She went on to recommend the second-hand trade to:

...the girl who likes poring over grubby bundles of books in the
Caledonian Market and does not mind being on her feet all day.
Once a firm know they can rely on her judgment they will send
her to country-house sales in search of rare books and valuable first
editions and even abroad, where she may have the thrill of staying
in monasteries and palaces and doing her book-hunting by air.

This surprising fantasy is printed next to a glamorous head-and-shoulders
photo of the writer seen in sultry film-star pose with a love curl falling on
to her right eyebrow.

In the year that this appeared Winifred Foyle was required to cease
working in the family business when she married Edgar Samuel. Bill, her
son, believes Winifred, good at figures and forgiving, was brighter than her
sister. She felt no resentment against Christina. A similar restriction did not
apply to Christina two years later when she married Ronald Batty, a childhood friend by then employed in the rare books department. They took,
as their London residence, an apartment on the top two floors of 119
Charing Cross Road. At what point brother Dick joined the family business is not clear. There is a photo of him in the centenary book wearing
top hat and tails at Christina's wedding but soon after he would have been
in naval uniform for most of WWII.

Foyles came through the grim thirties. The branches in the suburbs were
closed because the managers stole the takings and/or the stock. Shoplifting
and theft by employees are problems faced by all retailers; at Foyles they
were exacerbated by low wages and the untidy, dingy departments with
their ceiling-high shelving.

Most of Charing Cross Road escaped the blitz; none of its theatres or
bookshops was bombed, although there was an enormous crater in the road

outside Foyles. Over it a temporary construction was erected to keep traffic flowing; this became known as Foyles' Bridge. After the war, a young German bookseller related the story, probably apocryphal, of William Foyle strewing copies of Hitler's *Mein Kampf* on the roof to place them in the front line of destruction. Gilbert's war work was with the Home Guard, Golders Green section, 1940–5.

During the war the book trade, along with the other arts, boomed. Popular titles were often in short supply because paper was rationed and this brought further prosperity to the second-hand trade. By now a much higher percentage of Foyles' stock was designated 'new'. Not all of it sold, some of it remaining on the always over-crowded shelves where it came to look 'second-hand'; the profit margin on that which was genuinely so offset any losses made on certain 'new' books.

In 1943, William Foyle bought Beeleigh, a medieval abbey close to Maldon in Essex, where he installed his personal library. Gilbert and Ethel moved, in 1947, from Hendon to Eastbourne, where he became much involved in the life of the town. The company made significant purchases of property both in Soho and the London suburbs, some of it available at bargain prices before hostilities had ceased. The Foyles, related through Ronald Batty to the Eckert family, who were 'in property', took a chance on the Allied victory and bought what seemed appropriate.

Financially Foyles was secure after WWII. Cash flow was buoyant even allowing for large-scale embezzlement by staff. The boom in new books did not continue but the second-hand trade held up. William Foyle handed over virtual control, including shares, to Christina and her husband. FEL, under Gilbert, now joined by his sons, operated almost independently but shared the same premises which, in time, extended down to 111 Charing Cross Road. There was access, on several floors, for staff – and the public, if not apprehended – between the shop and the educational contractors. FEL staff filled orders from shop stock when urgently required, a practice which inevitably led to friction if a shop department manager maintained he could not spare the items needed. The gap had long been widening between the two brothers' spheres of influence, exacerbated by Christina's increasing domination, but large family gatherings took place periodically. There were smaller ones too at the Trocadero, Shaftesbury Avenue, where William held court over lunch on Fridays, having been chauffeur-driven from Beeleigh in his Rolls Royce. Business meetings were a rarity. William Foyle abhorred them. Penny Mountain quotes him: 'We seldom have any … son and daughter and myself decide on transactions running into thousands within a few minutes' – a rare reference by W.F. to Dick Foyle.

Neither of the founders fully retired for many years after their children had taken over. A settlement between the brothers gave a majority shareholding in W.&G. Foyle to William, and in FEL to Gilbert, though each retained a minority interest in the other's company until the mid-fifties.

Gilbert, in Eastbourne, was elected to the town council and became a general benefactor to the resort which had been a 'front-line' target for hit-and-run air attacks during the German occupation of France. He donated funds to preserve land near Beachy Head, plus £36,000 to provide the esplanade with a new sea lounge. He also formed the Gilbert Foyle Educational Trust to help needy students through university.

After the First War, Gilbert had returned to play a part of equal importance to his co-founder brother; after the Second, his offspring calmly prepared to take over in due course. William's son, on the other hand, scarcely received a hero's welcome from his firmly entrenched sister. Was there ever any question of Richard Foyle acquiring equal status, let alone seniority? Christina had already seen off any danger of her sister becoming part of the management but she was obliged at least to accommodate her brother Richard, who took on the role of buyer. Christina, famous enough by the 1930s to have featured in a series of cigarette cards, ruled from early in her career with her father's approval and admiration. She was confident, energetic, tough, intelligent and literate. She was born too late to become a suffragette and was never a militant feminist. She had no need to be. She had a natural authority and quelled interference from others. Richard, presumably given little support by his father, was not her equal.

Although book-trade mythology held that no one worked for Foyles for more than a few months, there were exceptions, including one-legged Mrs Turner, who operated the creaking lift installed at Trefoile House, and many more amongst the staff of FEL. Albert Hobbs started work with 'Gilbert' around 1935, and remained, attaining director level, for several decades. He and Ben Perrick, who came into particular prominence after the Second World War, were probably the two longest-serving employees of either company.

Ben Perrick played a more significant role in the company than did Richard Foyle. He was a shrewd, amiable man who knew how to cope with difficult women. He actually admired and liked Christina; he worked with her for so long that he became accustomed to her ways. As publicity officer, closely associated with the literary luncheons, he had far more rein than most employees; he also had a wife, Eve, who was a columnist in Fleet Street, although any stories he filed through her would have had to meet the requirements of the popular press. Just as a newspaperman must live with daily, or weekly, deadlines, Ben, in respect of the lunches, had monthly ones with only August off. Then the Battys visited their shops in South Africa, at Cape Town and Johannesburg (were they personal tax havens?) or went to the USA, which they did not colonise commercially. Ben enjoyed the razor's edge experience when the date for sending out a luncheon notice became nigh without a principal speaker having been engaged. But so did Christina. When the actress Dame Sybil Thorndike cried off with a broken leg and author-actor Robert Morley also reported sick, she remembered that Charlie Chaplin had said he would love to attend a lunch when in Britain. Ben learned he had just flown in; Chaplin became the leading speaker. (I had this story personally from Ben: in *Foyles a celebration*, Penny Mountain has a different version citing Noël Coward as the guest of honour who cried off.)

By 1984 Perrick had helped to mastermind 516 luncheons. Those who attended them arrived in chauffeur-driven cars and taxis to pay to hear authors talking about their most recent books. The speakers were not confined to those of mere literary distinction. Royalty and other heads of state, prime ministers, church leaders, film stars, sportsmen, foreign statesmen, military men, philosophers, newspaper editors, dukes and earls, cooks, crooks, horticulturists, museum curators, comedians – augmented the professional authors of fiction, biography, history and travel. Ill-printed and unalphabetical lists of speakers, their names crammed into tight columns, exist to prove that few major celebrities of the period 1930–2000 declined invitations to speak. They received no fee and were served the same indifferently cooked food, accompanied by white vin ordinaire, as those who had paid to hear them. The grand ladies who came in their hordes adored Christina. Large numbers of them bought copies of the books being celebrated. The luncheons became part of the London social scene, gracious gatherings held on the edge of Mayfair, far from the comparative squalor of the vast bookshop in Charing Cross Road. It is questionable whether many of the guests ever visited Foyles; probably their other book purchases were put down to accounts at Harrods or Hatchards.

In addition to those who willingly paid to be present, there was a large top table of Christina's personal guests who were served drinks beforehand at a private bar. She chatted with them but never addressed a luncheon herself. She had a number of favourite stories about speakers. One featured Sir Walter Gilbey, head of a company which sold gin. 'He spoke for one and a half hours', she recalled. 'A man in front of my father fell asleep, so he hit the chap with the toastmaster's gavel. The man said, "Hit me again. I can still hear him." '

Another anecdote concerned Bernard Shaw. She had overlooked the fact that he was a vegetarian and apologised for his having been served meat. 'You must come again, Mr Shaw,' she told him, 'and we will have vegetarian dishes served to everyone.' He declined gracefully, saying, 'Madam, I couldn't bear the prospect of hearing two thousand people all crunching celery.'

She once held a luncheon for ex-criminals borrowing, from Madame Tussaud's, a wax figure of the murderer Charlie Peace which was placed next to the chairman; it was approached by a guest who, believing it to be a certain living Secretary of State, wished to shake hands.

I knew Christina for nearly half a century during which period I met her infrequently – never on a daily basis, even when I worked at the 'World's Greatest Bookshop'. We met perhaps twenty or thirty times, not more. Yet she played a significant role in my entire working career. At first, as an employee, I hated her; later, in common with most of the book trade, I disapproved of her style of management. It wasn't until we met on equal terms that I began to mellow in my appraisal. Despite being an autocrat with a greater regard for animals than human beings, she was good company and loved, as I did, to exchange gossip about fellow booksellers and publishers.

In July 1949, when I became an employee at Foyles, the circumstances described by Christina in the 'thirties to readers of the *Manchester Evening News* had altered. Six months apprenticeship in the library had been succeeded by a form of slave-trade initiation, alike for both sexes, at plywood tables in the post room. Most of those around me, industriously opening the estimated 30,000 items of mail received each day, were girls.

Two weeks previously I had been interviewed by a severe, unsmiling, youngish woman. I had asked if I might work in the music and drama department, where I had been buying books for years, and was told, yes. When I hinted that £6 per week was too little, she had said, briskly, 'Six ten'. I was delighted. I had escaped from the dreary South Coast where few people had bought books at the shop I had tried to manage; now I was to sell plays and books about the drama in the heart of both the book world and theatreland. Then I found myself seated at a trestle table opening envelopes and being bullied by a masculine woman, with thyroid eyes, dressed in a belted tweed two-piece. On pain of dismissal she ordered me not to talk. Periodically the lady who had interviewed me stalked about. I glared at her accusingly until a fellow prisoner whispered, warningly, that she was Christina Foyle.

Early in the afternoon I was beckoned into the office where Miss Foyle informed me in her thin, whining voice that there were no immediate vacancies in music and drama so I must instead report to religion and philosophy on the top floor of the building across Manette Street, the one into which the founders had moved in 1912. (In the early 1980s it was to become Waterstone's; later still, a licensed sex shop.) I was so overjoyed at leaving the post table that I forgot my intense distaste for religion, also that I knew little about philosophy. It didn't matter. I was received cordially by the manager and set to work to arrange the great philosophers in alphabetical order, which upset regular customers unused to such a refinement. When I eventually reached music and drama, three weeks later, I did the same, so that at least *I* knew what was in stock. The customers didn't always believe me while Christina neither applauded nor held it against me. When she came prowling around in her tight, short-skirted dress, erect and matronly, she asked how I was getting on. I told her we had too much second-hand stock. She replied, airily, 'You must put the books on the shelves,' and continued her Progress, perhaps already subconsciously modelling herself on the future Queen.

The range of second-hand stock relied much on what members of the public brought in to sell. They were required to descend to the basement where buyers sorted through what was presented, selecting only certain titles. The disappointed owner would accept the small sum offered and request, 'Will you throw away the rest for me?' Once the deal was agreed, ALL the books were despatched to the appropriate departments, priced and, in some cases, sold at a total profit. When I had been working at Foyles for less than a month it was part of my duties to price second-hand stock in the music and drama department. I was not told what, if anything, had been paid for it. I judged what it might fetch or, if we already had twenty copies of the same book, I threw the additional one into a sack for waste, which was returned to the basement for disposal. Occasionally it reappeared only to suffer the same fate again.

We were all apprehensive about Christina's visits. She ruled by fear. Periodically, we heard about this person or that who had been peremptorily sacked. Sometimes a weeping lass would come to say goodbye on her way out. We were shocked when one – later to enjoy more congenial employment at Claude Gill Books – who had stood outside Foyles during the doodlebug raids selling from a stall, was dismissed while she was on holiday. It was an unsettling situation. There were four of us in music and drama, a department which turned over about £350 a week. The received wisdom was that to ensure some security one had personally to notch up

sales of £100 of this total. This led to trespassing on fellow assistants' territory, swooping in quickly to write out a bill while a colleague broke off to
find another customer a book. It brought out the worst in us all. Inevitably,
if one was not sacked one looked for an alternative job. By 1949, the wages
structure had altered since Christina wrote her newspaper article quoted
above. The assistant taken on prior to my arrival was paid £7. 15s. 0d., the
manager was on £5. 0s. 0d. plus commission; what the fourth, frequently
replaced person earned I never knew.

Christina, at this time, had not imposed the complicated procedure of
paying for a purchase, which was later to enrage customers and draw much
criticism from the press. This involved getting an invoice, queuing at a distant cashdesk to make payment, then taking the receipt all the way back to
the counter to collect the purchase. One commentator dubbed it, 'bookselling à la Kafka'. (The system was also used by the GUM department store
in Soviet Moscow.) In my time customers took purchases themselves to the
cashdesk or ran off with them. One ruse not unknown to assistants eager
for a particular title was to issue a bill for it at a knock-down price and sell
it to a friend who then legitimately removed it from the building. This may
have been the basis of a racket with second-hand dealers which could well
have led to Christina's notorious bureaucracy. The moral of this was that if
you chose to manage inefficiently, employing underpaid and constantly
changing staff, you were likely to be cheated.

Buying methods varied. Charles, our manager, bought gramophone
records (still 78s) and sheet music but the subscribing of new books lay with
Richard Foyle who did not consult anyone. In 1950 Christopher Fry was
the new white hope of the British theatre. John Gielgud had just concluded
a long run in *The Lady's not for Burning*, Laurence Olivier was about to open
in *Venus Observed*. The OUP was Fry's publisher. Richard Foyle subscribed
twelve copies, most of which went to members of staff at trade price; across
the road, at diminutive Better Books, Tony Godwin ordered a thousand.
The book was answered 'reprinting' almost at once, and in those days further supplies often took months to get to the shops.

Apart from Christina, who moved 'stately as a galleon', staff bustled, held
pens and clipboards, carried books. It was easy to differentiate between
them and customers. Ben Perrick darted in and out to check on a title he
was going to catalogue; John and Eric Foyle, from FEL, always looking
harassed, charged through to visit an office in a corner by the second-hand
plays; Gilbert was also sometimes seen, as was the genial, barrel-shaped
William – for all that they were supposedly retired. Girls from mail order,
as well as FEL, raided 'our' stock. I had no impression at that time that FEL

was a separate entity; it seemed a part of the whole awful, amorphous mess which was Foyles, existing in a micro-economy of its own and attracting thousands of customers in person or by post.

We worked a five-and-a-half-day week (no Saturdays off) from nine to six, we had to clock-on and -off and there was no staff room, although on a first floor in Manette Street, detached from the shop, there was a small canteen where cheap lunches were available. Morning coffee and afternoon tea breaks were taken on the floor; those of us who smoked locked ourselves in the loo. Men wore suits or sports jackets with ties; women did not wear slacks. There was a faintly relaxed atmosphere on Saturdays when the Foyles were at their abbey, although Christina's henchwoman, the dreaded Patsy Rosenstiehl, in her two-piece tweeds and brogues, might hone in to spy on us. She had a direct line to Christina who employed her from 1942–66.

I stayed for seven months before, for the sake of peace of mind, taking another bookshop job at ten shillings a week less. My only contact with Foyles during the next seven years came about when I was so short of money that I recalled I had not received any holiday pay in their employment. I worked out that I was entitled to two-and-a-half days and wrote demanding it. To my astonishment I received postal orders for about two pounds. Christina was probably amused by my cheek; she did not lack a sense of humour.

In 1954, then supposedly the golden-jubilee year, a thin celebratory booklet was issued. Less than 2,000 words, unsigned and presumably Ben Perrick's work, it is a shortened, less flowery version of Gilbert Fabes' silver-jubilee memento. It includes the statement: 'Today, 68-years-old William Foyle is still in control of his ceaselessly expanding bookshop and his brother Gilbert – now a youthful 67 – continues as his fellow-director.' Despite which, it is only Christina who has a full-page photograph to herself. There is no longer a love curl on her forehead. She looks away from the camera, coldly unsmiling, dignified, almost glamorous. She is wearing a low cut, short-sleeved buttoned blouse and a necklace. The founding brothers, sharing a page, are shown on the tandem they rode as very young men; it is the same snap that was used in the 1929 book and crops up again in the much smarter 2003 volume. The reader is also informed, '… the second generation is taking over several of the firm's activities ' and 'playing no small part in promoting the firm's progress'. (Richard Foyle's part was already diminished and he was to die, on a cruise ship, three years later aged only forty-five.) Total staff is noted as being nearly 600, thirteen of whom are credited with over twenty-one year's service. Four of these are designated, 'Foyles

Educational Limited'. Turnover was recorded as £2m; The organisation included a Book Club, with membership of over a quarter of a million, a publishing house, a nationwide lending-library chain (not destined to exist for much longer), a literary agency, an art gallery and 'Europe's largest lecture bureau'. The latter listed 'three hundred discussion groups and literary or luncheon clubs on its books' and boasted many eminent names among its lecturers.

Why Christina, at this late date, chose to have her role as effective head of at least William Foyle's side of the business played down is unclear. Only Ben would have had the answer; he was undoubtedly acting under orders. John Foyle's recollection of the golden jubilee is that FEL people, family or not, were cold shouldered on that occasion.

About two years after my spell in Charing Cross Road, George Depotex, later to become sales director for André Deutsch, Hamish Hamilton and OUP, was engaged by Christina to manage a department. On arrival, he was taken by Patsy to Department 31, on the first floor of Trefoile House, and introduced to the manageress as a new assistant. He protested about this status and was informed that everyone had to go through a test period of four weeks as an assistant. Writing to me in 2001, George recalled that on Friday afternoons Patsy toured all departments with a tray containing envelopes, 'Brown ones contained a week's wages, white ones two weeks' money and a notice to quit.' One day she bore down upon the new resentful assistant and snapped, 'Miss Foyle is making you the manager of Department 1. Follow me.'

Department 1 comprised the entire ground floor of Trefoile House, including second-hand books. One day Depotex received a large consignment of *The Concise Oxford Dictionary* which was in short supply. At closing time he could not account for many of the copies which should still have been in stock. He informed 'Miss Foyle' who instantly went into Manette Street and opened the boots of unlocked cars. In one, belonging to the chief store detective, the dictionaries were found. The security man was sacked but not prosecuted. Some weeks later, encountering Depotex in Charing Cross Road, he winked and said, 'I'm running my own bookshop full-time now.'

Depotex, writing fifty years later, remembered, perhaps not entirely accurately, that Richard Foyle bought for every department except his and had a simple system of purchasing three of every book offered; he also had to authorise all replacement orders but was never available after 12.30 when he had a liquid lunch followed by a visit to the cinema, where he slept until after the shop had closed. Long before Richard sailed on his last voyage, Depotex was instructed to take over his job, at £12 per week; this led to his being referred to as the 'general manager' although he was never officially given that position. Ronald Batty once instructed him to drop everything and do a complete stock take. The Inland Revenue had demanded it. After a week George, having made little progress, suggested he should value the length of one section and multiply the sum by the known number of shelves. Batty approved, saying he had already assessed the total value but that George's rough notes would be of great help ... 'especially if they were difficult to read or understand'.

On two occasions the law's demands on G.D. made Christina petulant. When he was called for jury service she said he must tell the court this would be inconvenient because the shop was too busy. He protested that this could lead to his prosecution, so she said crossly that he could go but she would not pay him during his absence. At the height of the Cold War, when ex-servicemen became liable to recall for fifteen days on what was called the Z Reserve, the nation again required Depotex's services. Christina's reaction was predictable. In fact, wages were not docked on either occasion.

G.D. insisted that 'Christina was not all *dragon*', also maintaining that Foyles had given him 'an education in bookselling' which earned him the managership of the book department at the Army and Navy Stores. When he gave notice, Christina and Ronald Batty wished him well and subsequently referred to him as 'our protégé'. Many years later, as sales manager to the Oxford University Press, George asked Christina for a literary lunch for one of their books, inviting her to join him and a colleague at a Soho restaurant to discuss the event. She arrived late, explaining that she had been delayed by a street fight in which one man had bitten off another's ear. 'She giggled,' George remembered, 'and said, "There it was lying in the gutter."' (In a broadcast version of this incident 'Miss Foyle' told listeners it was her detective's ear which was savaged on the shop floor.)

William Foyle, by then visiting the store only once or twice a week, lectured G.D. about disorder on the shelves, maintaining customers liked it and that it encouraged them to buy more than one book. George found William friendly, although he and his wife were never invited to Beeleigh as they were, by Gilbert's sons, to Eastbourne, for FEL's annual outing.

I had no personal contact with Gilbert but I met William Foyle on Friday afternoons if I made a staff purchase. The transactions, strictly cash, took place in his office. It was as though we were doing a private deal with him; perhaps we were.

I priced a second-hand set of the Choral Symphony at fifteen shillings, hoping for a 'third off'.

'Thirty bob,' he said.

'But, Mr Foyle, the selling price is only fifteen.'

'All right. Seven and six.' Then, in his still discernibly cockney accent and a twinkle in his eye, 'Shall I wrap them for you?'

Beryl Ennion, who was employed from 1956–60, echoes Depotex in believing that Foyles 'was an unparalleled training-ground for aspiring booksellers' with a turnover of staff so rapid 'that it was quite possible to be put in charge of a department within weeks of joining the firm! ... Working there was an unforgettable experience.'

Beryl's wage increased from £8 to £10 per week during her stint, by irregular ten shilling increments. She recalled that Christina would not allow a union, staff could be sacked for missing a day's work or chatting to a colleague, and that her unexpected appearance on the shop floor was dreaded. When this occurred ... 'Mr Batty always walked a few steps behind her (like the Duke of Edinburgh behind The Queen).' She 'had small, beautifully manicured hands ... wore pink nail varnish and spoke in that "little girl's" voice. Staff wore round yellow badges that read "Foyles for Books". C.F. gave Christmas presents of hankies or soap for women, after-shave or cigarettes for men.' (Not in my year!)

Clocking-in for a colleague who was late was a serious offence of which Beryl was once accused in respect of a German assistant. At the same time Christina believed, without evidence, she was implicated in the same person's theft of stock. Beryl protested her innocence but two week's later noticed in *The Bookseller*, 'my post as manager ... was advertised as vacant. So I moved smartly to Dillon's before the axe fell.'

Further evidence of the bizarre wages policy was given by German-born Lothar Simon who began a two-month engagement in January 1961 on £5. 15s. 0d. a week. He spent several days on the post table before being sent to the technical and scientific department where 'I could not understand the titles of the books, let alone pronounce them ... ' Learning that colleagues, equally underpaid, received commission, he good-naturedly allowed them to write bills for sales he had made. Quite soon he was fired for low productivity. He demanded to see 'Miss Foyle', threatened to report her to the German Embassy and the Ministry of Labour, for 'luring experienced foreign booksellers to fill the ranks of her underpaid staff' and, amazingly, won a reprieve. Shortly after Christina recommended him to Oswald Woolf, a London publisher and importer of German books.

Christina became notorious for employing foreign, mainly European, assistants with little command of English. This gave rise to comments such as, 'What language are they using at Foyles this week?' Stories of would-be book purchasers' experiences were legion, many of them true, some embroidered. My favourite concerned the bewildered customer who in reply to, 'Where will I find *Ulysses*, please?' was told, 'He's at lunch.' (As an anecdote it could be bettered only if the customer had responded, 'Tell him Penelope looked in.')

It was during Beryl Ennion's time that the company was so prosperous it could afford to buy the tax loss of the small London bookselling chain Alfred Wilson Ltd, which in the summer of 1956 had gone into receivership. Wilson's City and Victoria Street shops were sold along with its export and subscriptions departments but in order to benefit from the tax loss and offset it against Foyles' profits the Hampstead branch, which I was managing, had to be retained as a trading outlet. This was how I came to work for Christina again ... for seven years, not months. We traded as High Hill Bookshops Ltd but were registered as Control Nominees Ltd through a reputable firm of City accountants. I knew my employers only as 'Mr X'. When, in 1964, I became the chief shareholder the official records of the company had to be handed over to the new owners, so I supposed I would discover the real name of the vendors. Not so. Someone had neatly removed it with scissors from the company cash book. It was only when I ordered old pass sheets from the bank that, against two large sums paid to the receiver in 1957, I read the names Batty and Foyle. Had I known at the time I would have looked for another job but in fact I had virtually no interference from Christina during those seven years when the price of remaining anonymous caused her to lie low and deal through the accountants. I was paid generously, by bookselling standards, and encouraged to expand, allowed to publish books about Hampstead (for the first one we had a whole window at Foyles and I still had no suspicion of *her* involvement), acquire a branch at Belsize Park and open a Gallery. But, as 'Mr X', she did veto my plans for a shop at Highgate. Then she offered me what was virtually my own goodwill for £13,000. The City accountant was furious; he thought she should have given it to me. I was happy. I knew that 'Mr X' knew it was what I most wanted, and it was cheap at the price. When Christina learned that her cover had been blown she invited me to a literary lunch where, over drinks in the private bar, she said, 'I think we did you a good turn'. She did indeed. But who excised the names from the company's records? I cannot believe it was those highly reputable accountants. At another lunch she remarked, 'You're so lucky, you have children.

You've got someone to carry on after you.' This was in contradiction to her comment, heard more than once, that she was glad to be childless.

Richard's son, Christopher, joined the company in the early sixties and was sent to Germany, Finland and France to gain experience in Continental bookshops. He returned in 1965 in time to witness the annexation of the rest of the south side of Manette Street where derelict property was demolished to build a new Goldbeater's House, partly shop, partly flats, plus a penthouse for the Battys. Christopher saw the potential in the business and the need for modernisation but his aunt wished to continue running it her way. So in 1972, still on a modest salary of £1,600 a year, he left, first for the City, then to start an airline. The parting did not lead to an estrangement and Christina was heard to speak of him in a friendly manner as 'my nephew who went off to do things with aeroplanes'. Her attitude was different with Bill Samuel, Winifred's son, who was forbidden involvement in the business because he dared to criticise Christina's management methods.

When her father died Christina and Ronnie moved into Beeleigh Abbey, while retaining both the apartment above the shop and a house in Essex at the village of Cold Norton. At the latter they also owned a Georgian farmhouse where members of staff were sometimes accommodated for rest weekends. Christina's mother lived with the Battys until she died in 1976. The rare books department was also moved to the abbey where William's valuable collection was already housed. Sales of other second-hand books were discontinued, which surprised some of those who had thought the Foyle fortune was based on them.

In the *DNB, 1961–1970*, William Foyle was described as '...a very unusual and deceptive man. An adored if neglectful parent, overflowing with high spirits ... a considerable artist and pianist ... Although money was one of the last things Foyle thought about, he died a millionaire, a state which was due in some degree to his cautious daughter Christina... ' As recorded above, Christina was the author of this entry in which there is only one reference to Gilbert who is dismissed as the brother with whom William opened his first shop. Nor is Gilbert's life recorded individually in the *DNB 1971–1980*, or in the volume *Missing Persons*. It is surprising that the editors of the *1961–70* volume did not seek a more appropriate contributor than his daughter to write the entry about William and even more odd that the slightly revised entry for the *New DNB* (2004) does little to redress this injustice.

William Alfred may not have thought about money but he knew how to spend it. He bought for £20,000, in title only, various Lordships of the

Manor in East Anglia. His local paper, the *Maldon & Burnham Standard*, in its obituary, noted his love of angling, his presidency of the golf club and the delight he took in showing visitors Beeleigh Abbey and its grounds. It also referred to his being a millionaire and owner of a library 'reputed to be the most valuable private collection in the world'. *The Times* stated the library numbered ten thousand volumes; it was the only notice which mentioned the £250 annual prize for poetry Foyle inaugurated in 1949.

The Bookseller of 8 June,1963, carried an unsigned obit of William:

> …the book trade has lost its greatest 'character' … he not only created, in partnership with his brother Gilbert, one of the world's great bookselling businesses, but remained throughout the whole of his long life an original, and always an irresistibly lovable one.

The rest of the appreciation notes, with varying accuracy, the familiar success story but without a single reference to Christina or the literary luncheons. It ends by noting that in its sixtieth year Foyles' turnover was 'something in the region of £3 million' and that the store now boasted '30 miles of shelving, housing very nearly four million books'.

A family rift occurred in 1965, two years after William's death, when the bookshop staff – or part of it – went on strike for one month demanding higher wages and the right to belong to a trade union. The shop remained open but picketed. Deliveries were interrupted from publishers with union affiliations. This could have affected FEL which had staff belonging to SOGAT (a powerful union), so John and Eric Foyle insisted that their company, which had separate accounts with suppliers, was not involved in the stoppage at the bookshop. This enraged Christina and in the following year FEL moved to separate premises, with a retail department, in Upper Berkeley Street.

The strikers, not being part of USDAW, a union for shop workers which presented no problem to any retailer paying more than the derisory official minimum wage, received little or no support from fellow booksellers, although certain independent shopkeepers and publishers took pride in contributing to the collecting boxes manned at Foyles' doorways. Thomas Joy, a former president of the Booksellers' Association, was called in by the Battys as arbitrator. Neither side would give way. The dispute fizzled out when the strikers were forced to find work elsewhere, leaving Christina a little bruised but totally unbowed.

In 1971 Gilbert Foyle died. The founders each received (at different dates) twelve inches of formal, anonymous assessment in *The Times*. The obituarist(s?) made little attempt to note contrasting characteristics in the brothers or in their individual contributions to the company. Apart from naming their wives and children, and dates of birth and death, the notices might have been interchangeable; reading them, without prior knowledge of the company, one would be entitled to assume that an entity – 'W.& G.' – had founded, maintained and expanded its brainchild without ever dismounting from that tandem.

The anonymous *Bookseller* obituary of Gilbert quotes at length Ben Perrick and also R.C. Phelps, a long-term senior colleague at FEL. Perrick notes:

> It would be difficult to imagine two men less alike than William and Gilbert Foyle ... William was a jovial extrovert, given to great guffaws and practical jokes, a great showman and incurably gregarious ... Gilbert was quiet, reserved and serious-minded ... a very friendly and warm-hearted man ... it was his habit to call in at various departments at Foyles and extend kindly greetings to every member of staff – enquiring about husbands, wives and children and showing a genuine concern for their welfare ...

R. C. Phelps described 'Mr G.' as 'the ideal governor' who 'performed good deeds in a quiet and unobtrusive manner'.

The *Eastbourne Herald* printed three head-and-shoulders photographs of Gilbert, all revealing a high forehead, broad smile, rimless spectacles and even teeth. It refers to him as 'a true Cockney born in Finsbury' and notes that he was life-president of the Eastbourne Dickens Fellowship, a founder member of the Eastbourne Society of Londoners, also of the Forest Rambling Club, a freeman of the City of London and a freemason of London Grand Rank. It did not have space to mention his association with the Astronomical Society (to which he presented a building and a telescope), several other bodies concerned with allotments, gardens, preservation and Rotary, or that he founded the Eastbourne Silver Band.

Following Gilbert's death, FEL moved to Sussex and continued to operate until the mid-nineties. Unifoyle Ltd, 1978–94, developed export trade in schools but closed because margins became too narrow. (In 2003, John Foyle's son, Robert, based in New Zealand, developed an internet company using the domain name, foyles.com. This brought him into dispute with his second cousins in Charing Cross Road who won a legal action against him.)

• • •

Christina played little part in trade affairs. She and Ronnie occasionally graced the annual Booksellers' Association Conference (which was always attended by as many publishers as booksellers because the former never held one of their own) but rarely if ever went to meetings of the London branch, or sent a representative. She was opposed to the Net Book Agreement by which publishers imposed fixed prices, but while it remained legal Foyles recognised it. She endowed a bungalow at the Booksellers' Retreat in Hertfordshire and became a director of the Book Trade Benevolent Society which administered it. She also twice hosted the annual outings my wife and I organised for the residents at the Retreat, inviting us all to lunch and tea at Beeleigh Abbey, by then closed to the public due to vandalism. We descended upon her estate in a fleet of cars. Beeleigh, which is mentioned in Pevsner's *Essex*, is not easy to find. Not only is the entrance off a country lane which merges with grassland but the lane is reached along a truly rural road lacking signposts. We were regally received, given a lavish alfresco lunch, with wine superior to that then served at the literary luncheons, allowed the freedom of the beautiful gardens, and were conducted through the library. 'It's a bookseller's library,' Christina informed us, without further definition. Did she mean it consisted of volumes her father had been unable to sell, borrowed from stock, sold to himself preferentially on Friday afternoons or thought too precious to offer to the public? I don't know. I only remember her demanding imperiously, 'Ronnie, have you shown Mr Norrie the first folio Shakespeare?', before I was whisked off to the banks of the River Chelmer, forming part of the abbey boundary, where she pointed out land she had purchased so that her view should not be spoiled by some creature building upon it. Back on the lawn, tea was served while the sun obediently continued to shine. She was the perfect hostess, in total control. The visit was repeated a few years later, in 1987, but by then she, partly stricken, welcomed her guests while lying on a chaise-longue. Illness prevented my being there so my wife sent the letter of thanks, to which Christina replied, '... The little Persian cat you saw is called Shelley ... We have twelve cats, nearly all strays and I love them all.'

By the 1970s the Battys were beginning to wind down. They spent only the first part of the week in London returning on Wednesdays to the abbey with mountains of paperwork, according to one observer, Mrs Jan Wise. She was employed as a part-time cataloguer in the rare books department, now Beeleigh Abbey Books. Nigel Traylen, son of a well-known dealer, was in charge and responsible for issuing three or four catalogues a year. Most transactions were by mail although some customers were received at the abbey where overstock was stored in a nearby farm building. Mrs Wise recalls crossing the courtyard leading to and from it with her arms full of valuable works while trying to fend off the attention of fierce geese. Her fright and concern for what she was carrying amused Christina who, she says, collected any stray animals or birds which took her fancy regardless of whether they were suited to the habitat.

Jan Wise also typed correspondence and adverts. In one letter dictated to her Christina refuted a charge of having unfairly dismissed an employee. She informed the complainant's solicitor that the sacked assistant had been rude to her, laying on thickly the image of herself as poor, defenceless, little old woman. The adverts were destined for the local paper to attract domestics to work at the abbey. All applicants were required to send a stamped addressed envelope; if their 'CV' did not appeal to 'Miss Foyle' the stamps were used to frank other correspondence; the sender received no reply. Turnover of staff, says Mrs Wise, was frequent. She herself – unusually, perhaps uniquely – received a redundancy payment of about £500 when she was asked to leave. Nigel Traylen had already departed and following Ronald Batty's death in 1994, Beeleigh Abbey Books closed down. (It was later reinstated at Charing Cross Road.)

Jan Wise had also experienced Christina as a neighbour at the village of Cold Norton when the Battys lived there at 'the haunted house'. During that time Christina 'had been President of everything in the village', including the Young Wives Association which was invited to tea at the abbey, where William Foyle and his wife were then living. Tea was served in cracked cups, which outraged the young wives much as the glassware proffered by William years before to visiting Indian friends of mine had them. My friends were conducted round the abbey by Foyle père and then served sherry. He told them, 'These glasses are never washed. It helps to keep the flavour of the wine.' Surely one of Willie's leg-pulls?

After the Battys moved to Beeleigh, De Laches, the house at Cold Norton, was not sold. They slept there once a week 'to keep it aired'. When it had been burgled in 1987, Christine wrote to me '…absolutely everything was taken – carpets, pictures, all furniture. Never have two houses. The only thing they left behind were the books.' Peter Underwood, an author who was an expert on ghosts maintained that phenomena were experienced at both dwellings, and Christina had no doubt that Beeleigh was haunted. From the room where a priest had been executed in the sixteenth century there was heard, every twenty-second of August, 'a weird and inexplicable wailing sound'. She slept there one night and suffered two teeth marks on her neck. 'Doctors,' wrote Underwood, 'told her she had been infected by a germ unknown for more than a quarter of a century.' She insisted that no one should sleep there again. (Ronald Batty told the local press he had ignored her edict and rested there undisturbed.)

Christina was active in extra-mural activities in her home environment. She was a member of the court of the University of Essex from which she received an honorary degree; chair of the East Anglian Region of the Royal Society of the Arts, on whose national council she sat, and president of the Chelmsford District, National Trust, 1979. In the country she assumed a different persona. The *Maldon Standard* in 1975 quoted her as telling a local society that Foyles 'was more like a library than a bookshop', and that it had always been 'a public service where people could come to study or to buy books'. With spider-like expertise she wove fantasies which recurred in her broadcasts, once projecting the image of Foyles as a charitable concern, run self-sacrificingly by the family for the benefit of the nation. Her father and uncle she said in 1964, 'gave their lives to it'. (It was permissible to allow Gilbert sacrificial status.) She declared herself (1971) devoted to the staff whose '…salaries are the highest in the book trade … ' Shoplifters, she told listeners (1962), were men more than women, '…clergymen, teachers, not the ordinary type of thief … ' They were not prosecuted but made to buy what they had stolen. She returned to the subject at a lunchtime discussion at the City church of St Mary-le-Bow, with the vicar, the Reverend Joseph McCullough, 'We catch about eight people a day … we get a tremendous lot of conscience mail. It always happens after a visit by Billy Graham.'

In 1982 there was a further involvement with USDAW when an industrial tribunal ordered Foyles to pay compensation and costs to sacked staff who had dared to demand their right to join a trade union. Victor Stimac, then general manager, told the court, 'I don't think she'll accept it … she is capable of shutting the business down.' The *Daily Mail*, reporting, did not say who won. According to Dennis Barker, writing in the *Guardian* in 1990, the company was fined £23,000 for infringements of fire regulations, due to 'crass, eccentric management'. Christina, who did not attend tribunals, commented about one of them that it was a shame how '*people*' let their political feelings 'spoil things'.

Yet the more that Foyles was castigated in the press – the *Evening Standard* led a campaign, voting it on one occasion, 'the worst shop in London' – the better pleased she seemed. She was taken to task for refusing orders by phone, for the complicated procedure of paying for goods, for the layout of the stock and other shortcomings. She thrived on publicity and welcomed competition, leasing part of her premises at 121–125 Charing

Cross Road, to the newly formed, formidably expansionist group run by Tim Waterstone. With New Goldbeater's House long since added to Trefoile House and the departure of FEL she had all the space she needed under one roof. She also welcomed the arrival of Books Etc in very large premises on the opposite side of Charing Cross Road.

In *The Bookshops of London* (1993), the authors noted of Foyles that 'The travel department on the ground floor at first sight looks as good and as comprehensive as anywhere else.' But: 'Look closer, take your eyes away from the peeling paint and poor lighting to discover that … every section is ordered by publisher … to make life easy for staff and suppliers. … Foyles has every foible that Waterstone's and Books Etc have done much to eradicate from bookselling.'

Christina kept a commonplace book for much of her life. Selections from it were published by André Deutsch in 1984 and given to those who attended the eightieth-anniversary dinner of the founding of the company. On this occasion she did speak, throwing down a gauntlet by claiming, 'It is said that I have a bad record as an employer; that no one works for me for long.'

Everyone laughed nervously.

'What about Perrick?' She almost raised her voice. (Applause for the ever popular Ben.) 'What about Mrs Turner?' (Less applause; few remembered the disabled woman who had operated the ancient lift at Trefoile House.) She didn't mention anyone else. FEL, with its old retainers, had flown out of orbit; they were none of her business.

The commonplace book was recorded on cards which she riffled through in later life for her own pleasure. It was published as *So Much Wisdom*. On its first page there are quotations from Rebecca West, Walt Disney and Erasmus. In a short preface she relates:

> Very early I found great comfort in my books. I was three years old when the First World War started and saw little of my parents until it was over … but I had Mrs Molesworth, E. Nesbit, Peter Pan and Andrew Lang … I began to copy passages which gave me particular pleasure … .

In a section entitled, The Conduct of a Business, she quotes H.P. Kraus (antiquarian bookseller) from whom she learned: 'Never leave employees alone and presume they're working.'

• • •

During Christina's lifetime there was little question of modernisation. An escalator was installed only, some believed, to enable 'Miss Foyle', who suffered increasingly from arthritis, to continue prowling around her domain to spy upon her minions.

Until the 1980s credit cards were not taken by Foyles, nor was there any question of evening or Sunday opening. Moreover, apart from the luncheons, promotional programmes such as author signings, which became the norm for most booksellers, were scorned. Christina rested on her laurels dangerously too long, losing sales to vibrant new competitors, one of whom advertised mockingly on lampposts in Charing Cross Road, FOYLED AGAIN? TRY DILLON'S.

When the eightieth anniversary of Foyles became imminent I suggested in *Publishing News* that, after her death, the large site in Charing Cross Road might become a permanent national centre for the book, commemorating the family name, incorporating general and specialist departments and providing facilities for conferences, training and social events. She said she didn't want a memorial but in response to a comment I made she wrote: 'If you were only 20 years younger I would hand it [the bookshop] over to you. We need a real bookseller, that is a bookman, but also somebody very capable as well – the two things seldom go together.' I protested that I felt at least twenty years younger than I was and invited her to lunch. She declined. (When I mentioned this to Gerry Davies, sometime director of the Booksellers' Association, he replied, 'I've also got one of those letters.')

In the last years of Christina's reign, not only were she and her husband milking the firm, for half a million annually, but turnover was falling – in 1999 it was less than it had been twenty years previously; attendance at the literary luncheons, once numbered in thousands, was now between 200 and 500 and the worldwide mail-order business had flagged. It was probable that the property was worth more than the business. And property prices were zooming. *The Bookseller* published Foyles' annual figures. For the year ending 31.12.98 – the last full one before Christina died – they showed an operating loss of £82,597. The previous year's net profit had been more than £1m. The auditors, Kidson's, had once again noted, 'We have not obtained all the information and explanations that we considered necessary … ' There was no annual stocktake. Each year, apparently, the Inland Revenue accepted a signed certificate by an independent bookseller confirming the value.

In 1988 Christina had rung me (unusual for her because she hated the phone) to ask if I would take on the task of stock valuation. 'We'll pay you well,' she said. 'I'll put you over to Ronnie.' Ronnie assured me it would not take long, making it clear (as with George Depotex years before) that I would have only to make an assessment – 'It usually comes out at £Xm', he told me. Next day came a follow-up letter from Christina:

> Dear Ian
> It would be really sweet of you if you do our stock valuation. Nobody knows better than you. Do let me know if you would like to take it on. It won't take very long as we can give you helpful guidelines …

I declined this chore (previously undertaken by ex-bookseller Thomas Joy) but someone must have been found because each year the accounts continued to be published.

In old age Christina became aware that many people were speculating about her will. At the last Park Lane lunch I attended she was not at the reception because she could not manage the stairs. I found her alone in the dining-room. She looked at me suspiciously. Who was I? How had I reached her through the outer guard of flunkies? Her memory rallied. She knew she knew me. I spoke my name, mentioned Hampstead … High Hill Bookshop. It all clicked into place. I told her I wished to record her for the National Life Story Collection, asked if I might visit her at Beeleigh? Soon we were into anecdotage and, as she repeated the GBS/celery story for the second time, we were interrupted by relatives, come to wish her well. When they'd been politely rebuffed, she said, 'They're all after my money.' adding, 'I never think about money.' Then, looking only slightly abashed, she laughed and remarked, 'I suppose you only have to if you haven't got enough.'

A year before her death, on my last visit to Beeleigh, I asked Christina if she was going to sell Foyles. She drawled flippantly, 'Oh, no – o … Where would I get my books? I'm a great reader, you know.' She said she slept very little and read for much of the night, when she and her several dogs were alone at the abbey. (Her caretakers lived in a cottage nearby.) During the day the abbey swarmed with staff who were literally at the beck and call of 'Miss Foyle'. I tape-recorded her in a smallish, crowded ground-floor room within hailing distance of the kitchen. It was crammed with furniture and books. She offered me champagne at mid-morning but permitted me to have tea instead. The bubbly followed at lunch (ritual smoked salmon and a cold chicken dish) which was taken – just the two of us – in a medieval chamber into which little light penetrated. Talking about staff, pensions and job security (contentious topics with her) she said disingenuously, 'I like to feel staff are free to come and go.' We then got down to serious book-trade gossip and she asked if I had known a certain famous *Sunday Times* literary critic and author. I hadn't. 'He used to steal books from us,' she threw in casually. (I can relate only things she told me, unrecorded, over lunch; the trustees of her will have closed, indefinitely, the tape, which is at the British Library.) In a letter sent soon after she wrote:

> Do you remember Clarence Hatry,* He was very fond of books, also very religious, which led to his writing a book called *Light out of Darkness*. When it went out of print he called at Foyles, seeking a second-hand copy. He was horrified to find we had it classified under Crime. Aleister Crowley† was always asking me if we knew any famous person with something mucky in their background so that he could blackmail them. He said he would make it well worth my while. The Book Trade is great fun!
> Yours,
> Christina

Her cynical remark about where she would obtain her reading matter if she sold up was the joke of a woman who knew that whatever happened she would remain rich. She could not envisage life without regular trips to the heart of her domain; equally, she was resigned to the fact that it would not outlive her. In 1994 she had said, 'When I'm gone, this marvellous bookshop will have gone.' It was as though her ego needed to hope for this. She had turned it into the spoilt child she never had and it could not answer back. By then she spent most of her week at Beeleigh, where she kept fifteen cats, six tortoises and four peacocks and indulged her love of birdwatching and gardening. Yet on Mondays London still called. She was driven there to perform what she saw as the essential task of engaging staff. This was sheer force of habit. Some of those she employed were taking advantage of an antiquated accounting system and an overall lack of surveillance to swindle the company out of millions. Nephew Christopher, not a director but with a vested interest himself in the family business, was uncovering an inside racket which she told me about, even naming one of

---

* A financier who had spent some time in jail, he became owner of Hatchards, the Piccadilly bookshop with a royal warrant.
† He was known as 'the Great Beast' and dabbled in black magic.

those involved. I was surprised when, in her will, the same man was revealed as a beneficiary for a five-figure sum; she had obviously forgotten to amend it when his misdemeanours came to light. Towards the end, the famous memory faltered and she repeated anecdotes she had only just related. The memory but not the bank balance. That, despite the inroads made upon it by the embezzlers, remained sufficiently healthy to finance the post-Christina refurbishments and modernisation.

When Ronald Batty had died his widow was advised that she should appoint another live director but for five years she made do with one of her subsidiary property companies instead. Nephew Christopher was partly back in orbit helping with the literary luncheons, but he was also heavily engaged with his air-transport enterprises. Christina took to phoning him day and night requesting him to 'keep in touch'; then, a week before her death, she called him to Beeleigh and made him a director.

Christina's death was more widely reported than either her father's or her uncle's. There was coverage in *The Times* and *Daily Telegraph*, plus a diary piece in the latter from Peterborough; the *Guardian* with a news story and obit; the *Independent*; the *New York Times*, the *Maldon & Burnham Standard* (quoting local resident John Lodge's description, 'a dear and gracious lady'); plus follow-up articles in the *Financial Times* and *The Times*. The book-trade press was by and large critical but affectionate. Tim Waterstone, in *Publishing News*, recorded that 'Her personal manner was … rather regal'; the *Telegraph* described her as 'striking looking, with grey-blue eyes that could sometimes glint with impatience'. Her shortcomings as an employer were not glossed over but the portrait primarily was that of a dominating, eccentric running a bookshop which was in a time warp. The public tends to admire millionaires and the fact that she left just on £60m. prompted, at the very least, respect. Waterstone named her 'an eccentric and ungenerous employer', stating that she and Ronald Batty had 'destroyed all prospects of growth' by bleeding Foyles 'year after year', adding that under their own-ership, it 'became a physical and financial mess', yet concluding, '…her stock … was the best and most varied of any big bookshop in the world and she loved books and authors. Christina was a proud and steely-willed woman. I liked her very much indeed.'

The *Guardian* obituary misreported the deal between Christina and Tim, stating that she 'kept Foyles … alive … even when it was challenged by Waterstone, who opened his flagship shop next door to her in Charing Cross Road'. The premises – not his flagship – she leased to him because it amused her. He had been astonished. The *Guardian* also quoted

Waterstone's anecdote about a drunken old woman who had a fruit stall in Manette Street. 'She was Christina's exact twin and the two had known each other all their lives.' Christina kept her in brandy. When he bought some plums from her one day she told Tim, 'You'll be all right, dear. Miss Foyle thinks your shops are quite good.'

Roger Tagholm, of *Publishing News*, concentrated on the shop which he adored, stating that staff running their own departments chose to stay because they had no interference from management ... had a free hand to buy and sell what they liked, no problems with budgets and, as one put it: 'You have your own shop within the shop.' (He wrote this before news broke of the multi-million-pound fraud.)

None of the obituarists referred to Christina's act of kindness to a member of staff in the early 1950s. A girl named Buttercup who worked in the mail-order department had a chronic cough which her employer noticed. In one mood she might have sacked her for being ill on duty. In fact she sent her to a private doctor and settled the bill. Buttercup was treated for tuberculosis and cured; she subsequently married Christina's cousin John.

Norris McWhirter, who with his brother founded the *Guinness Book of Records*, was an in-law through Ronald Batty's family. He referred, in the *Independent*, to Christina's well-fed peacocks admiring themselves in the polished panels of visitors' cars and pecking their owners; the same guests were often bemused by the slowly moving lights in the gardens, shining from the candles which Christina had affixed to her tortoises.

The tortoises featured in Chistina's will. She left £100,000 to her former gardener at Beeleigh, Tony Scillitoe, with instructions that he should care for them and her collie, Bobby. He told the *Daily Telegraph* that 'Miss Foyle was good to work for. She could be a bit strict and we heard some stories about how she sacked people in London. But down here in the countryside she was quiet and kindly.'

At her death Christina owned 60% of Foyles, including much property in Soho as well as Essex; Christopher Foyle and his brother had 16% each and sister Winifred 8%. Most of Christina's share was left to a trust without specific instructions for its use. Christopher subsequently purchased from it Beeleigh Abbey but not William Foyle's library which was auctioned over several days at Christie's and fetched £12m. Christina's ashes were buried alongside those of her husband at Beeleigh beneath, so Peterborough of the *Telegraph* reported, a statue of Sir Robert de Mantell, founder of the abbey.

Potent criticism of Christina's role at Foyles came from her nephew Bill Samuel who joined his cousin Christopher on the board in late 1999 to assist him in transforming Foyles into a bookshop fit for the twenty-first century. Gradually, one department at a time, and without closing for a single day, new shelving and fittings were installed, new flooring was laid, opening hours were extended, the staff were given contracts, better wages and pensions. In an article in *The Times* (31.7.01) Samuel was quoted as saying his aunt had been a wealthy woman yet when she died '…in real terms the business was probably worth no more than it was when she was given it … She was in charge for forty years and it was grossly mismanaged.'

Within two years of Christina's death Foyles had become a shop to be recommended not only to customers but also to would-be booksellers. I became a customer, taking special delight in finding stock arranged alphabetically by author or subject. New departments were opened, the feminist Silver Moon Bookshop, due to close for personal reasons, was absorbed, so was Ray's Jazz, featuring live music, a café was opened, the gallery renovated and, in its centenary year, Foyles was awarded a Nibbie, by *Publishing News*, whose readers voted it Independent Bookshop of the Year.

The centenary was brought forward to 2003 when inspection of what were rumoured to be rooms full of unsorted archives proved this to be the correct year. *Foyles a celebration* was published to mark the event. In essence, it is a memorial to Willie featuring many photographs of him in genial mood, highlighting numerous of his quips, recording some of his practical jokes and quoting Bill Samuel, who remembered him 'as a wonderful grandfather', giving 'us a love of books and mischief in equal measure … ' It is a typographical disaster area, assuming a reader attention span of under two seconds, but Penny Mountain's text, once excavated, is rewarding to read. Willie gets full value and it deals more fairly than its predecessors with Gilbert. It is unlikely that Christina would have given it her approval.

Christina Agnes Lilian Foyle, born Highgate (Hampstead?), 30 January 1911, younger daughter of William Alfred and Christina Foyle. Married Ronald Batty, 30 January 1938. Died Beeleigh Abbey, 8 June 1999.

Seven

ALAN HILL

My other subjects all became wealthy, some of them multi-millionaires by their own efforts or through inheriting family firms. Alan did neither. He never owned the company he created; for long he was employed on a monthly-salary basis. His background was lower-middle class; he won a scholarship to Cambridge; he died comfortably off, a middle-class publisher with a good pension, living in Hampstead Garden Suburb.

Probably, rather than possibly, the most innovative and successful British publisher of educational books, at secondary and tertiary levels, in the entire twentieth century, A.H. (as he was not known) also saw himself as a general publisher of some standing. Although founder of the Educational Publishers' Council (EPC) and champion of what he saw as a non-establishment, even below-stairs, branch of his profession, he prided himself on having a list rich in biography, drama, poetry and fiction. He was born 'a completely-packaged product of the English Nonconformist Conscience' (his words to me, eighty years on) in the Midlands village of Barwell, where William his father was the schoolteacher and a pillar of the Wesleyan chapel. May, his mother, was the daughter of a Baptist missionary in the Cameroons. Africa, and particularly West Africa, was to become a dominant theme of his publishing life.

William Wills Hill was a Fabian, a disciple of Bernard Shaw and admirer of Ramsay Macdonald, MP for the nearby constituency of Leicester. He was a Labour Party worker, a teetotaller and, until the death from meningitis of his eldest son in 1913, a devout Christian. He renounced his faith but not the Protestant work ethic which remained embedded in his descendents, motivating the publishing life of his third son, the medical life of his second, and the political life of both.

In 1928 Alan met Enid Malin who was two years his junior when they were attending Wyggeston Grammar and High Schools respectively in Leicester. They realised they were kindred spirits and agreed one day to marry. They were equally academic, adventurous, left-wing. Enid was down-to-earth, scholarly, hockey-playing; Alan was impulsive, impressionable, quick-witted, with a penchant for travel and an innate though hidden capacity for leadership. Both came to maturity in the 1930s. On coming down from Jesus, Cambridge with an honours degree in History, Alan had a brief career as a teacher, and also worked at Harrods, before joining William Heinemann publishers, in 1936; he had a lifelong attachment to Jesus College which was to be reflected in his publishing and by his ritual attendance at reunions. Enid, an Oxford graduate, also became a teacher. The couple wed on 4 August 1939 in a ceremony which took place late in the morning after Alan had been to the office to keep his work up to date. By the law of the time Enid, now a married woman, was required to cease working as a teacher.

William Heinemann, a second generation immigrant, had founded his imprint in 1890 and quickly become successful with both literary and popular fiction. This enabled him to fund translations of European, especially Russian, authors and to introduce their work to English readers. Within one decade his was a major list. Moreover, many of his most important authors, such as Somerset Maugham and John Galsworthy, remained loyal to it long after his death. He made a disastrous, childless marriage. His cousin, trained to succeed him, was killed in the First World War. Heinemann never recovered from this loss, learned Braille because of failing eyesight, then died unexpectedly in 1920.

The company was bought by the American publisher, F. N. Doubleday, who promoted one Charles Evans to take charge of it, later foisting upon him journalist Alexander (A.S.) Frere as a senior colleague. During the depression ten years later Evans and Frere achieved a kind of management buyout, also establishing a public company, Heinemann Holdings Ltd, in which they had shares. They were the virtual owners of the business which Alan Hill joined as assistant to R. Welldon Finn who ran the education department, started in 1931. Five years on it had an annual turnover of £4,000 most of it due to two textbooks. Holderness and Lambert's *School Certificate Chemistry*, almost unaided, doubled total sales by 1939. It was just sufficient to pay both men's salaries, of which Alan's was £350 per annum. Even at this early stage of his career it became his ambition to outshine the established leaders in the field. In 1936, while visiting a school, he was patronised by a Longman's representative who gave him a lift in his car. This man had two hundred and fifty titles on offer; Alan had only six. He resolved, 'to surpass Longmans, however long it took.' Half a century on he recorded, 'It took exactly 43 years.'

In 1926 the American owners of Heinemann had taken a step into the future by removing their warehousing, accounting and all activities apart from editorial, on to the Surrey Downs. At Kingswood they bought spacious gardens and land on which the Windmill Press was built to print their own publications; they also found room for a company sports ground. When war was declared in September 1939 the editorial department was temporarily evacuated there from London and the Hills set up home at nearby Tadworth. Regulations forbidding married women to teach were relaxed. Enid returned to the classroom and in the following year Alan was called up into the RAF. By this time because of paper rationing the educational department was not publishing any new titles and the slender list all but disappeared over the next five years.

Hill's poor eyesight disqualified him from aircrew duties and he became a trainee armourer, aircraftsman 2nd class, the rank of all new recruits. He was subsequently commissioned, ending the war as a squadron leader responsible for ensuring thorough maintenance of aircraft on his station. He had what was called 'a good war', enjoyed the companionship, flirted with authority, worked with planes but seldom flew in one and lived to relate hilarious tales of days when things went wrong. He was already an entertaining raconteur, an embroiderer of good stories.

Alan inherited from his father an enthusiasm for the Labour Party, claiming, as an old man, he had belonged to it for most of his life. He did not mention in his memoirs that he and Enid had also been Communist Party members in the 1930s. At that time many socialists, as leftish democrats then liked to call themselves, turned to the CP as the only possible alternative to the fascism which was overrunning much of Europe. Many of Alan's contemporaries, including his brother Cedric, fought against Franco in the Spanish Civil War, a few became spies and remained undetected for decades. By 1945 the Hills had presumably left the CP and Alan took seriously the notion that he might enter Parliament for Labour. On his father's nomination he was listed for selection and thereby became eligible to be considered by any constituency party seeking a candidate, but this plan was side-tracked when he was invited to an interview at Heinemann's. A.S. Frere had already been released from service with the Ministry of Labour before the European war ended on 7 May 1945 because Evans had died. He had become managing director and wished Alan, once demobbed, to revive the education department. An election had been called but Alan accepted Frere's offer albeit with some regrets – there was politics in his blood – because he believed, along with millions of others, that the nation was unlikely to reject its wartime leader Winston Churchill. He and they were wrong; Labour won a landslide victory and Alan had he stood for Parliament might well have become a backbencher MP. It would not have been a role suited to his temperament or abilities nor, as a potential minister, would he have found it easy to toe the party line. It was fortunate that he opted for educational publishing under the benign auspices of Frere, financial director H.L. Hall and Dwye, son of Charles Evans.

Hill returned to 99 Great Russell Street, Bloomsbury, in January 1946 – it had proved impractical to run the editorial side of publishing from Kingswood – on a salary of £750 per annum with, for five years, annual increments of £50, which would take him to the then magical sum of 'a thousand a year'. Frere, to his credit, understood that with continuing paper shortages and the greatly changed conditions of a nation scarred by a six-year war careful planning would be necessary for Alan to build a feasible, saleable list in less time. His grateful acolyte wrote:

> I re-started my publishing career with a table and chair, a shared telephone, a handful of pre-war books and an annual sales revenue of £15,000, most of it coming from three titles. Nothing else: no staff; not even a secretary for my first eighteen months. Certainly not a company car. I had to use my own pre-war Ford Eight and provide my own portable typewriter. In my first year I published nothing.

Although at this early stage of his return Hill's list was not actually growing the process of seeking new titles demanded assistance. Employed at that time on the trade counter, down the area steps at 99 Great Russell Street, was Edward Thompson, a young man who when not serving bookseller customers, read Kafka and Dostoevsky. Frere recommended him to Hill who gave him some poems to report on and told him he needed 'an assistant to learn about education, visit schools, look out for authors', as well as attending to office work, accounts and the mailing system. 'But what you will really have to be,' Hill concluded, 'is a missionary.' Thompson accepted and, apart from twelve months off combating tuberculosis, stayed for forty years, becoming editor of the Drama Library and sales director. In 1947, the two men published six books before Edward fell ill: on recovering he insisted for his health's sake on working from Kingswood where he contrived not to be deemed 'in isolation'. He was the first of an all-male team which remained intact for several decades, room being made for each new senior person as expansion demanded.

The writer James Reeves, who had been at Cambridge in Hill's time, became prominent on the education list, leading off with a poetry anthology which sold in hundreds of thousands. It was he who recommended Alan's next senior colleague, A R. (Tony) Beal, a scholar who wrote a critical study of D. H. Lawrence and became, as deputy MD, a perfect foil to Alan. The latter wrote of himself, Edward and Tony, 'We three effectively created HEB' (Heinemann Educational Books, as it was to become known).

In HEB terms 'educational' was to be interpreted in the widest sense. The creators were appalled at the stuffiness of the average school English literature courses on which twentieth-century writers were virtually unrepresented. This led to the New Windmill Series starting with C. Day Lewis's *The Otterbury Incident*, an imaginative, adventurous and amusing novel for young people which adults could also enjoy. Tony Beal became responsible for this series in collaboration with the writer Ian Serraillier and its bounds were soon widened to include such masterpieces as Harper Lee's *To Kill A Mocking Bird*, Solzhenitsyn's *One Day in the Life of Ivan Denisovich*, Schaeffer's western, *Shane* and John Steinbeck's *The Pearl*, which sold more than a million copies. 'Educational' also meant biographies such as Robert Gittings' *Life of John Keats*, Robert McKenzie's *British Political Parties* and Fred Hoyle's science-fiction novel *The Black Cloud* (with Alan proudly in the role of editor) as well as his *Frontiers of Astronomy*. Under Edward's guidance, 'educational' was not only the Drama Library of actual classical and modern plays but also Gordon Craig's *On the Art of the Theatre* and memoirs by star actors John Gielgud and Michael Redgrave.

So Alan had every right to consider himself a general as well as an educational publisher although the William Heinemann list was not actually as confined to adult and children's fiction as he sometimes claimed. In the immediate post-war period, while Alan was building his list, the founding company had formidable successes with *Boswell's London Journal*, rediscovered and decoded by an American academic; with *I Believed*, the recantation of his Communist faith by Douglas Hyde, a former news editor on *The Daily Worker*; with volumes of autobiography by Richard Church; a biography of D. H. Lawrence by Richard Aldington; and a title the HEB men might well have coveted, Aneurin Bevan's *In Place of Fear*, the Labour Health Minister's justification of the welfare state.

For HEB the success of the general titles was none the less always dwarfed by the schoolbooks where six- or even seven-figure sales were not limited to the few years following publication; they continued for decades. In a short while Alan found not only the books but the colleagues he needed. A characteristic he shared with Allen Lane was the inclination to appoint people with little or no experience to senior positions. He claimed to have found Hamish MacGibbon 'languishing in the production department of William Heinemann'. It was 1960; Hamish (son of another publisher, James MacGibbon) had but recently graduated – in History.

'I winkled him out,' wrote Alan, 'and put him in charge of our science list.'

To find more bestselling books in science – and maths, which was added to Hamish's brief – was a formidable undertaking, especially when arch rivals Longmans and Penguin were preferred as publishers by the newly formed Nuffield Foundation Project. This became a blessing in disguise, thanks to HEB author A. J. Mee and rep James Watson, who were au fait with the Scottish Education Department's new curriculum in these subjects. Hill and MacGibbon were soon convinced of the enormous potential and launched the Scottish Primary Maths Project alongside a rich vein of science books including Jardine's *Physics is Fun*, which sold in huge quantities for the next two decades.

Another trait Hill shared with Allen Lane – with Stanley Unwin and Billy Collins too – was a love of travel. In his case he liked it to be spiced with adventure and recreation. He climbed, trekked, flew, drove, sailed, entrained, not solely to satisfy his curiosity and to encourage indigenous authorship for school and university texts but also to sponsor creative writing. Yet although he became most closely identified in his 'missionary' work with Africa, it was Australia with which Hill first fell in love, when he went there in 1956. He revelled in the absence of class and flirted briefly with the notion of emigrating. Instead, he opened an Australian office and became friends of, amongst many others, Don and Thelma McLean. Don was a teacher and already on the Heinemann list. He and Thelma came to live in Hampstead for some years where Mavis and I also enjoyed their company. Don succeeded in doing what none of the hundreds of Hampstead authors did in my thirty years of trading there – he intimidated me into stocking copies of his own books, which *he* supplied, allowing me a mere 10% commission, terms worse than those offered to booksellers even by educational publishers.

Alan also visited New Zealand and Malaysia, setting up agencies and branches wherever he went, invariably choosing the right man (rarely, if ever, woman) for the job, one who would remain loyal to him over a long period. From Singapore he journeyed north through dangerous territory where guerrilla warfare raged in search not only of authors and selling points but also because he wanted to see the Malaysian peninsular for himself. In Africa similar exploits were to land him in life-threatening situations. Once, by unwittingly having bought a hat in Kenya which in West Africa instantly branded him a public enemy, he was arrested. Enid had already been waved through immigration control. His captors became menacing. Alan proclaimed himself a friendly publisher, demanded a lawyer, possibly dropped the name 'Achebe', finally, in desperation, asked for his wife to be called. Enid explained in her blunt Midlands manner, 'Of course he's not a spy; he's my husband.' It could only have been her utterly transparent honesty that saved the day. Alan lived to relate the story, spun to ever greater and more hilarious length, for many a year. It was his own apparent lack of guile in admitting to having been a Communist Party member, when applying in person at the American embassy for a visa, that gained him admission to the USA. (This happened to the man who so often insisted that there was no such thing as 'good luck!')

In his determination to make HEB international, Alan remained conscious of the immense advantages enjoyed by Longmans and OUP, who had been publishing for the educational market before William Heinemann first opened his door. He especially believed he had made a mistake in not employing Tim Rix, of Longmans, although those who knew both men expressed doubt that a good relationship would have resulted. Until the 'seventies, Longmans, Green and Co. (founded 1724) was the oldest established, and one of the largest remaining, independent family publishers; along with the Oxford University Press it established EFL (English as a Foreign Language) known also as ELT (English Language Teaching) as a major category. Others were in the market too – notably Thomas Nelson, Cambridge University Press, Macmillan, plus Evans Brothers who, as early as 1947, had been ahead of competitors in exploring the West African market, although not in ELT.

Yet, great though the prestige of the older imprints was, certain of them did not display in Africa the vision which was to make HEB's progress so impressive. On his first visit, in 1959, Hill quickly understood that British publishers thought of that continent primarily as a dumping ground for their schoolbooks, usually the work of British authors and printed in the UK. Chinua Achebe's first novel, *Things Fall Apart*, initially published in a small edition by William Heinemann, had opened his eyes to the potentials of indigenous publishing at every level. The French, in their former colonial territories, were at least in fiction ahead of him in this respect and the African Writers' Series was to use some of its titles, in English translations, to enhance HEB's offerings.

In establishing the AWS, Alan was assisted by Van Milne, head of Nelson's Overseas Department who, having rowed with his overlords, defected to HEB to help build the series. Later, in 1962, when Milne resigned to rejoin Nelson because he did not get on with Alan, Tony Beal was despatched to Nigeria to persuade Achebe to become 'editor on the ground', a role the writer undertook for ten years. At HEB Milne was succeeded by his former deputy, Keith Sambrook, who played a vital role in Africa, having to endure the hair-raising experience of driving with his new employer through jungle to a small town where one Aigboje Higo was headmaster of an Anglican school. Higo was offered and accepted the job of manager of HEB's Ibadan office. Keith, who was told by Alan, 'You're not a publisher but you're good at setting up other publishers', stayed to become part of the inner team and, when not on overseas posting, a neighbour in the Garden Suburb where he played tennis with his boss. He too was Leicestershire-born, and a graduate of Jesus College.

Most of Alan's team had experience of Africa. In 1970 Hamish MacGibbon was sent out to win a contract for the Nigerian Integrated Science Project, known as 'NISP'. This involved commissioning, printing and delivering tens of thousands of copies of each of six textbooks in little over a year. He sought the help of HEB author A.J. Mee, who had ten years previously put him on to *Physics is Fun*. Catching him at London airport, about to fly to the Caribbean on a British Council mission, he persuaded him to create the series. Mee joined fourteen authors assembled at Ibadan for a three weeks' workshop; the books, based on the Scottish project, were completed and ready for the 1971 year. Fifteen years later they were still selling 250,000 copies per annum.

All senior colleagues of Alan's endured the rigours of travel as part of their mission. 'At any moment during the late 1960s and early 1970s,' he wrote, 'Hamish, Keith Sambrook or myself could be found in some far corner of the globe … ' Also David, his younger son, who had been, or was still, a member of the far left International Socialists (later the Socialist Workers' Party), was sent to Nairobi to set up local publishing. Alan said of him that his 'anti-colonial attitudes were so pronounced … I was concerned that he might alienate the local white community!' David's choice to manage the project was Henry Chakava, a Kenyan educated at a progressive school run by Quakers. He subsequently became MD and chief publishing editor of HEB East Africa Ltd, a company in which, in accordance with Alan's policy, 60% of the equity was locally owned.

Another even more senior 'African' colleague was James Currey, ex-Oxford University Press, who took charge of the whole of HEB's school and university publishing on the continent and had overall daily responsibility for the AWS from 1967–85. This took 20% of his time; he also inaugurated the Caribbean Writers' Series. At home Keith Nettle, an English graduate with publishing experience at Penguin, was recruited to develop an English and Modern Language list. This Keith, wrote Alan, 'showed that it was possible to be commercially successful while still retaining educational idealism.'

The other leading member of the team, which for long remained intact, was Paul Richardson, whose appointment illustrates the manner in which HEB was run. For Alan, private life, work and holiday were one, inseparable parts of an ongoing, enriching experience; it was an attitude which could be perplexing for the person on the receiving end. Hill had approached the Cambridge University Appointments Board in search of a history graduate who was an aspirant publisher with teaching and writing experience. Preference would be given to someone who had taught in grammar as well as secondary modern schools. Paul Richardson not only met all these qualifications but could claim classroom experience as well at the prestigious (private) Dragon School in Oxford.

The job specification was to build a list of textbooks on history, geography and economics. (It is only surprising that Alan had not insisted on someone with a degree in mathematics or biology.) The interview took place, crucially for Paul, on the day before the final date when he could give notice to the Manchester Grammar School in order to be available by September. Its first session lasted for most of the morning, taking place in Alan's office while he made and took numerous telephone calls, signed letters, gave instructions to various underlings, scrutinised documents placed before him and paid as much attention as he could spare to the applicant. No actual offer had been made by the time he took the now disconcerted teacher to lunch where, at the coffee stage, they were joined by Hamish MacGibbon. Late in the afternoon, back at HEB, an actual employment proposal was made and Paul presented with a typescript to read and comment upon. There was no mention of remuneration, but Paul had promised his wife he would not accept any job unless he was offered an immediate salary increase and good prospects. He now had less than twenty-four hours in which to decide. He mentioned how much he was currently earning but Alan brushed the subject aside, saying there would be a letter in the post; Paul was not to worry. The would-be publisher boarded the train for Manchester and decided to chance his luck, telling his wife he expected at least £200 p.a. more. When the official offer came it was £500 more. (In 1967, £1500 p.a. in publishing was not wealth but it was 50% more than one earned as a teacher at a top grammar school.)

Soon after he started at HEB Alan enquired how the book Richardson had written, for Cambridge University Press, had sold. 'Not very well,' the author admitted. Alan instantly phoned R.W. David, London manager of CUP, and said, 'Dick, this book you have by my new young man. It's not

doing very well, is it? OK. Why don't you transfer it to us?' David thought
the suggestion sensible. On the HEB list the book sold twice as many copies.

Alan could get away with such unorthodox tactics. No manual of management would have dared authorise them or the personal, often eccentric,
manner in which he conducted the affairs of HEB, even though he was not
in control of the purse strings. That he was allowed to behave so was due
to the faith that successive overlords had in his ability. His prime aim may
have been to further the cause of education in Britain and its former
empire, but in so doing he chanced upon a gold mine. It sounds too good
to be true, like a Victorian moral tale of virtue rewarded, with all the ingre-
dients of the classic success story, including a lasting, happy marriage, three
bright children, a pleasant house in one of the more agreeable parts of
London, a second home in the Lake District, a passion for, plus the means
to enjoy, Shakespeare, Bach and endless travel. Could such good fortune
(and good health) in one man make for interesting biography? In fact, the
amazing expansion of HEB took place against a background that was constantly threatening and distracting. The Heinemann ship was holed.

Frere, as post-Second World War chairman, ruled the company with a certain laissez-faire grandeur. Board meetings were treated as casual, social
occasions. H.L. Hall, once company secretary, later finance director, was
permitted to be secretive about the manner in which he employed the
company's resources. That was his job; the task of Frere, Dwye Evans, Alan
Hill and Phyllis Alexander – who ran a subsidiary, The World's Work
(1913) Ltd – was to publish. Frere also had an expansionist side. Heinemann
already owned the above-mentioned World's Work and Peter Davies, a
general list acquired in 1937. To these were added Secker & Warburg, The
Naldrett Press, Rupert Hart-Davis and other imprints needing financial
assistance; towards them Frere maintained a policy of non-interference at
editorial level. Heinemann was buoyant with its plethora of bestselling novelists headed by Somerset Maugham, J.B. Priestley, John Steinbeck,
Graham Greene and Nevil Shute, its impressive backlist and the non-
fiction triumphs already mentioned. To accept the protection of its financial umbrella at the same time as publishing independently was as attractive
to Fred Warburg and Rupert Hart-Davis as it was to Alan Hill. The latter's
contribution to the success of the group was recognised when he was
elected to the board of William Heinemann in 1955. (Heinemann
Education was still then a department, not a company in its own right.) It
was sensible of Frere to make this gesture of recognition and Alan appreciated it, although he must have felt slightly less honoured when he discov-

ered that one of his duties was to take the minutes, which were never circulated in advance of the next meeting. He had become a director but was less equal than some of his fellows. He did not, because of Hall's cagey procedures, find himself privy to the details of the finances, although thanks to his aunt Cecilia's modest purchases on the stockmarket he came to own a small shareholding.

Thomas Tilling Ltd, a City corporate, with greater means than Alan's aunt, owners of a transport firm and much else, had also begun to buy shares. These probably became available partly through the cost of taking over Secker & Warburg and others, partly because the shareholder-directors were rewarding themselves too handsomely. Sales and profits began to decline; cash flow was poor. Tillings had a policy of not owning a minority interest in other companies but in the case of Heinemann, because of one man's devotion to literature, they made an exception. The son of a butler, Lionel Fraser, a banker as well as chairman of Tilling's, was a Christian Scientist, teetotaller and member of the Garrick where he met Frere. He loved the idea of being connected with publishing. It was also a principle of Tilling's that they did not interfere with the management of businesses they bought; they judged only on results. It was only once Tilling's had acquired a majority of Heinemann's shares that they looked closely at what to their surprise was an ailing enterprise. It was over trading, short on liquidity, stock was not written-down, its printing press at Kingswood had been left unmodernised while Hall's archaic management structure sometimes allowed financial considerations to take precedence over publishing priorities. The educational-book department almost alone was prospering partly because Hill was placing print orders outside the group to avoid using the inefficient Windmill Press.

Fraser called in a City colleague R.O.A. (Reg) Keel to investigate and appointed Alan Hill managing director. This was flattering for the junior member of the board but he could have done without the promotion because he was still expanding his own department and enjoying the experience. It speaks well of the senior colleagues to whom he had delegated at 'HEB' that the list was unharmed during the two years that Alan was required to give part of his attention to the group. It was not a task he was especially fitted for and although he understood himself to be caretaker MD he could not totally distance himself from Keel's damning report to Fraser.

Fraser did not allow his love of 'being' a publisher to cloud his business instincts. He put feelers out in America and got a response from the long established, internationally minded McGraw-Hill. He then behaved extraordinarily by inviting their negotiators to a secret Sunday meeting in

London to which neither Frere (now chairman) nor Hill was invited. Heinemann Group people at this meeting included Rupert Hart-Davis, Fred Warburg and others who were fiercely against being taken over by McGraw. They indicated this so forcefully that the Americans withdrew and Fraser was forced to think again. He called a board meeting and, in Hill's words, 'told us that he felt that the firm had been run in such a dis-orderly fashion that it almost merited a Board of Trade inquiry'. Frere was immediately pushed upstairs to become president, Tilling's became sole owners and Fraser embarked on a scheme to merge Heinemann with The Bodley Head, 51% owned by a merchant bank but effectively under the direction of Max Reinhardt. This deal foundered partly due to Alan Hill's opposition and led to Frere's resignation and defection to The Bodley Head along with authors Graham Greene, Georgette Heyer and Eric Ambler.

At this time (as mentioned in Chapter Three) there had been an abortive bid, by directors of Michael Joseph in alliance with Allen Lane, for Jonathan Cape Ltd. Charles Pick, ex-joint MD of Joseph, was 'looking around'. Fraser, on the advice of Fred Warburg, invited him to join Heinemann. Alan Hill had already been permitted to form HEB as a separate company within the group while relinquishing his role as managing director of William Heinemann. His friend Alan Steele, London director of the Somerset printers Butler & Tanner, offered to raise backing to allow Hill to become independent. Long after, Alan excused to me what he called his 'excessive caution' in remaining with the devil he knew as being primarily due to the fact that both Frere and Fraser had left him 'completely alone to publish as I wanted'. He told Hamish MacGibbon that it was also due to having grown-up during the thirties' slump.

Alan asserted his independence within the group although retaining a respectful attitude towards Fraser when he called at Tilling's Mayfair head-quarters, the elegant eighteenth-century Crewe House. This mansion was close to Heinemann's new, bleak 1960s premises in Queen Street which Alan found unsympathetic as offices and architecturally offensive. He toler-ated them only briefly before leasing a Georgian terrace house in nearby Charles Street. There he saw out most of the rest of his career, with Enid, who had for many years been managing the London end of the Loeb Classical Library, awarded a cramped work area partly beneath the stairway to the first floor. (Loeb, with its dual texts, founded by William Heinemann in 1912, had been owned by Harvard University Press since 1938.)

The relationship between Alan Hill and Charles Pick who became MD of William Heinemann in 1964 was neither close nor, at least on the surface, particularly unfriendly. Alan insisted he was inefficient at having enemies and had never hated anyone; Charles is unlikely to have believed the same of himself. Both men accepted the new overall financial director, Peter Range, another City man who, in Keith Sambrook's words, 'knew how to manage the relationship between publishing and Tilling's'. Pick was a masterful publisher of middle- and lower-middlebrow fiction who had begun his career as a rep for Victor Gollancz. In 1935 he joined the new imprint of Michael Joseph where he soon manifested both a genuine publisher's nose for bestsellers and a keen business brain. Fraser made no attempt to hide from him the parlous state of Heinemann. Charles instantly saw that the backlist, a potential gold mine, was so grossly underpriced that it was contributing only a fraction of its true value to the profits. He was conscious of what the loss of Graham Greene and other authors loyal to Frere meant, but soon attracted John Le Carré from Gollancz and made a major discovery in Wilbur Smith. He also nurtured non-fiction and held on to the technical and professional list which, at tertiary level, published across a wide spectrum of subjects from cookery for chefs, wig-making, ship construction and management to manuals for accountants and journalists. This belonged naturally to HEB but had come to the group through the purchase of the Naldrett Press, so it was part of William Heinemann Ltd. Its commissioning editor was John St John, resident and borough councillor of Hampstead, later official historian of the group. He was much closer to Hill than to Pick but accepted the status quo. Dwye Evans, then chairman, offered it to Alan who refused it, later admitting that this had been a wrong decision.

Pick swiftly reversed Heinemann's fortunes while Hill took HEB from strength to strength, spreading across the Commonwealth, creating subsidiaries which were granted near dominion status, mirroring the inevitable fragmentation of the British empire, while remaining close to base. He recruited on the spot, on whichever continent he happened to be, or delegated to a colleague. After 1968 he went no more to *South* Africa, he and Enid finding the political climate too oppressive, 'preferring to leave responsibility for our educational business out there to Tony Beal'. It is the right of a chief to behave thus to his No. 2. Beal made no complaint on that score, although he objected to the racist attitudes of the local William Heinemann staff which then represented HEB in that area. As a result Alan grandly withdrew 'our business from them and in 1978 set up our own HEB branch under Anita (Wolfe-Coote) – the first woman to get to the top in our worldwide educational organisation'.

That other women had not attained director level was partly due to the men, who had not moved on. There was no anti-feminist policy, although

Alan had rationalised male domination in his firm by saying that women often had to leave to bear children and to look after their families. There were actually two or three who stayed for some years – Heather Young, who from being Tony Beal's secretary became editor in charge of English-language books, and Susan Ault, another editor so dedicated to her work that, on the day of her marriage in Oxford, she insisted on attending a meeting at HEB first. Alan then drove her to the wedding, stopping en route at a tin hut in a layby where she changed into her trousseau. A third was Gillian Dickinson, who moved on to the British Council to preside over admirable work concerned with providing low-priced books for emergent nations. Even so MacGibbon maintained that Alan primarily welcomed women as middle-managers but employed secretaries who did not hesitate to pronounce aloud about his foibles. Paul Richardson noted that until 1975 the annual climbing outings in the Lake District were strictly excursions for the men, the women being given a day off in lieu for Christmas shopping. It has to be wondered what 'the old Neen', as Alan customarily referred to his wife, thought of this, but by the mid-1970s HEB had introduced gen-erous maternity-leave payments and inaugurated a trainee scheme for out-standing graduates seen as potential leaders. Two of the first four were women. Alan referred flippantly to this as the time when his company 'became bisexual', although it remained predominantly male with the men tending to like and respect each other. Hamish remembered that there was no back-biting between any of them; Paul said there was trust and that the weekly editorial meetings were robust events, when all present scrutinised rigorously each other's recommendations for publication. MacGibbon recalled that, surprisingly, on these occasions Alan did not talk all the while, nor fall asleep for long periods. He listened and asked pertinent questions, such as, 'Why do you want to do this book? Convince me.' His three cri-teria for publishing were – always do a good book even if its sales potential isn't great; even do a bad book if it has a definite market and will make money; never do a bad book with no sales potential. Sambrook recalled that Alan was sometimes indulged by his fellow directors if they thought little loss would be incurred. Then they let him have his way about a title they didn't much like as a kind of 'thank you' for giving them all so much rein. Alan, he said, had a weakness for what he thought of as 'big names'. This was part of his pleasure in being seen to be a 'general' publisher, a side of HEB which Tony Beal tolerated but did not relish.

Alan believed strongly in readers' reports and, when in doubt, in send-ing out a typescript again. He also insisted that 'if the ultimate outcome is a book I want to publish, then the author can be as difficult, greedy, insulting, as he wishes.' On occasion, he allowed his hunches to rule. He received two unfavourable reports on a physics textbook and ignored both. This was Nelkon and Parker's *A Level Physics* which sold 850,000 copies under his aegis.

Turning down authors came more easily than dismissing unsatisfactory staff. Hamish remembers that Alan '…just made life difficult for them' so they took the hint and resigned. Nor, although he and his management team were politically left-wing, did he relish the introduction of a National Union of Journalists' chapel which was established at Heinemann in the late 1970s. His son David, then a commsisioning editor, was a particularly radical member of the chapel whose existence made Alan so uncomfortable that he tended to leave delicate negotiations to senior colleagues.

As head of HEB Alan was democratic in principle yet maddeningly feudal, remaining supremo at the same time as opting out (as instanced above) or delegating. Hamish, Tony, Paul, the two Keiths and others learned to get on with their jobs while keeping a weather eye open for sudden interference that might arise from his sharp eye for detail. For instance, he insisted on being shown proofs of all company advertisements which he might amend in his neat, legible hand. He was vague, unpunctual, infinitely divertible, infuriating and disarming, a man with a fertile mind through which his own and other people's ideas coursed. Sambrook told me, 'Alan always knew what you were doing … it was never any good trying to outwit him.' Paul Richardson wrote, 'When things went wrong excuses cut no ice but a full admission of the problem brought not just forgiveness but usually a supportive solution.' 'By the time I gave up the reins in 1979,' Alan declared proudly, 'all my original appointments were still there and running successful Heinemann enterprises.' (This was not quite true.)

My experience of Alan was mostly at a social level but also on committees. There was no male domination in either case. He was fond of the sometimes ferocious Norah Smallwood, of Chatto & Windus, and delighted in the company of Kaye Webb, of Puffin Books. The Hills were generous entertainers, hosting frequent luncheons, dinners and parties at their home, at one of Alan's clubs or at restaurants. At Northway, in Hampstead Garden Suburb, there was little formality. Alan when he opened the front door might well be wearing carpet slippers; if a meal lasted longer than his attention span he would probably leave the table and watch the television news. I recall a Sunday lunch when, following the starter, he went to the sideboard to operate the loudest electric carver ever and all conversation was suddenly drowned. One person present, noticing he had left the table but with her back to Alan, remarked, 'What a time to go pruning the hedge!'

Alan had a naughty habit of ignoring the existence of those whose presence had not immediately engaged him. For Mavis, and for me, the chemistry worked at our first meetings; for Martyn Goff, a close friend of ours, it did not. This was embarrassing, as it was for Edward Thompson, a neighbour of Martyn's and a customer at his Banstead (Surrey) bookshop. Edward often dined with the Goffs. Meals were invariably interrupted by a phone call starting with an imperious demand, 'May I speak to Edward Thompson, please?'

'Good-evening, Martyn Goff here. Who shall I say it is?'

'Alan Hill.'

Martyn, one of the most courteous people I have known, after several such incidents, was affronted. It took a lot of persuasion on Mavis's and my part to insist that Alan was actually a super person, a fine publisher and someone Martyn would like; I have little doubt that Edward made the same points. Finally I brought them together at a Christmas drinks party at my bookshop. They never looked back; for the next few decades they lunched and dined each other regularly; when Martyn became director of the National Book league Alan joined the executive council; Martyn wrote a book on social problems of youth for HEB ; Alan introduced him to J.W. ('Mac') McGregor, his lawyer friend, who gave advice to the NBL. He put Martyn up for the Athenaeum because he thought that would put him in touch with significant people in government departments. Thereafter, both swapped contacts, each having a vast source of them.

I was less successful in breaking the ice between Alan and Trisha Nunn, a senior colleague of mine who had previously been personal assistant to Alan Steele, the printer once ready to raise backing for Hill. This Alan and Joan, his wife, bought a 40% holding in my Hampstead bookshop. They were close friends of us all yet when Alan Hill visited the High Hill Bookshop he never acknowledged Trisha. Alan Steele begged him to remember her next time they met. I made a point of referring to her as 'Joan and Alan's great friend'. It made no difference. Even at the reception after Alan Steele's funeral, when we were all present, Alan Hill still did not recognise her. It made a difficult situation for those of us who were fond of them both.

Mavis and I were urged by Alan to arrange a dinner party at which our neighbours Edward and Nancy Blishen would be present. Edward was a regular broadcaster to Africa on the BBC World Service. It surprised me that the two men had not met but we invited them, their wives and others. At pre-dinner drinks Alan could not wait to be introduced to Edward; on an upright chair, like a child playing trains, he manoeuvred himself across the sitting-room floor to confront him. When we ate, accepting that these two would become centres of conversation, I sat them at opposite ends of the table, hoping this would encourage other guests not to feel they were part of a planned audience. It did not work. As soon as we were seated Alan began to address Edward, six places distant, by shouting to make sure he was heard.

Alan was master of sotto voce too, guaranteed like a trained actor of old to be heard at the back of the gallery. At this same dinner party, away from table at the coffee stage, he gave Edward a moment's respite, nudging me while indicating our friend, the author and teacher Joan O'Donovan, to whisper, 'WHERE'S HER HUSBAND?' Frequently at the Garrick he acted similarly, enquiring as a fellow member left the table but was still in ear shot, 'WHAT'S THAT CHAP'S NAME?'

The dinner party certainly brought Hill and Blishen together. Edward is quoted thus in Alan's memoirs, on the publication of the hundredth AWS title:

> I shall tell my grandchildren that I owe most of what education I
> have to Penguin and that through the African Writers Series I saw
> a whole new, potentially great world literature come into being.

It was worth enduring a bizarre social occasion to have brought them together.

Once Alan Steele called at the Charles Street offices to take Alan Hill to lunch. They chatted while the latter cleared his desk. Then Hill excused himself, saying he would return in a moment. Steele examined the splendid array of HEB titles on the walls, noting appreciatively how many had been printed by Butler & Tanner, then found himself at the window overlooking the street, where he saw Hill entering a taxi and being driven off. Later that afternoon, Alan Hill had the grace to jump into another, directing it to the B&T offices, off the Strand, to make his apologies. He had simply 'forgotten' and gone off to one of his clubs. Hamish's version of this incident is that Hill had gone to Heathrow *en route* for Nigeria. (He also remembers him bursting into a meeting with overseas publishers clad sportingly for a game of squash.) On another occasion, Keith Nettle asked him to meet a visiting American publisher with whom he was doing business on HEB's behalf. 'Wheel him in,' responded Alan, 'I'll shake the old hand.' Nothing of the sort happened. Alan became instantly engrossed with the telephone and his post. The American was outraged.

Against this can be related Alan's own anecdote of a visit to Canada where, at a hotel in Montreal, 'I was so repelled by the insensitivity of the American businessmen – who were addressing the French-speaking staff in

loud and aggressive English – that when my turn came I spoke in French.'
Disarmingly, he added, 'I had stumbled on a way to soften the hardest anti-
British atttitude'. He warmed to Canada and the Canadians, praising their
academics who '…had all the prestige of North America without the stigma
of the USA'.

When Alan dropped bricks they splintered as alarmingly as a cluster
bomb. Once, while helping to organise a retirement dinner for him, I had
to complain about the inordinately long list of invitees he had supplied. I
told him we had room for a maximum of eighty, not eight hundred. It
should be restricted to close friends and colleagues. As illustration, I mentioned it included one of my colleagues whom he hardly knew and usually
ignored (not the lady mentioned above). A day later he came sweeping into
the shop with a heavily subbed list, referred by name to my colleague, who
happened to be standing beside me, and cried, 'I've cut out the dross.'

Why was he so well-loved? Was it charisma? If so, how does one define
that easily bestowed label? He was certainly charming, friendly, self-confident,
amusing and stimulating; he could also be boorish, inconsiderate, exasper-
ating. Mavis likened him to 'Pooh Bear'. In our household, he was known
by our children as 'Alan Fitzbad', whereas the kindly, impeccably mannered
Alan Steele, was 'Alan Fitzgood'.

'Fitzbad' shared with all Heinemann directors I knew an intimate relationship with everyone else's telephone. (What would they have been like
in the mobile age?) Alan frequently called at High Hill on his morning
journey from the Garden Suburb to HEB, marching across the shop to my
office, not then protectively situated on an upper floor, cigar smoke bil-
lowing, to request use of a phone. I can only think that the urgency of the
message he transmitted to a colleague was something so important that he
was afraid he might have forgotten about it once he was at his desk. He was
forgiven. Somehow his visitation made us part of a larger book world and
it was due to him that we supplied Hampstead's University College School,
an independent where his and James MacGibbon's sons were educated. (I
sold hundreds, possibly thousands, of copies of Brookes' & Dick's
Introduction to Statistics, published by HEB, to the school but nary a one over
my actual shop counter; Mavis and Het, Brookes' wife, worked together in
their local Labour Party. There were many cross references in our associated
worlds, a lot of them to do with Alan.)

While Alan Hill and I were respectively chairman and secretary of the
Society of Bookmen (the honorary treasurer was Alan Steele) I was even
more at the mercy of Heinemann-induced telephone habits. The day
before a meeting Alan would call me late in the evening asking me to drop

around. (We lived only three miles apart.) When I arrived and Enid had
directed me to the den Alan had contrived for himself in the eaves of the
house, we would go over matters we had already discussed and resolved.
The actual meeting could be a nightmare for me as secretary because often,
at the moment the guest of honour was expected, when it would be Alan's
duty to put him at ease, he would announce, 'Ian, I've left my reading
glasses at the office, won't be long,' or, 'I'm just slipping out to buy some
cigars.' Yet he was a good chairman, witty, disarming, never pompous or
ponderous. Among the speakers he persuaded to address us (they were not
paid) was the rebel ex-Tory Minister for Education, Enoch Powell, and the
novelist John Le Carré.

Alan chaired, or sat on, numerous committees and trusts of the PA, the
British Council, the National Book League, UNESCO, the Nuffield
Foundation, London University, the Friends of the Lake District, the
Prehistoric Society (he was an enthusiastic amateur archaeologist), the
Keswick Amateur Athletic Club (I never heard that he was an athlete but
he was a climber), the International Publishers' Congress, and dozens more.
He had at least two clubs; he was highly gregarious.

His bêtes-noires were accountants. He was contemptuous of any publisher who permitted them a whip hand. He once told a country-house
conference of visiting Americans, 'If you make six good publishing decisions a year, you can throw your accountants out of the window.' Another
comment (in his autobiography) was '…A company headed by an accountant is a company that will asssuredly go down to bankruptcy with the books
in perfect order.' Only someone totally dependent on City finance yet confident of his own publishing prowess could have got away with the outspoken views he expressed against a profession which was taking over not
only the book trade but much of the commercial world. The all-pervasive
insistence on the inexorable creed of 'the bottom line' had to be taken seriously by unsubsidised organisations. Alan understood this as much as his
backers did. He could read balance sheets as well as literature and this
enabled him to talk to accountants in their own language. He abhorred the
very idea of being in debt; all he asked of his sponsors was to share his belief
that the publishing of educational books was, as well as a profitable exercise, a social necessity.

He made one of several exceptions to his low view of accountants in the
case of Reg Keel, paying him this tribute:

> His comprehensive rescue package was particularly generous to our
> long-suffering staff. He not only reorganised our management and

finances … he rationalised the salary structure and brought the staff
into the Tilling pensions scheme.

Alan also approved of Keel's successor, Peter Range, 'who proved unusually sympathetic to the idiosyncratic and highly demanding needs of the
publishers'.

Although Alan enjoyed globe-trotting, those who had to accompany
him were not always so enamoured; he was not a good traveller. Paul
Richardson in this context described him as 'a complete nightmare'. He
regularly insisted on changing his bedroom; he abhorred air-conditioning.
At Edinburgh they once stayed together at a hotel where breakfast was not
served until 7 a.m. by which time they needed to leave for Dundee. Paul
was required to phone HEB's Scottish manager to 'bring over a couple of
eggs cooked to a very specific prescription' before they set out. In Hong
Kong, Alan refused to stay at the Mandarin Hotel and chose instead one on
Repulse Bay, to which he moved in the middle of the night. (Or was Paul
confusing this with the incident in Melbourne where Dwye Evans met
Alan, dressed in pyjamas overlaid by trousers and dressing-gown, moving
out of the hotel 'because of the din'?) At another establishment Tony Beal
was once required to lie for a while in the corner of a bedroom to 'test the
noise'.

Hamish MacGibbon's experiences illustrate both the benefits and the
irritations bestowed by Alan. Hamish on his honeymoon, generously designated 'business trip' by the boss, was booked into a luxurious hotel in
Barbados; Hamish, on a tightly scheduled promotional tour of Malta, had
to endure Alan flying in suddenly and taking him sailing. When the junior
director insisted on keeping an engagement with the Maltese Minister for
Education, Alan complained, 'You're a bit of a snurge, Hamish.'

By 1970 Tilling's believed that the Heinemann Group was in such good
shape that it should again become expansionist. It was axiomatic in commercial circles that 'bigger' meant 'more secure and powerful', although
those beamed into an acquisitive groove often overlooked the associated
vulnerability to takeover. While supposedly concentrating on HEB Alan
was asked by group chairman Dwye Evans to sound out independent publishers who might be willing to sell. Walter Neurath, founder and head of
the art-book publishers, Thames & Hudson, had recently died. Two years
before Hill had met, on a PA Far-East trade mission, Tom Rosenthal then
MD of its international company. To test the waters, he invited him to
lunch at the Garrick. During the meal Tom said he realised why he was

there and, without waiting for a reply, added, 'You want me to become managing director of Secker & Warburg.' Alan was flabbergasted, but aware that a successor to Fred Warburg (due for retirement) was being sought, he saw an opportunity for keeping the prestigious S&W imprint within Heinemann. So the highly improbable attempt to buy privately owned Thames & Hudson, which was not for sale anyway, did not get discussed. Which was how, according to Alan, Tom Rosenthal was offered the top job at the Heinemann subsidiary. Tom accepted and in doing so frustrated Chatto Cape's negotiations to lure Secker into their new group.

Seven years on – by which time Alan had become group managing director on the understanding that Charles Pick would succeed him – the old-established educational publishers Ginn & Co, then owned by the American Xerox Corporation, was offered to HEB for £1.8m. Tilling's wouldn't budge beyond £1.75m the correct sum, they said, for a company forecast to make an annual gross profit of £450,000. Alan viewed this stance as a typical, hidebound accountant's view and, exasperated at the thought of losing Ginn for the sake of fifty grand, argued his case successfully. In its first year under HEB it made £750,000. (In the previous year HEB Ltd had made a profit of £1.5m on turnover of £8m whereas the fiction and general companies of the group had done slightly better with £1.4m on a turnover of £6.6m. Both could be said to be performing well.)

By now Alan had reached the official retirement age and Charles Pick was becoming impatient for the crown. Relations between the two top men deteriorated, although Alan contrived to remain group MD for two more years. Some saw warning lights. Paul Richardson, offered a lucrative position by Macmillan, decided with some regret to accept it. This provoked a memorable episode in the Hill saga. It was summer. Paul, with holiday due to him, was to work out much of his notice while in Brittany with his family. Deliberately he left no address but Alan was proof against this. He discovered the location of the Richardsons and sent a telegram to the relevant gîte, which was delivered by the local postmistress on her bike, and read: 'It is a very bad thing for you to move. You must rethink things.' Paul replied, 'No.' Two days later came another cable from Alan. 'I've been talking to Charles. You could become Group Marketing Director.' Richardson insisted his die had been cast. The third telegram announced the imminent arrival of both Alan and Charles at Quimper Airport, to which they flew in an ancient ten-seater airplane. Paul lunched them. He was urged to stay on with Heinemann. He said he would think it over. Then, because there was no available flight home from Quimper, he felt compelled to drive the other men to Brest – fifty miles to the west. Next day, he telegraphed a final 'No', which was accepted. (This was not though to be the end of his association with Alan.)

In 1979 Hill did officially retire as MD of the group but remained chairman of HEB (Nigeria) and HEB (USA). To keep himself fully occupied he accepted academic appointments with Chelsea College, King's College, London and the Nuffield Curriculum Trust. Even they were not sufficient to take his mind off what was happening at HEB, which moved about this time from Charles Street to Bedford Square, and it was rumoured that he did not hand over his actual office to his successor, the ever-patient Tony Beal, for many months. By 1981 he was actively involved as MD of a new subsidiary, Heinemann Computers in Education Ltd, the progress of which was disrupted when Hamish MacGibbon left to set up a computer-software company. This was in 1983 when Tilling's fortunes nose-dived and it was absorbed into BTR, an international company 'with interests in rubber ... and everything from toy balls to submarine escape suits'. A year later Alan and Hamish formed Hill-MacGibbon Ltd to publish educational software for home computers. The vast expected market did not materialise. The firm was sold to Collins where, on Alan's recommendation, Paul Richardson had moved to run the educational division. Briefly the three men were associated again until Hamish resigned to form his own company and Alan accepted an offer to return to HEB as 'an adviser to Nicolas Thompson, the new publishing head of all Heinemann', occupying the office recently vacated by Enid on her retirement from the Loeb Library. The appointment ended with his death in December 1993. By then BTR had sold Heinemann to Octopus (owned by Paul Hamlyn), which soon after merged with the Reed Group (for which Paul Richardson was then working). HEB, as the foremost educational publishing business in the UK, survived these traumas as a relatively independent unit, becoming based on Oxford where Alan was a regular visitor. By 2000 it had become part of the Harcourt Educational Division of Reed Elsevier, yet even then, as Paul Richardson recalls, '...into the twenty-first century there were still elements of the company in terms of both style and product that bore Alan's imprint'. Elsewhere in Oxford, another ex-colleague, James Currey, had set up his publishing company dealing in African Studies.

(Charles Pick's reign over the Heinemann Group saw him through two new owners into the mid-1980s when he took retirement, nearly as active as Alan's, to become literary agent for his 'discovery' Wilbur Smith; he died in 2000.)

Alan Hill's memoirs were published, according to the jacket and spine, under the John Murray imprint in 1988; John St John's history, under

Heinemann's in 1990. Johnny died, as the result of a routine operation, before he could complete his detailed and meticulously researched centennial account of William Heinemann, which is why the final brief chapter, anonymously contributed, reads like a bland, corporate company handout. On the title page of Alan's book the imprint reads 'in association with Heinemann Educational Books' suggesting that there was a gentlemen's agreement between publishers.

As part of celebrations for his 80th birthday, I interviewed Alan for *Publishing News* at his home. Enid tactfully went out. The only interruptions came from the man who delivered fish weekly from Grimsby and the television when Alan wished to know the latest test-match score. That interview is on tape at the NLSC; it includes a reference to his musical tastes and to his publishing friends. Alan was passionate about Bach but dismissed Beethoven as 'too soupy'. When I asked him to name the publisher he most admired he replied, unhesitatingly, 'Ian Parsons' – of Chatto & Windus.

In answer to queries arising from the interview, Alan sent me four handwritten pages of A4 making, among others, these points:

> RELIGION – This is important in its influence on my publishing style … My parents transmitted the Non-conformist ethos to me … Although I abandoned institutionalised religion, the morality remained … (it) was highly motivating to my team of collaborators, producing a dynamic which carried HEB from point zero to the top of the educational publishing league. My brother was similarly influenced … it was our love of music which led [us] to take an interest in the Church of England service, which seemed far more attractive than Methodism . . .Throughout my life there was a steady cultural shift from Matthew Arnold's … 'undeniable provincialism of English Protestant Conformity' … towards … 'contact with the main current of national life' … if you describe all the above as 'being a Christian' then I accept the description.

(His crematorium service at Golders Green was secular, presided over by a member of the Humanist Society, with moving family contributions; there was also a memorial service at a church in Lakeland.)

Alan expressed schoolboyish delight at being profiled in *PN* and bought many copies of the issue in which it appeared. On his death the following year he was widely obituarised. Jessica, my younger daughter, who had thought of him only as one of my eccentric friends, reading Hamish

MacGibbon in the *Guardian*, was impressed and chastened. She phoned to tell me, 'I didn't realise old Alan Fitzbad was so distinguished.'

Hamish paid tribute to Alan's 'crucial role' in developing the careers of 'the many fortunate individuals' who were encouraged to take 'maximum participation … in decision making'. Tony Beal, in *The Bookseller*, quoted the advice Alan gave him soon after he had joined Heinemann: 'Always keep a piece of paper and a pencil beside your bed, in case you wake up in the night with an idea for a book.' He noted that Hill was interested in participation more than power and ran 'a charismatic democracy'; he also wrote the piece in the *Independent*, recording that, on the day before he died, Alan 'enjoyed the Christmas lunch of the Educational Publishers' Council, and was 'as ever … the life and soul of the proceedings. Later he went to a meeting of the Society of Antiquaries, of which he had just been elected a fellow.' Robin Hyman, fellow publisher and neighbour, also had space in *The Bookseller*, where he quoted Chinua Achebe: 'Alan was a "visionary" … who proved that educational publishing can be "high-minded, adventurous and profitable". ' These three obituarists, plus the anonymous writer in *The Times*, emphasised the immensely important role that Enid played in Alan's life. That lady, at a memorial meeting held at King's College the following year, when eulogies were poured forth from several speakers, remarked to a friend, 'I sometimes wondered who they were talking about'. Enid, who survived Alan by just over two years, was a forthright soul, kind, friendly but not prone to displaying emotion in public. When Alan was offered a CBE her instant reaction was, 'You'll refuse it, of course!' To her regret, and that of at least one of their children, he didn't, taking his elderly father's advice – 'I see no harm in it.' She would have hated to become 'Lady Hill', but might have tolerated it for his sake and he would have rationalised it by saying, 'It's not for me but for Educational Publishing.'

If there were real honour in the honours system Alan Hill would have been awarded an earldom or a peerage, although both would have landed him in dubious company; the absurd companionship of a long lost empire belittled him. The high regard and affection in which he was held by publishers, writers and teachers worldwide was the truest tribute accorded to him.

Alan John Wills Hill, CBE, born Barwell, 12 August 1912, third son of William Wills and May Frances Hill. Married Enid Adela Malin, 1939. Died Hampstead, 17 December 1993.

Eight

ANDRÉ DEUTSCH

André Deutsch exemplified one of two vibrant strands of 'English' publishing which had for over two hundred years thrived on contributions made by immigrants from Scotland and Central Europe. He imposed himself on to the publishing establishment of the second half of the twentieth century by the sheer brilliance of his performance. He was Jewish-Hungarian, without academic or any other educational qualifications except that he could speak English. He was the son of a Budapest dentist of Guggenheim descent and a mother of Hungarian, French and Turkish stock. He had worked briefly in a factory owned by an uncle, had dabbled in photography and studied political science in Vienna before arriving in London in 1939 with the intention of enrolling at the LSE. Instead he lived briefly as a playboy until war broke out and his father's allowance ceased. His first job was as a bird scarer in Shropshire, his second as a van driver delivering pâtisseries in London, his third as either a receptionist or floor manager (myth inevitably intrudes and who now knows?) at the Grosvenor House Hotel, where, in 1941, he was detained as an enemy alien because Hungary had entered the war on Germany's side.

He was interned, first in the parrot house of Manchester Zoo, then on the Isle of Man, where he took part in a poetry recital, reading a range of Hungarian verse to which he was devoted. Among his fellow prisoners was a publisher named Aldor, a relation of Arthur Koestler, who offered him his company, his flat and his mistress when he was released. Following his return to London, Deutsch met a fellow refugee at a party. George Weidenfeld was working at the BBC, as was their hostess, Diana Athill, a young, upper-class Englishwoman who was to be André's publishing colleague for more than half a century. The Aldor commitment did not last long. André took a job at Simpkin Marshall, the principal trade wholesalers whose premises had been destroyed in the Blitz, where he remembered being paid '£14 or £15 per week', a good wage for the time. Precisely what he did to earn this is not clear from the NLSC tape made when he was terminally ill, but his boss there, Arthur Minshull, recommended him to return to publishing and to try Nicholson & Watson. The caretaker for that small imprint, whose owners were absent on war service was John Roberts who desperately needed assistance. At Nicholson & Watson, chiefly distinguished for having published the memoirs of David Lloyd-George, prime minister during the First World War, André voraciously learned his trade; he learnt partly from other members of staff but for the most part was self-taught. Thereafter he was to expect others to become proficient in the same manner and as swiftly. He also reviewed books for *Tribune*, a weekly magazine whose literary editor was the author George Orwell, who lamented the fact that leading publishers, for ideologically correct reasons to do with supporting 'our gallant Russian allies', had rejected his *Animal Farm*. André wanted it for Nicholson & Watson but was overruled by Roberts, which led Orwell to urge the young Hungarian to found his own imprint, making his book its lead title. André, though tempted, declined, while remaining resolute about becoming independent. He asked Diana Athill to join him when the war was over and he started a new publishing company. She accepted.

In 1945, Deutsch raised £3,000 – the minimum amount thought necessary at that time for starting a publishing company was £15,000 – from various sources including Cambridge bookseller Reuben Heffer and Haddon Whitaker, publisher of *The Bookseller*, and registered the name of Allan Wingate. His father, who had survived the war in Budapest and was now in London with André's mother, thought that Deutsch was too German-sounding a name and should not be used. (The Wingates were a distinguished British military family.)

The meagre capital was inadequate. André survived by charming his creditors into waiting for their dues, by underpaying his tiny staff (a characteristic which did not alter significantly for the rest of his career) and by persuading those whom he thought of as 'English gentlemen' to provide additional funding. When the latter obliged – and there was a succession of them – he neglected to secure their investments with written agreements to protect himself, a cavalier attitude which led to his undoing. This in due course occurred despite the overwhelming success of Norman Mailer's *The Naked and the Dead*, the sales of which were boosted by the octogenerian editor of the *Sunday Times* calling, on the front page, for it to be banned – of *Operation Cicero*, a sensational account of wartime espionage in Istanbul, and of the satirical *How to be an Alien* by André's sometime school friend, George Mikes. The backers wished to become more involved in what was proving to be a successful venture but André saw this as interference. As they clamoured for more control he soon realised that he could not work with them. He told Diana Athill that they must leave Wingate to start a list using his name. Following his departure Wingate did not prosper. André Deutsch Ltd did, and for several decades. Its first title, in 1952, was *Books are Essential*, a symposium to which booksellers, publishers and authors contributed. It was not a bestseller; the successor to *Operation Cicero* was.

The veracity of *Cicero* had been endorsed by Germany's wartime ambassador to Turkey, von Papen, who was engaged in writing his memoirs. André signed him up … but for Wingate. He had to fight for what he saw as 'his' book and only won when the author insisted that unless the English translation were published under the Deutsch imprint it would not appear at all. The book gave the new young firm instant financial credibility when André sold the newspaper rights for £30,000. From then on, through thin years and thick, André Deutsch Ltd annually made a profit and seldom while the founder was at the helm had an overdraft at the bank. He became notorious for running a tight ship. His premises were scruffy – although immeasurably superior to those of Victor Gollancz – and lit by low-watt bulbs. He economised in every possible way although he was prepared to pay a large advance for a book he really wanted. He accepted advice from Diana about certain fiction titles and listened eagerly to the opinions of others on anything 'too British' for him to comprehend. Diana has recorded that he just did not understand other people's opinions when they differed from his own but another colleague maintains this was true of business matters rather than of literary ones. He was a hard taskmaster, impatient of those who couldn't instantly master all the skills of publishing, and taught by example, being highly critical of his underlings though quarrelling with only one at a time, which was a mercy for the others. Peter Moxey, his London rep for decades, who had followed him from Allan Wingate, was frequently sacked for alleged shortcomings. Whenever this occurred he stayed away from the office for a few days and sent in orders before reappearing to be taken on board again.

André respected Diana's expertise as an editor and as his mentor in the use of correct English but this did not deter him from treating her parsimoniously. She has left vivid portraits of him which emphasise his conflicting characteristics. She bore with him because the ambience was exciting and because she liked him. In her memoirs, she relates that they went to bed 'without … much excitement on either side', adding that she had 'gone blurry about the kind of affair' they had had. She was an undoubted lady who had perhaps never expected to have to earn a living but who found she had a gift for editing. For the company she also carried out other tasks which fell to her, filling whatever gap there was, undertaking publicity, designing adverts, whatever was needed. She played a significant role in building the Deutsch fiction list and was particularly associated with the work of Jean Rhys, Molly Keane and V. S. Naipaul. She did not have exclusive control of fiction. There were always other editors and there was always André, who was determined to build an essentially quality list. He turned down *Peyton Place*, *Valley of the Dolls* and other titles of huge sales potential although, much later, on the advice of Piers Burnett, he published Peter Benchley's *Jaws*.

André tended to be friendly more with American than English publishers. He made frequent trips to New York which was where he signed up John Updike. His list became one of the brightest and the best of the immediate post-war generation of British publishers. And naturalised British was what he became. He liked also to be a publisher of his own time, one who was, in the parlance of the day, 'with it'. Jack Kerouac's *On The Road*, a seminal American novel of the mid-1950s, brought both kudos and sales; the western *Shane* by Jack Schaeffer had a further incarnation with Heinemann Educational Books (see Alan Hill); his other leading American writers of the time were John Updike, who stayed with him, Norman Mailer and Philip Roth (*Goodbye Columbus*), who came and went. So did the Canadian Mordecai Richler (*The Apprenticeship of Duddy Kravitz*) and the Ulster-born Brian Moore, although after a long stay. And there were Wole Soyinka from Africa and V.S. Naipaul from Trinidad. There were even some English novelists (Roy Fuller, etc.). Naipaul stayed the course for a long period and brought him a Booker Prize winner with *In a Free State*. There was too Leon Uris's *Trinity*, a copy of which was inscribed by the author to the publisher with the words, 'For André – from one great Irishman to another … Leon'. (It may be found in the Deutsch archive at Oxford Brookes University which also holds a copy of Patrick Leigh Fermor's *The Violins of St Jacques*, published jointly with John Murray in 1953, following André's acquisition of the short-lived Verschoyle list.) I name these authors, these titles, as evidence for readers in the twenty-first century that André Deutsch, Hungarian-born immigrant publisher, was not a maverick but one of that distinguished band of refugees from Hitler's Europe who added lustre to the British cultural scene. The reason he lost so many of his authors was his reluctance to pay large advances and his meanness about full-colour jackets.

The other early working director was the cartoonist and writer Nicolas Bentley who illustrated most, if not all, of George Mikes's books. 'Nicolas Bentley drew the pictures' was displayed on their covers and title pages. He was a quiet, self-effacing man, almost an éminence grise, who, like Diana, conferred a certain respectability on André. André liked to have him present

at interviews with prospective staff. He did some editing and he was officially in charge when André was abroad. This led him on one, but only
one, occasion to paying several printers' bills before they had become due
because 'the money was there'; André only approved such a policy if he
could claim a settlement discount. Another backer of his new company was
Gwen Winham, the lady who was to be his partner for the remainder of
his life, although they did not marry and always maintained separate estab-
lishments. ('Not being married', he informed me, 'is a moral responsibility.')
His relationship with Gwen was private; she did not become part of his
social life in the trade – few of us knew her – but they seem to have been
essential to each other.

The list was by no means confined to middle- and upper-middlebrow
fiction. It welcomed the eminent American diplomat and economist J.K.
Galbraith, who liked to share his books between André and Hamish
Hamilton. (The latter tended to get the plums, such as *The Affluent Society*.)
It had a range of cookery books for which, in the beginning, the adviser
was Elizabeth David. It was strong in humour, the core author being
George Mikes with whom André had a love/hate relationship going back
to childhood in Budapest. I frequently lunched with George who could
hardly wait to take his place at table before coming out with details of the
latest confrontation with his publisher. 'I took him my new book today,'
George would say (he did not employ an agent), 'and he suggested, rather
he told me, "Shall we have the same contract we had for *Italy for Beginners*?"
How would I remember what that contract was?' Yet the two trusted each
other and there was never any question of George seeking another publisher. It was possibly due to his identification with Mikes, whose early
books remained with Wingate until the demise of that imprint, that André
began to be thought of as a publisher of humour and satire. The list also
became rich in titles which emanated from the weekly satirical magazine
Private Eye, for which Deutsch acted as distributor.

Although it always remained relatively small, André's list was regularly
featured on literary pages because he tended to publish titles to which literary editors and reviewers were attracted, books such as Eric Berne's
Games People Play, an amusing though serious item of popular psychology,
and Helen Hanff's *84 Charing Cross Road*, letters exchanged between an
eccentric New York book collector and a second-hand-book dealer in
London. (Some believed she wrote them all.) He had a special relationship
with The *Sunday Times* through Leonard Russell, its literary editor, whose
wife Dilys Powell was a respected film critic and author of books about
Greece. Through this connection the Insight Books were published, the

hardback versions of investigative journalism into crucial social and political issues in the news. The first – the only one in which Russell was involved – concerned the uncovering of the spy Kim Philby, a cause célèbre of its time. He sold the book rights, for which Weidenfeld had offered £10,000, to André for £20,000; and André sold the paperback rights for £60,000. Deals such as this one kept André Deutsch Ltd very much afloat. Thereafter, Harold Evans, editor of the paper, dealt with Insight and became a crony of A.D.'s, although his own books on journalism went to Heinemann.

André became notorious for his turnover in sales managers/directors. This was partly due to the Deutsch philosophy which ruled that when a book failed to sell there had to be a scapegoat. When in 1961 George Depotex, recruited from the Army and Navy Stores where he had succeeded Tommy Joy as buyer for the book department, had been with Deutsch for only a week, a fellow Bloomsbury publisher met him one lunchtime in the street. 'I'm with André now,' said George affably. 'Still?' queried the publisher.

George Depotex, who remained friendly with Deutsch to the end of his life, was aware that most of his acquaintances gave him three months at the most because André was known to be impossible, ruling dictatorially over a difficult, disaffected staff. 'Doom and unhappiness … was on every lip,' he wrote. At the end of the first month he found the staff were happy, enjoyed their work and were helpful to him. The ambience was in deep contrast to the Army and Navy where all employees addressed each other formally however long they had been working together; at Deutsch, even by the early sixties, everyone was on first-name terms. André he described as 'mercurial, unpredictable but always immaculate', Diana was 'very county, and with a penetrating voice … was so unpunctual and forgetful that it drove André mad, but she knew her authors. Nick Bentley was in the office only of an afternoon after he had drawn his pocket cartoon for a daily newspaper.' He told George he had designed the Deutsch colophon, a bow and three arrows in a circle. The central arrow, slightly ahead of the other two, represented André. George thought stories of André's meanness were exaggerated. Bonuses were generous and staff, when ill, were well looked after by the standards of the time. He maintained that it was the cashier, not André, who turned off the lights in empty offices. Others who have published their recollections of working at Deutsch are at variance with this opinion. Leo Cooper, whose 1965 letter of engagement did not actually specify the role for which he was to be paid £2,000 p.a., described him in his often hilarious memoirs, as resembling 'a boiled canary'. The two did not click but Leo concedes that André was 'a very good publisher with an eye for a book'. Tom Maschler, employed much earlier as an unpaid learner over Christmas received 'a bonus of £25', and was later offered £6 a week to become production manager, a role for which he was totally unqualified. In his autobiography he accused André of cadging cigarettes from him, which was one reason why, when he read Colin Wilson's *The Outsider* in typescript, he recommended it to Gollancz where it became a bestseller.

To revert to Depotex. On his arrival from the Army and Navy, George was astonished to learn that the annual turnover of Deutsch was slightly less than that of the store's combined book department and lending library, which was just into six figures.

Deutsch, like its founder, was small but soon to be growing apace. George was involved in the move from Carlisle Street to Great Russell Street which would be more able to accommodate it. This was organised by André. 'We all,' recalled George, 'moved our papers and possessions in our own cars; afterwards the removers moved the furniture. All this on a Saturday morning.'

Norman Mailer who had been lost to Cape for a couple of books returned to Deutsch with *An American Dream* on terms which gave George Depotex doubts:

> The advance was for those days very high and had the book not been a success we might have gone under. It was a very Hungarian deal involving advances for serialisation ... paperback rights and book club deals. Pre-publication sales were not enormous. At that time the 'f' word was not accepted by all. Smiths were difficult, the libraries and many country booksellers equally reluctant to give big orders.

Mailer came for a promotion tour. André prepared to meet him at Heathrow. As he left George advised him to suggest to the author 'that if the book had fifty per cent less fucks it would be twice as fucking good'. André told George the following day that he had passed on the message and invited him to guess the reply. George got it in one.

Although almost obsessively committed to his imprint, André did not forgo relaxation, enjoying regular skiing holidays with Gwen. Once he left on a tour of Australia which was both business and pleasure. On that occasion Nick Bentley informed George Depotex, 'When André is away, we all take it easy – we do not come in on Saturdays.'

André regularly attended the BA conference in company with his sales manager and sometimes other colleagues. At Gleneagles one year accommodation was so limited that André and George D. found it necessary to share a room. George recorded, 'I would go to bed late but André was nowhere to be seen. The following morning his bed had been slept in but again, no André.' The explanation is up to the reader. Another time in Amsterdam, on returning from the Frankfurt Book Fair, George went to his hotel to change and wash while André guarded the car against being moved on by the police. They then swapped roles but when the room key was handed in the concierge was disapproving. '" Sir," he said, wagging his finger, "this is not that sort of hotel – one man, one room."'

When Depotex took his summer holiday he was encouraged to combine it with at least some business, even though he might be going with his wife to a quiet Mediterranean resort to get away from it all. One year, before I had a car of my own, André thought it a good idea if George gave Mavis and me a lift to Provence; another year he was requested to drop off in Paris for a couple of nights to call on booksellers who sold English titles and visit Sonia Orwell, who edited an arts magazine distributed by Deutsch in the UK. André was generous on these occasions. Mavis and I travelled free; George, of course, was paid expenses.

Several times I was invited to endorse André's choice of a new sales manager/director. Once, in the interests of the person concerned who was a good friend – one more vulnerable than his would-be employer – I advised André against it. On other occasions I thought the candidates could stand up for themselves. André was fulsome in his thanks for my help; I was sent a case of claret as a mark of his appreciation. It was delivered by the departing manager. Despite which, eighteen or twenty-four months later, the new boy was out. A limited number left of their own accord. Peter Wolfe, wittiest of copywriters with puffs for the books he published, went on to found his own imprint. George Depotex, following a chance encounter with Ken Wilder, who had that morning resigned as sales manager for Hamish Hamilton, moved along Great Russell Street to take his place; he may have felt he had skated on thin ice for long enough.

One who has left a vivid and slightly mocking account of working editorially for André in the seventies is Jeremy Lewis, whose autobiographical *Kindred Spirits* has a chapter, 'Deutschsland uber Alles'. His portrait is complementary to Diana Athill's. André is the small man with the large desk in an office on the first-floor front where he sits with his back to the window. The desk is piled high with books, opened and closed, proofs, letters, memos, trade journals, spring and autumn lists, all the paraphernalia and detritus of the publisher in action. It contrasts starkly with that of a competitor (who has to be George Weidenfeld), whose inner sanctum is as lacking in evidence of work in progress as that of a bank manager. Trevor Moore, a rep for Deutsch in the late 'seventies, confirmed the appearance of André's desk on which, to him, 'it seemed sometimes that a letter from V.S. Naipaul or John Updike might just be pointing towards the visitor'. Once he was present when one of the telephones rang, instantly involving André in a disputation with Tom Maschler, by then of Cape. Trevor made to leave but was motioned back to his seat 'as André proceeded to give Tom the benefits of his elder status and superior wisdom – I could not help but feel,' he added, 'that it was, albeit in small part, also for my benefit.'

Jeremy Lewis humorously described André's infuriating habit of constantly moving the offices of lesser members of staff from attic to basement, or second floor to first, operations in which most able-bodied members of staff were required to hump filing cabinets and other items of furniture in the intervals between being asked to report to the chairman's office or responding to the demands of their own secretaries. If André was in the building, noted Lewis, his presence was felt everywhere.

Whatever he might be engaged upon, the telephone took precedence, no matter who faced him across his desk, be they American publisher, printer, literary agent, reviewer, author, bookseller. André could never resist talking to the caller.

On Jeremy Lewis's first day André required him to give a report on the typescript of a novel about which all of his colleagues were abuzz. He read it with increasing dislike. In the late afternoon André asked for his opinion; Jeremy believed it would be held against him. On the contrary, André alone among the others loathed the book. Next morning it was formally rejected.

Lewis maintains that, despite the leftish ambience apparent in the Great Russell Street offices and the fact that André had published such dissidents, famous at the time, as Daniel Cohn-Bendit and Bernadette Devlin, he later confessed to having voted Conservative in 1970. He also related how André's father, seeking to give his son a break from work, took him to Highbury to watch Arsenal. André spent the entire game engrossed in reading a proof.

In the spirit of the age, André became acquisitive, taking over the short-lived list of Derek Verschoyle and the old-established company of Grafton. Verschoyle, a small literary list of little distinction, he bought for a nominal sum for the sake of inheriting their offices just off Soho Square. This enabled him to move from Marylebone High Street which was not a good publishing address. He later passed on the premises to Secker & Warburg when he bought his Great Russell Street headquarters, close to the British Museum, in about 1960. Grafton specialised in books on librarianship. It was innately dull and its premises opposite the British Museum were so gloomy that I can almost persuade myself they were lit by miners' lamps, but the backlist held worthy perennials regarded as necessary reference tools by the profession it served. Clive Bingley, who was later to buy it and start his own imprint, came with Grafton and was regarded by André as 'a wonderman'. André had a series of wondermen throughout his career. He selected them with loudly expressed enthusiasm, then usually found them wanting. Linked to the acquisition of Grafton, although an innovation of his own, was the Language Library, edited by Eric Partridge, a revered Australian character, one of whose early books André had reprinted. Partridge compiled dictionaries of slang, unusual words, clichés, children's names, etc., and became an expert on matters philological. In 1927 he had founded Scholartis Press which he directed until 1931.

In financial terms, more important than any of the sidelines noted above, was the children's list which started with the delightfully illustrated *Madeline* titles by Ludwig Bemelmans. André knew and cared little about juveniles, as the trade named them, but had the good sense to engage Philippa Pearce (who wrote *Tom's Midnight Garden* and several bestselling Puffins) as editor. When she took maternity leave, a secretary, Pam Royds, was asked to hold the fort. Pearce didn't return; Royds went on to develop a range of great appeal to the young. I once asked her how she got on with André. She replied, 'Splendidly. He never interferes because he is no judge of what I do.' The children's list was to become almost the tail that wagged the dog. The *Postman Pat* series, despised by many for what they saw as its downmarket values, was a big money spinner.

André valued his African connections, two small publishing houses in Nigeria and Kenya producing indigenous work. They did not substantially compete with HEB or OUP or other major British publishers on that continent but they gave him great satisfaction and brought him authors who were eminent Commonwealth leaders at the time. When I interviewed him for *Publishing News* in 1987 he asserted with pride, 'Both will succeed and will contribute towards the development of their respective countries and, although we are out of both, and lost money on one, I still consider these two ventures the highlights of my publishing career.' Once again he may have considered it brought him close to the British publishing establishment which, in the person of Stanley Unwin, did not accept him. As already recorded (see p.52) Unwin blackballed him from the Society of Bookmen to which André was elected only after the other man's death. He then became a regular attender and during my chairmanship I had difficulty in coping with his eagerness to suggest speakers – all of whom happened to be his authors.

Diana Athill has recorded that Stanley Unwin prevented André from being elected to the Garrick Club, also stating that this led to her colleague campaigning to become a member. She must be wrong about this because Unwin was never a member of the Garrick and it is highly unlikely that anyone who lobbied on his own behalf would ever get in. In fact André was elected in 1978 and his candidature was strongly supported. I can find no record of his having been previously blackballed. As a member he frequently invited guests and held private parties, but George Mikes and I only once persuaded him to drop in by himself and be clubbable with other members. André confessed to me, 'I wouldn't have the nerve to walk in alone and sit at the long table.' Nor in fact did George, who invariably placed himself at the so-called 'publishers' table' and waited rather anxiously for other members to join him there. On his initial visit he had found himself in the company of Daniel Macmillan who was holding forth to Ian Parsons and others about the iniquity of 'bloody foreign publishers who had invaded gentlemanly British publishing'. Suddenly aware of the presence of a new member with a central European accent Macmillan felt he should be more welcoming. He sought to redress the balance by remarking, 'All I mean to say is that I wouldn't trust Deutsch any farther than I could throw Weidenfeld.'

As inflation grew alongside increasing turnover and overheads the difficulties of the Deutsch imprint remaining independent were taxing. Above all André had to be in command. Yet he was always dickering with the notion of selling-out or merging despite knowing that final decisions must lie with him. So when Lord Beaverbrook, the Canadian-born press baron who owned Express Newspapers, invited him to develop its tiny book-publishing department, he refused. No press baron tolerates interference and André was aware of it. He was not so resistant to Time Life of New York when they showed willingness to purchase 40% of his equity. According to a colleague 'he was always looking for security', which was not surprising for one from his background, and he saw this as a golden chance to gain fresh capital and perhaps more influence over American publishers while remaining the majority shareholder. After a while he might consider selling out to them for a huge sum and then start all over again.

It was not a long partnership. Time Life began to irritate André by persistently wishing to call meetings and asking for budgets and management accounts. Once they sent a cable demanding a 'Fiscal Forecast'. Deutsch replied that the sales figures were compiled by a man in a North London garret, the precise location of which was not known to him. Time Life began to lose interest and finally accepted André's offer to buy back their shareholding. Not only that but they sold out for less than they had paid.

On a later occasion George Weidenfeld suggested that they should merge their imprints. George, ennobled by Labour PM Harold Wilson and the first publisher to become a peer (apart from Mervyn Horder who inherited his title) was admired by André but seen as a rival. His lordship tended to move from one office block to another south of the Thames. One day, in expansive mood, he proposed, 'Let's bring our resources together, move into Great Russell Street, then sell our freehold.' 'MY freehold, George,' André told him, and that was the end of the matter.

Despite becoming known as a penny-pinching and capricious employer, André in fact had long-term working relations with many others beside Diana Athill. Philip Tammer, even more diminutive than himself (Leo Cooper has a story about one standing on the other's shoulders to fix in place a light bulb of low wattage), became company accountant. They addressed each other as 'A.D.' and 'Mr Tammer'. One day the latter announced his intention of resigning to which André responded, 'You can't. I love you.' Tammer replied, 'I love you too.' He stayed. There were also Piers Burnett and Bill McCreadie who were to become crown princes. Piers joined in the early sixties as a general dogsbody and became editorial director. Bill came much later (significantly from Collins for whose marketing André had great respect), as sales director, and did not suffer the fate that had befallen so many of his predecessors.

In the early days Piers, who had succeeded a series of banished wondermen, had no job description. He was told he might be sent 'to look after Africa' or, possibly, 'Grafton', or attend to this and that. Once he shared publicity with Janet Whitaker, wife of Ben, a Labour politician; she was to deal with authors whose names were alphabetically A–M; he with N–Z. So she had to promote Norman Mailer's *An American Dream* for which there was no watertight agreement. André's laxity in this respect led to his losing the author who had brought him his great initial success. Whitaker, who was not to blame, in due course left and later became a Labour peeress. Piers found his face fitted. His first desk was in a small office without windows, which he shared briefly with a lady who said she was leaving so, 'You'll be doing advertising' (Diana helped him initially with layouts); later, another lady advised him she also was on her way, 'So *you* are going to do foreign rights.' Subsequently he was given an editorial role with a nudge in the direction of natural-history books which led to *Where to Watch Birds*. Peter Giddy, manager of Hatchard's, Piccadilly, was invited to lunch. He ordered a thousand copies.

Piers was offered an editorial position by Edmund Fisher at Michael Joseph. André promptly gave him a rise. He was sent to America on what he called 'a sabbatical' to get books. 'Once he trusted you,' Piers told me, 'you could buy what you wanted.' In New York, having read Benchley's *Jaws* he phoned André to recommend making a bold, pre-emptive offer although this writer had previously published only a volume of essays. Tom Rosenthal of Secker & Warburg had put in a bid although he had not read the book and withdrew when informed by the negotiating agent that the company interested in the paperback rights thought it too expensive. 'Let Deutsch have it,' said Tom. All good publishers make mistakes. Although not a work of outstanding literary merit, *Jaws* became a popular bestseller of the type which every list needs.

At sales conferences and editorial meetings André was impatient, fidgety and had a low attention span; he had a habit of interrupting with an incisive question or comment which deflated most of what had been previously said. Trevor Moore found him variably benign and irascible, taking 'a perverse pleasure in the disagreements that would often take place between Bill McCreadie, Kitty Samson (publicity director) and Piers Burnett. Diana Athill always appeared to be sublimely indifferent in such disputes and concentrated simply on presenting her own books with erudite and dignified wit and charm.' By Trevor's time such meetings were sometimes held in a hotel in Great Russell Street. 'At one of them', he recalled, 'when McCreadie had banged on about the iniquitous habits of some booksellers, André remarked quietly, "You know, Bill, your attitude towards booksellers reminds me of that of a sex-maniac who cannot stand women."' In fairness to Bill it should be said that André had made mincemeat of several of his predecessors so he was probably covering himself; my relations with Bill, as bookseller and author, were always open and friendly both at Deutsch and, later, at Aurum Press.

The top floor of the Great Russell Street premises was mostly given over to a directors' dining room and a small kitchen. Here André entertained authors, booksellers, literary editors, American publishers. I was invited many times, on some occasions to discuss a particular problem or project. It was usually a foursome with Bill and Piers present, never Diana, although she sometimes lunched in an adjoining room with one of 'her' authors. The cook/waitress was the widow of the composer Constant Lambert. Her cuisine, seemingly prepared in an alcoholic haze, was superb. André and his colleagues took it for granted and were, in my view, often dismissive of her. They were amazed when I insisted on praising to her face a dish she had created; she was sufficiently sober to enjoy the compliment. One lunch was called because Bill and Piers were keen to have my backing for opening a bookshop on part of their ground-floor premises. André was dubious about it. So was I. I felt similarly to Jeremy Lewis when he was the only one who didn't like the novel which all of his new colleagues wished to publish. We discussed the matter for a course or two until André remarked, 'You haven't given one positive reason why we should do this.' 'Then perhaps you shouldn't,' I replied. The premises were subsequently let to a dealer in second-hand books. I think I may have saved André Deutsch Ltd a large sum of money; it was in earlier times the business of publishers to both originate their own books and sell them and those of their competitors. By the start of the twentieth century the division of publishing and bookselling had long been almost complete; by the time of this lunch in the 1970s, it was the business of publishers to publish and of booksellers to retail, although there was ever the example of Blackwell's performing both roles profitably. Piers and Bill were accustomed to being overridden by André; they remained friendly to me after I had dished this plan. When Bill, from Collins via Macdonald, took on the sales hot seat it seemed for a long while that André had found the man he wanted; as with Piers Burnett the face fitted.

In 1982 when Mavis and I took a five-month sabbatical travelling across Europe André expressed interest in the itinerary. 'You must stay on a Greek island,' he said emphatically. 'I will get Helen Vlachos to help you.' Mrs Vlachos was the proprietress of an Athens newspaper and had written a memoir for André. She took her commission seriously, invited me to tea at her London apartment and arranged with the British Council's librarian in Athens to rent us a house on Aegina for a month, taking much trouble for someone she never met again. André and George Mikes both insisted that in Budapest we should stay at the Hotel Gellert but we must make reservations well in advance. When we arrived we received red-carpet treatment. How was Mr Deutsch? How was Mr Mikes? And what of Mr Deutsch's mother? Had we brought any of them with us? Years later, when my bookselling friends Martyn Goff and Rubio Lindroos told André that they were having difficulty in booking at the Gellert he personally phoned the manager, demanding and getting the best suite for them – at standard prices. Both André and George had long been British citizens. They visited

their homeland with impunity at a time when it might have been dangerous for them to do so on Hungarian passports.

It was a blow to André when, in 1980, Bill and Piers decided they could
wait no longer to succeed him. Piers and his wife developed their own list
on the social sciences; Bill joined the Gordon Fraser Gallery, as managing
director, to sell greetings cards and later ran a stationery company of his
own. André became aware that days were numbered for his style of independent, literary publishing but soldiered on, engaging Dieter Pevsner,
with a good track record from Penguin and elsewhere, as editorial director.
When the appointment was announced André was quoted in *The Times* as
saying how fortunate he was to take on this scholarly and experienced senior colleague. It soon ended in tears. Dieter was not accorded the carte
blanche which Piers had enjoyed. He was not permitted to buy the books
of his choice.

I played a small role in bringing him into disfavour. When Dieter was
part of Wildwood House, it had published jointly with my tiny imprint,
High Hill Press, a book of mine and Dorothy Bohm's about Hampstead. It
sold a few thousand. At Deutsch, Dieter, with André's approval, commissioned me to write a companion volume on London, illustrated again by
Dorothy Bohm's excellent photographs . On publication day we gave a
small dinner party at the Garrick for André, the Bohms and the Pevsners.
André said to me, 'Dear boy, none of my authors has ever done this for me
before.' The book did not sell well. André became distantly polite when
we met. Giles Gordon, my agent, had pushed him to a larger advance than
I actually wanted by calling him mean. I asked George Mikes if he knew
why André was being unfriendly. George replied promptly, 'You must be
losing him money.' Ironically, when Tom Rosenthal joined Deutsch he
gave the book another breath of life in paperback with a new, brighter jacket
and, because Dieter had made a deal with an American book club, my royalties continued for some years, so I did well out of it. I think André too
made a profit. In any case good relations were restored.

André was not one to bear grudges. Had he done so, he would have had
so many fewer friends. His forgiving nature was never better expressed than
at the huge party he threw at Camden Lock, North London, in 1977, for
the 25th anniversary of his company. Every single person he had employed
(including all those he had sacked) was invited. At my suggestion he
widened the list to include others who had turned down the jobs he had
offered them. Which was how Mavis and I came to be present. (In 1955,
soon after our marriage, he offered me the position of trade manager at

£600 p.a., 40% less than I had been earning, and said he would require me,
'Mind, body and soul.' Reluctantly I had declined.) The hospitality at the
Lock was lavish in wine and food for about three hours. Someone insisted
the occasion demanded a focal point. André was dragged to his feet and
spoke with a brevity which amounted almost to ungraciousness. It wasn't
that. He was shy and did not wish to be applauded. (As Diana Athill wrote
of him, '[He] … was never a conceited or arrogant man. He never
bragged.') Then a Cinderella motif was heard. When the clock struck nine
the bar would remain open but thereafter guests would have to pay. You
could almost hear the command, 'Turn that light out!'

Following Dieter's departure, André, possibly with the ubiquitous Lord
Goodman – éminence-not-so-grise to the British book trade – hovering,
opened negotiations with Paul Hamlyn who had entered an acquisitive
phase, although how either of them envisaged Deutsch as a tentacle of
Octopus we may never know. No deal was done but in 1984 Tom
Rosenthal, then of Secker & Warburg and William Heinemann, suggested
to André that he should acquire the list. Agreement was reached that Tom
should buy 50.1% of the shares immediately and the remainder after three
years. On day one the two men became joint chairmen and joint managing directors, continuing as such until 1987 when Tom would become sole
MD, although André was to remain joint Chairman for two further years,
following which he would be president, with salary and expenses.

Rumours of the deal flew around the trade with many people doubting
that the two could tolerate each other on a daily basis. Diana Athill was
astonished when told of the proposition. In her memoir, *Stet*, she wrote,
'André had always seemed to dislike him … (André) had been rude – not
to him, but about him'. She described the two men:

> André was small and dapper; Tom was large,with the slightly rum-
> pled look of many bearded men, though he was far from being
> among the seriously shaggy. André was a precise and dashing driver;
> Tom was too careless and clumsy to trust himself to drive at all.
> André, without being prissy, was nearer to being fastidious in his
> speech than he was to being coarse; Tom evidently liked to shock.
> And above all, André abhorred extravagance, while Tom enjoyed
> it … They were not designed to be friends.

André believed the arrangement would suit him and that although he
might officially become retired he would not actually be required to give
up his beloved desk or his personal authors such as George Mikes. He

derived pleasure also from the generosity of about four hundred friends who contributed to pay for a portrait Leonard Rosoman painted of him, for his 70th birthday. In fact they over-subscribed and the balance went to the Royal Literary Fund. But the fact remained that the new set-up at 105 Great Russell Street was unfeasible, as was proved when Tom, in 1989, long after buying the remaining shares, found he could no longer tolerate the older man's presence and insisting on moving him out of his office. Tom maintains that André took book-trade dignitaries out to lunch, at the firm's expense, to complain about him and that he 'fomented a number of hostile articles in the press'. David Whitaker backed Tom and told André he was harming his own reputation. Diana Athill became aware that André having realised that the company really was no longer his was behaving outrageously. Spiteful paragraphs about Tom began to appear in the press and inevitably the two men parted acrimoniously. (Diana, who although a director, was never told by André the financial details of the sale, was invited by Tom to remain and did so.)

The situation, largely of his own making, embittered André's final years. Without his publishing firm he had lost his raison d'être, even though, as he had confessed to Diana, 'it's no longer fun'. He was comparatively well-off, so was Gwen. He had no children. He had benefited greatly from being one of the original shareholders in the Groucho Club (the best investment he ever made, he claimed), he would still have owned a freehold property in Bloomsbury. He could have remained in command just as Ernest Hecht of Souvenir Press, who was in a similar situation, did. He chose otherwise and watched the imprint bearing his name pursue an unsteady course until it was sold off.

During his years in control Tom Rosenthal broadened the base of the list to include a series of books on film and one on cricket and introduced new mainstream authors such as Penelope Lively, Elias Canetti, Malcolm Bradbury, etc. He was an experienced publisher but he had used all his available capital to pay what he believed, at the time, was a fair price for André Deutsch Ltd. Then, when recession struck in the 1990s, he was forced to sell first the children's titles, then the archives, finally the entire adult list.

After my retirement in 1988, before the final rift with Tom, André gave me lunch one day at the Garrick in gratitude for my supporting his list over the years. I was touched, and even more so, when he recited a poem in Hungarian which, translated, was thanking me for my friendship. André revealed surprising talents, when least expected. At a Society of Young

Publishers' pantomime in the late eighties he made a guest appearance as a clown. He was not billed on the programme; others in the cast did not meet him until the dress rehearsal. At one performance he sat between Diana and Gwen in the audience until it was time for him to make-up. When he left them and failed to return they worried that he might be ill. At his appearance on stage they didn't at first recognise him. He excused this indulgence with the words, 'I loved Grock.' He also loved theatre. It was one of his few distractions from publishing. (He bequeathed over £100,000 to the National Theatre.)

Years later, I was present at the Gay Hussar (the Dean Steet restaurant deemed Hungarian but actually founded by a south Londoner famous for his brocaded waistcoat) to celebrate André's 80th birthday. We met for lunch, a dozen or so of us, at Peter Mayer's instigation and with Paul Hamlyn donating the wine, at a large round table in the small top-floor room. Others present included Ian Chapman, senior, Paul Scherer, George Weidenfeld, Philip Joseph, Ed Victor, Graham C. Greene and Piers Burnett. In retirement André, with Greene, Victor and Edmund Fisher (by now ex-managing director of Michael Joseph), started a company, Libra, whose motivation was to sell publishers' overstocks (as distinct from remainders) to Hungary for the benefit of students and others who, following the collapse of the Communist regime, were thought to be finding it difficult to obtain British books. In fact such books were not those in demand so the policy changed to dealing in EFL titles which were. Each man invested £200 and the venture was successful. While negotiations were continuing for Libra's foundation André often visited Graham in his Albany apartment. There his lifelong habit (whatever George Depotex claimed to the contrary) of switching off lights had to be curbed in the interest of preventing accidents to residents in the gloomy courtyards and passages. Graham was an old associate whose first wife, Judy, had been one of André's publicity managers. (The tempestuous Carmen Callil was another; that didn't last long.) When Chatto Cape was formed André had hankered to join them, according to Graham, but it was thought better (possibly Tom Maschler especially thought it so) that he should remain independent. I believe that was a wise decision.

André also became associated with Aurum Press which had been bought by Bill McCreadie, Piers Burnett and Sheila Murphy (another former Deutsch publicity manager) on Bill's return to publishing. He and Piers had first attempted to buy back the Deutsch imprint from Rosenthal but this was not pursued when Tom sold the valuable children's list. Aurum was formerly owned by the Really Useful Group and had daringly published Tom

Bower's biography of Robert Maxwell against the tycoon's wishes. André became president and carried out such tasks as flying to Barcelona to collect an outstanding debt.

André was widely obituarised here and abroad, with *The Bookseller* allotting a whole page to Diana Athill, whose tribute came largely from the text of her forthcoming memoir. In mid-article she summed him up perfectly: 'For all his drive, he was a modest and unpretentious man both personally and as a publisher. He was not an academic; he was no kind of specialist; he just wanted to publish books he liked.' Her account of him in *Stet* and, afterwards, in *Logos*, have to be the basis for any longer study of the man.

André Deutsch, CBE, born Budapest, 15 November 1917, son of Bruno and Maria (née Havas) Deutsch. Educated Budapest, Vienna, Zurich. Unmarried. Naturalised British subject. Died London, 11 April 2000.

Nine

PAUL HAMLYN

The first words of Paul Hamlyn's I can recall hearing – more accurately, overhearing – were in the bar of a crummy Blackpool hotel where the 1957 Booksellers' Association conference was being held. He was standing, pasty-faced, in an uneasily poised group, saying, 'But there is nowhere you can eat in the Caribbean.' It was Cowardian and untypical. The last word of Paul's registered on my memory was when I sat next to him at a private lunch at the Garrick in 2000 to honour André Deutsch (who was too ill to attend). By then I had met him many times over the intervening years and, although never a close friend or even acquaintance, I knew about his total lack of small talk. There was no observation he wished to make to me so he remained silent. He was probably, even at that late stage of his dazzling career, formulating a deal; I was simply thinking that one of us should say something. So I asked, 'Paul, if you were starting out again, would you do anything differently?'

Instantly he replied, 'No.' End of conversation.

Inevitably, during the course of lunch, we did pass remarks (and even the salt) to each other but I have no recollection of them. In fact I had had exchanges with him before I eavesdropped on his comments at the Blackpool bar because the previous year he had interviewed me at his austere premises in Spring Place, Kentish Town, when Tony Godwin, then a bookselling whizz-kid, had recommended me to him as a likely bright young man seeking employment. Tony thought he owed me a favour; I was grateful but knew I was unlikely to prosper in the Books for Pleasure organisation because I didn't truly, deep-down, believe in selling. It was an embarrassing interview. Paul was shy. I felt awkward. I admired a print (Dufy, I think) on his whitewashed wall. He grinned but said nothing. No job specification was mentioned. I said, pointlessly, I knew his rep Bill Jackson (whose wife became Paul's secretary) and what a nice chap he was. I forget what else was remarked upon between us but he did offer employment of some sort which I didn't accept. We would not have suited each other whereas by becoming a bookseller in nearby uphill and upmarket

Hampstead I became a small (by his standards) but healthy account while also learning to admire what he was doing for the trade. He had an influence on it over the next four decades that was surpassed only by Allen Lane's and which, in its global significance, could stand beside Stanley Unwin's and Alan Hill's.

I empathised with Paul's rebellious nature and found myself frequently on his side. I revelled in his diatribes when, at a conference or a Society of Bookmen dinner, he lambasted the die-hard attitude of so many publishers and booksellers speaking, despite an inherent strain of shyness, fluently, amusingly, iconoclastically.

Paul was born in Berlin in 1926, the fourth and youngest child of left-wing, middle-class, academically inclined parents. His brother Michael wrote to me, 'We did not know we were "Jewish" until Hitler made us Jews.' Their father, who was named Hamburger married a certain Fräulein Hamburg. He, a paediatrician, was an agnostic humanist; she, from a banking family, became a Quaker. It was a bookish home and Michael remembered, 'We had chamber music in the house and musicians like Lily Kraus and Max Rostal.' Paul rebelled against the bookishness but loved music, especially Italian opera. The family moved to Britain in 1933 shortly before the Nazis came to power. Paul was educated first at the Hall School, Belsize Park, afterwards in Letchworth, Hertfordshire, where he boarded at St Christopher's, a Quaker establishment which he recalled as 'full of sandalled, earnest, vegetarian pacifists' whereas he was 'carnivorous and pro-war'. He left at fifteen – his father's death having caused a family cash crisis – to become an office boy, on the verges of Covent Garden, at the magazine *Country Life*. It was wartime. There was a staff shortage so he also found himself working in an editorial capacity, both 'writing and answering "readers"' letters'.

As a naturalised Brit, Paul became liable for call-up to the armed forces but instead of donning uniform he was drafted to work in the coal mines, becoming a Bevin Boy, so-called after the Minister of Labour who devised the scheme. The pit he dug was in South Wales where he contrived to double as a reporter for the *South Wales Argus*, covering football matches and weddings. Either before or after working in the mines – perhaps both – he had his first jobs in the book trade, at Samuel French, play publishers, whose offices faced *Country Life*'s in Southampton Street, and at Zwemmer's art bookshop in Charing Cross Road. His experiences there led to his first self-employed job manning a bookstall in Camden Town market, having set himself up in business with about £350 inherited from his grandfather. A later colleague recorded, 'Paul was a great success from his first barrow … he wasn't a reader; he was a trader.' By then, having suffered the ribaldry of schoolboys who had dubbed him 'Wimpy' and 'Sausage', he had changed his name to Hamlyn. His elder brother, an academic who became a prolific poet and translator, did not. They had little in common. Books became vital to each of them but in markedly different ways.

Paul was not a literary person. He read few books and his collected letters would make only a slim volume. He would probably have achieved wealth whatever occupation he had undertaken. Selling came as naturally to him as breathing and he wished to afford the luxuries of life. Possibly it was his admiration for Allen Lane as the founder of Penguin which directed him into publishing.

He began his career by buying and selling publishers' remainders at bargain prices; he closed it by selling his company for more than £500m. His achievement, measured in sales of books and the rapid accumulation of a fortune several times over, was spectacular. His motivation came from the triple wish to be rich, to flout social convention and to attack the foundations of the particular industry in which he worked. Why were so few books sold? Why were they highly priced? Why wasn't distribution more efficient? Which markets were unexploited? He was a doer not a talker; his was a restless nature. Charing Cross Road was thick with bookshops – why weren't the centres of other cities? Publishers relentlessly churned out new titles – why didn't more people buy them?

He made effective use of his limited capital. André Deutsch with whom he enjoyed a long friendship related of him, 'He bought five books from us for sevenpence each, crossed the road and sold them for elevenpence, then came back and bought some more.' A basic illustration of how money makes money – Paul Hamlyn's career in a nutshell.

By 1948 the wartime boom in books was over. The years when almost anything published found a purchaser were ended; shops and warehouses became choked with unsaleable volumes. Even so there were not sufficient suitable for the market that the young Hamlyn was tapping. The annual total number of new titles was around a mere 15,000 compared with the 100,000 plus fifty years on. So Hamlyn began to manufacture his own remainders by reprinting cheaply, in Czechoslovakia and elsewhere, some of the 'failures' he had bought. This led to a deal with Artia, the Czech state publisher/printer, giving him exclusive English-language rights in their books. One of them was a ten-shilling volume on Rembrandt which outsold, collectively, all other books about the painter over a five-year period. In

1949 he had founded his company Books for Pleasure but was not content to deal solely in publishers' mistakes. He became a publisher himself and originated titles, then series. Books for Pleasure was joined by Prints for Pleasure, Records for Pleasure and, in association with EMI, Music for Pleasure. He and his first wife Bobbie, who came from an Irish Roman Catholic family, went on buoyant selling expeditions together, often to woo the buyers at department stores. Their marriage in 1952 underlined Paul's break with his upbringing; he was to remain a rebel for much, though not all, of his life. The Hamlyns also employed a sales force dealing with traditional trade outlets, while reserving the right to market in any way they chose. Rep Bill Jackson, mentioned above, remembered a sales trip with Paul when there was a gap of some hours between appointments. They booked into a cinema but Paul couldn't tolerate the inactivity so they abandoned the film and went in search of unscheduled potential customers.

Traditional publishers on both sides of the Atlantic were at first wary of Hamlyn but as they found that his emergence as a major competitor did not lessen their own share of the cake he was at first accepted, later welcomed. In Britain, he did not threaten that prize sacred cow, the Net Book Agreement; he simply ignored it. He did not net his publications; he sold to the trade at a recommended price without worrying whether or not the retailers stuck to it, which on the whole they did; he did not join the Publishers' Association though he mixed with its members on his regular but brief visits to the Frankfurt Book Fair. His business grew prodigiously, he became associated with several series of art books printed on the Continent. These, particularly in the early years, did not always compare in quality with what was later – thanks chiefly to another brilliantly innovative immigrant, Walter Neurath, founder of Thames & Hudson – to become the norm, but they were acceptable for their time, and they were cheap. By the mid-sixties he had moved on to Landmarks of the World's Art, slim, handsome volumes printed in the Netherlands which drew praise from his sometime employer Anton Zwemmer. These, along with reference works from Hachette, were titles of quality which no one was ashamed to display on their coffee tables. In 1958 he was elected to the Society of Bookmen. Its treasurer, the printer Alan Steele, remarked, 'We thought it better to have him on the inside rather than the outside.' The printer also told a story against himself concerning Paul. It was Alan's brief not only to obtain orders daily and weekly from London publishers to keep his company's presses in Somerset active but to ensure that those who became customers were solvent. When the young Hamlyn burst upon the scene and placed an order for 100,000 or more of a title – Paul always dealt in large print numbers, it was the way his style of business worked – Alan politely turned it down. (This was not held against his firm, Butler & Tanner, which later did work for Hamlyn. Although British printers could not usually compete on price with their rivals in the Far East, or behind the Iron Curtain, for certain titles a home-based company was the answer.)

Becoming a member of the Bookmen was by no means unhelpful to Paul and for some years he often attended its dinners. A small part of him always wished to be accepted. There is an instance of how he conformed during a National Library Week in the 1960s when, for the local Camden group, he manned a stall in the market on a Saturday. The barrow boy in him re-emerged when he found himself bartering with a prospective customer. He couldn't resist knocking down the price to make the sale of what was a *net book*. Having concluded the deal he contributed the difference out of his own pocket. Being on the 'inside' also helped in his search for new talent to employ.

One of the first senior trade figures recruited was Philip Jarvis, the book buyer for Boots, the pharmaceutical retail chain with long-established subscription libraries in most branches, which, under him, had 140 book departments. Jarvis had become notorious by daring to suggest that 'books can be sold like soap'. To make the fullest impact he kept the message short though he must have known he should have said, 'some books'. Many pillars of the trade snorted with disbelief; others thought he had made a valid point. Paul recognised a kindred spirit. In fact he already knew Philip because he and Bobbie were still calling on major accounts at that time. Jarvis was a member of the BA council with many useful contacts, who became, according to Lionel Leventhal, his erstwhile personal assistant, one of a 'small tight-knit management team' which 'went out to lunch each day'. Another colleague of the time remembers him as Paul's speech-writer. In 1959, he became managing director of Hamlyn Publishing. Two years later Paul invited Ralph Vernon-Hunt, highly esteemed sales director of Pan Books, to join them; in his turn Ralph brought in Paul Scherer from Penguin.

Paul needed 'likely lads' (and lasses) to join him for the sake of the inspired suggestions they might contribute. He aimed to form a team of men who were respected within the established book trade. Some of those enlisted were frustrated by not having their jobs defined, and found themselves treading on the toes of others, such as Lionel Cordell and Bill Dancer, who had been with the firm from near the start.

Ronald Whiting, with a track record of successful selling at Allen & Unwin, Putnam and Dobson, was flattered but guarded in his reaction when approached by Hamlyn's remainder buyer, Richard Asher. He wasn't sure he wished to change jobs. This was reported to Hamlyn who invited him to lunch at Boulestin, in Southampton Street, 'one of the most OK restaurants in London'. There Paul persuaded him '...rather stupidly, rather foolishly, very regretfully', recorded Whiting, to leave Dobson and join him at 'a ghastly old warehouse' in Kentish Town. 'From the word go I was really like a fish out of water ... it was a different world, not my world ... ' He did his best to come to terms with it, wrote papers, as requested, about merging the Hamlyn approach with bona fide traditional publishing but they were all ignored. He lasted six months. Paul was generous to him, allowed him to keep his company car for a while and told him, 'I don't know how long it will be before you get a job but ... you can come in here and use the phone because it's easier ... if you seem to have one.'

Lionel Leventhal, also recruited from general publishing, was another misfit. He wrote long after that despite being Jarvis's deputy Philip wasn't capable of deputising or perhaps he, Lionel, 'couldn't be deputised to'. The situation was at first resolved when he was suddenly placed in charge of Music for Pleasure, a joint venture with EMI which, although it turned over £12m in long-playing records in three years, was in a state of appalling disarray.

Overall, Paul's staffing policy worked as the founder moved inexorably towards not only his first million but also the first takeover. The practical side of his left-wing political beliefs was shown in his treatment of employees. Not only did he pay well and give bonuses, he also encouraged staff to invest in the company for which they worked so that a great many of them were beneficiaries when he sold out. He even loaned them the means to buy the shares. He could be a hard taskmaster, was undoubtedly impatient and sometimes, it seemed to others, pig-headed, but his enthusiasm and powers of innovation were contagious. There were few who did not feel that they were part of an ongoing success story with the future ever brighter. He was a born leader who stimulated debate. He did not involve himself overmuch in minutiae but, when he did, he had the ability to read upside down what lay on others' desks. On Paul Scherer's he once noticed orders from booksellers which he tore up, remarking, 'We don't supply single copies.' He used the phone endlessly, preferred a low couch to a desk and was an obsessed gadgets man, one of the first ever owners of a pocket calculator. He was a good mimic and a practical joker who found it amusing to phone friends using a fake voice.

Hamlyn acquired several foundering imprints, like: Peter Nevill, the Batchworth Press and Andrew Dakers, but why? Did they bring him

remainders? He also founded Spring Books, but all under the umbrella of
the Books for Pleasure Group, until he chose to use his own name.

Philip Jarvis and a later colleague, Sue Thomson, were to relate how
Paul evolved a totally different approach to publishing a book from that of
previous generations of practitioners. The traditional method was to accept
a manuscript/typescript and then decide how it should be printed, bound,
jacketed, sold. Not so for Paul. As early as the Books for Pleasure days, once
a subject had been decided upon, his team began with the look of the book,
the format, the mechanics of it. Only after that were a writer (editor) and
illustrator engaged.

Having toned-down a strong remainder image, Paul embarked on publishing creatively, as he saw it, not only for the still inward-looking home
trade and other retailers but for the wide world beyond. *Cookery in Colour*
by Marguerite Patten was the forerunner of many on the same subject,
notably the Hamlyn *All Colour Cookery Book*, which doesn't actually have
an author and sold in millions. There had from Mrs Beeton to Elizabeth
David long been successful cookery books. They were already prominent
on the Penguin list – and paperbacks had the added advantage that there
was no taboo about soiling them with flour and sauces. Hamlyn cookery
books and cookery cards went beyond this market to a vast new one
reached on television, one which had always been there but Paul tapped it
as none but the BBC (with a natural built-in advantage) had before.
Increasing prosperity brought millions into the middle-class bracket in a
western world becoming dominated by superstar chefs. Hamlyn books met
its demands, even helped to create them. Similarly, with gardening, house
plants and DIY, although, especially in the latter category, the Readers'
Digest, seemed to retain the edge over Hamlyn. Travel he perhaps wisely
neglected. Travel books require regular, often annual, updating and there is
no remainder market for last year's Michelin Red Guides. Surprisingly,
Hamlyn also steered clear of sport, which is a great leveller and one would
have thought a perfect subject to dangle in front of the partly-educated
market which he unveiled; he also avoided almost entirely contemporary
fiction, biography, history, philosophy and the social sciences, categories
wherein perhaps one title in a thousand, or ten thousand, might prove to
be a bestseller. But he did have a massive impact on children's books and
especially on those for the very young.

If I were to name the top selling books from all categories during my
thirty-two years of bookselling in Hampstead – along with Chelsea, probably the most literary and author-strewn area of Greater London, even of
the UK – I would include Richard Scarry's *The Best Word Book Ever* in the

first ten. It was one of many titles for children which originated with the American Golden Pleasure Books imprint, of which Hamlyn was 50% owner. He bought exclusive rights to 'translate' it into English spelling and to sell it anywhere except in the United States. It cut across all class and social barriers and was adored equally by adults and children. There was a certain irony attached to its title and popularity; it probably had more illustrations than words.

Another book, for toddlers, was printed in Czechoslovakia in vast numbers. Its text amounted to fewer than 100 words but there were two literals. Paul, for whom offering bargains was an essential part of his creed, had noted that a competitor was selling a *First Dictionary* for 3s. 6d. so he must publish a better one at 2s. 6d. The books duly arrived in the railway sidings at Kentish Town. Copies were distributed to all senior personnel. Within minutes of examining them they rushed out of their offices and gathered in a corridor, each pointing out the errors – A for Appel, Y for Yatch, or whatever. The crisis was resolved when Eric Warman, one of Hamlyn's early senior associates, pointed out that the books had not been jacketed, the covers were unlaminated and they lay in the sidings in another wagon. 'Get them round to a local printer,' he suggested, 'with instructions to sticker them with a message reading – 'Children, there are two deliberate mistakes in this book. Can you spot them?' 'The book,' recorded Ronald Whiting 'sold and sold and sold. The errors were corrected in the next edition.'

It would not be quite true to assert that primarily Hamlyn books were produced to be looked at more than read but the theme has some validity. A young art historian, Trewin Copplestone, who had written the commentary in the ten-shilling Rembrandt volume, became editorial director, putting together, amongst other works, the lavishly illustrated *World Architecture* which in Hampstead I piled high and sold. There was also the *Larousse Encyclopaedia of Mythology* which, in 1959, I named in the *Ham & High* as one of my choices of the year, praising it as 'the sort of book to which one turns to verify a point and stays browsing in for hours'. The so-often reticent Paul actually phoned to thank me. I had penetrated his armour a little. That tiny Achilles heel of his allowed him not to despise being the publisher of learned books. In the case of Larousse he had the best of both worlds because, to quote his sometime colleagues, Jarvis and Thomson, 'he bought outright English-language and Scandinavian rights' to both their *Mythology* and their *Gastronomique*, plus 'two other encyclopaedias, for less than £1,000 – a sum which he was later to turn into millions'. *Gastronomique* gave rise to a problem because the jacket featured a recipe for rhubarb showing that fruit's poisonous green leaves attached. A warning sticker had to be prepared, or maybe a whole new wrapper, but this brought not unwelcome publicity. Not only did Paul have the Midas touch but much that he did became news.

Speaking to the Society of Young Publishers in 1960 he claimed that most people were terrified of going into a bookshop and that new outlets must be found. Young people in publishing were eager to work for him, as Joan Clibbon, an editor from 1958, recorded in a *Bookseller* article, because it was exciting and stimulating. Soon he amassed his first million, an event which was celebrated by his staff producing a one-off volume for him in which the £ sign was printed one million times. (Who counted?) It was a slightly moronic gesture which nevertheless expressed their feelings of elation about the company for which they worked. Many of them were to benefit when, in 1964, Cecil King, chairman of the Mirror Group (known as the International Publishing Corporation), successfully bid £2,275,000 for Hamlyn Publishing, which by now was turning over £3m annually. The deal allowed Paul to retain his job, and to head a division of Mirror book publishing which already included Odhams Press, Ginn, George Newnes & Pearson, Country Life (the magazine had spawned an excellent list of illustrated books), Collingridge (gardening manuals), Dean's Rag Books and Hulton's annuals.

It was no doubt satisfying to Paul to become head of Country Life where twenty years earlier he had been the office boy, but having control of these lists, almost all of which published in a style utterly different from his own, threw him off course. There were thousands of backlist books in print which he did not wish to know about. Leventhal, instructed to move these disparate elements out of crowded premises near Drury Lane and into one corporate building, found a newly constructed skyscraper at Feltham in west London, not far from Heathrow. A greatly reduced staff, all woefully suffering from the effects of restrictive practices undertaken by the unions, moved into what was named Hamlyn House, although Leventhal himself resigned. Paul remained in offices, next to Cecil King's, on the top floor of another new skyscraper just off Fleet Street. He was not happy but whilst there he brought off a deal with Robert Maxwell which rid IPC of *Chambers' Encyclopaedia* and other titles sold door-to-door which had led to the Newnes Pearson division making a loss in 1964/5. Maxwell paid £1m. It was the only business encounter, according to Eric de Bellaigue, between the two men, although in 1968 both became contenders, on behalf of their companies, for the highly esteemed legal, medical and accountancy list of Butterworths. Maxwell lost out on that one. The *Butterworth Gazette*, an in-house journal, recorded Paul Hamlyn, 'dressed in a [for then] dazzling concoction of greens, liberally sprinkled with purple polka dots', entering into possession on behalf of IPC, 'facing the grey-suited ranks of the Butterworthians', dramatically symbolising the change which had overtaken a run-down old family-owned firm. H. Kay Jones, a former deputy managing director, acidly commented in his official history that 'Hamlyn may have thought he was taking over but it was from Cecil King and other directors … that Butterworths took their orders'. Not, though, for long.

The Hamlyn – King relationship does not seem to have brought much joy to either man. Paul actually claimed to be in awe of the Mirror chief. When he agreed to approach him on behalf of the Society of Bookmen to speak at a dinner he became like a prima donna. He said Cecil wouldn't stay if the room got too hot, he might leave if he didn't like the meal, and so on. He was as nervous as an actor on a first night. In fact the evening went swimmingly. Cecil King spoke well and behaved impeccably. In retrospect Paul's behaviour was even more surprising because when, not long after, King was the victim of a boardroom coup, Hamlyn was revealed as the largest single individual shareholder in IPC. This fact did not, though, help him when the re-formed board of directors decided to sell the book division to the Reed Paper Group plc. Paul informed the Australian bookseller Michael Zifcak that he was bitterly upset at losing the company which bore his name. He resigned, Philip Jarvis took a major appointment in the USA, Ralph Vernon-Hunt returned to Pan, Paul Scherer joined Collins.

It was at this time, in 1969, that according to one source Hamlyn waited for a summons to Harmondsworth. Allen Lane had hinted, or even said outright, when Paul visited the Old Mill House driving his pink Rolls-Royce, that if ever he sold he would offer Penguin to Paul personally although he was not willing to consider IPC. As we know, he acted differently (see p.92).

In the immediate aftermath of leaving IPC, Paul seemingly did little. His marriage to Bobbie, by whom he had a son and a daughter, had been dissolved following her affaire with a TV presenter. Despite this they remained friends and he phoned her every day until in 1971 she took her own life. By then he had married Helen Price Guest who was said to have organised his lifestyle as first a millionaire, later, a multi-millionaire. Neither she nor his children by Bobbie were to play much part in his publishing although she was to be a dominant factor in the Hamlyn Foundation (set up in 1972) which benefited the arts, education and the third world. Helen gave his life a new dimension 'in which a private plane, a helicopter and two châteaux played their part' (Jarvis & Thomson).

That was in the future when Sue Thomson, who had first joined him at Hamlyn in 1966 (following service with Foyles and Thames & Hudson), was invited by Paul to a small party in a house he had just bought in Old Church Street, Kensington. It was yet to be furnished so champagne was served to guests seated on orange boxes. Their host announced his intention of returning to publishing but 'it was going to be quite small'. Sue was invited to become one of an unstructured team. She believed this to be unrealistic and persuaded Paul to appoint her managing director and grant her two and a half per cent of the equity. This was agreed on a handshake and without a written contract. Bill Dancer, also offered a share in the new company, stayed with Hamlyn Publishing and thereby lost a fortune. Derek Freeman accepted employment, maintaining he had been hired because 'I knew nothing about books.' (Shades of Allen Lane.)

Soon after Paul's second wedding his new colleagues were advised of a change of plan. He surprised them by joining News International, owned by the Australian newspaper tycoon Rupert Murdoch. This did not seem a recipe for the independence which was essential to Hamlyn, but he was already deeply attracted by Australia and things Australian; also he liked Murdoch.

Rupert Murdoch, who was to become proprietor of *The Times* and the *Sun*, and of publishers William Collins, in London, and Harper in New York, was much disliked across a wide spectrum of the media and the book trade. For a while he and Hamlyn were joint managing directors which, wrote one commentator, was ludicrous, 'a doubly bizarre linking of two supreme individuals'. While it endured, Paul pursued his intention, with Murdoch's blessing, of starting a book-publishing subsidiary. Twelve months on, he had bought it from News International from which he resigned as MD, although remaining a non-executive director for fourteen years.

Thomson, who also had doubted that Hamlyn and Murdoch could work together, was happy about the future value of her small share of the equity, and assumed her role of MD of the book company in a small room in the Aldwych. Paul was a quarter of a mile away in Bouverie Street in an office designed by Helen in 'several shades of beige ... ' Sue recorded that he 'never had a desk. He would work at a coffee table ... he didn't really write ... he dictated ... made notes ... ' but 'he'd write down an order all right!'

The first day of the new venture began with more champagne. The company then did not even have a name, let alone a book. It was to become Octopus. Asked why, Paul said because that was the name of 'a loving, cuddly creature not unlike himself'. To some in the trade Octopus, with a staff of one dozen, seemed, at least at first, a rerun of the original Hamlyn. There was the same emphasis on cookery and other subjects known to command massive sales. There were the same books with the same authors (or lack of them) and almost the same formats but it was not to stay small for long.

A year later the staff moved to an elegant eighteenth-century house in Grosvenor Street, Mayfair, where Helen Hamlyn again set the scene with her designing skills, although this time more lavishly. 'Paul had a plain cream room with Tantric art, antique looking glasses and a curved sofa with a low table.' Sue Thomson remembered it as 'a lovely working environment'. The staff appreciated the garden in the summer; there were two annual parties. Paul was now sent to nearby Savile Row for his suits. Helen entertained tirelessly and joined him on his travels; Sue protected him and some of his staff from each other in the interests of the whole operation running smoothly. If really useful employees found themselves over-promoted she tactfully rewrote their job description and they moved sideways on the same salary. Octopus was small and prosperous enough to make this feasible. Her job, she recorded, was to sweep up after Paul, also at times to point him towards directions in which he might choose to go.

Paul had stated at the outset that he was determined to have fun; *it was only really a hobby*. It was nothing of the sort. Following the familiar early titles came series on film, the arts and classic cars, with Octopus moving well beyond the confines of the book trade to produce up to fifty a year own-brand titles for Marks & Spencer, including *Microwave Cookery* whose sales ran to almost seven figures. It made deals with the broadcaster David Frost, the retailer and designer, Terence Conran; there were forays into stationery and other commodities. And it became global, undertaking books for foreign publishers in their own languages, setting-up subsidiary companies in Australia (where a revised *Microwave Cookery* sold another 100,000) and other parts of the Commonwealth. Paul set out again on the fast track to make more millions by improving a proven formula. 'He was not reinventing the wheel but making a better one' (Thomson). This time round, however, he would not involve himself in problems of distribution, warehousing and representation to the trade. It was a new, streamlined Hamlyn with W. H. Smith taking on the less colourful but necessary secondary roles in return for a 60% discount. This Octopus had at least as many tentacles as a natural one and Paul went to work on it with the fierce drive and relentless energy he had shown with Books for Pleasure and Hamlyn. At Frankfurt he was reported as arriving 'clad overall in his chocolate-coloured

Rolls, presiding over his stand with décor in the royal purple'. The centre-piece, designed by Helen, was a great silver model octopus.

Paul had a taste for fast and stylish cars, owning a Rolls and a Bentley. His estate manager at Edgeworth, Gloucestershire, would drive him in one vehicle to Heathrow; Colin, his chauffeur, would meet him in the other at Frankfurt where he stayed at the five-star Frankfurter Hof, booking in for a week, as required by the management, although his visit might last only two nights. (An earlier chauffeur, Peter, had once objected to the splendid vehicle he drove displaying a VOTE LABOUR poster. 'OK,' said Paul, 'move over and I'll drive until after the election.') Speed boats were another of his luxuries. The printer Robert Gavron when invited for a weekend to Paul's second home at Cap Ferrat was met at Nice airport by his host wearing a white suit. He was offered a choice of transport – the Rolls, parked on a jetty, or a Riva moored below it. The two men had been introduced by a financial journalist who correctly surmised that they would become close friends. Gavron took an interest in Octopus, becoming a director in 1975 and his St Ives Press occasionally printed for Paul. The two families took holidays together although Hamlyn invariably spent the first part of every morning working. Once assured that his empire was properly functioning he would relax, play ping-pong, swim, enjoy meals. Cookery books featured prominently on his list; enjoyment of food rated high among his personal predilections. The lunch habit was one thing he shared with establishment publishers although he was not clubbable. Martyn Goff, when director of the National Book League in its Albemarle Street days, recalls attempting to host him on three occasions at the Savile. He would call at the Octopus Mayfair office where Paul would ask, 'Where are we going?' When told, he protested that he hated clubs and asked his secretary to ring the Savile. 'Tell them Mr Goff wishes to cancel his table, then book one at Claridge's.' His entertaining could be lavish; it was said that for special occasions he had oysters flown from Sydney Bay to London.

David Whitaker, while editor of *The Bookseller*, was invited to Grosvenor Street by Paul who wished to be interviewed. Whitaker said he never visited publishers for such a reason but would make an exception in this case. Arriving at the Mayfair offices he remembers that his feet sank into the deep pile of the carpet. The room stretched the forty-feet depth of the house to the garden beyond. He was confronted by Paul seated behind a desk which was a 'sheet of plate glass supported by two stainless steel tripods. The glass shone, there was not a paper on it, nor a fingerprint.' David raised an eyebrow mischievously. 'Do you think it's getting to me?' Paul asked, meaning had he contracted megalomania. His visitor's look having confirmed this, he then enthused about the project he was about to launch on a personal worldwide sales tour for which he was seeking publicity. David returned to his office to write a partly acidic piece about Hamlyn producing a new series which, despite its being identical with previous ones, would no doubt sell like mad. When Paul read this he sent his chauffeur to buy as many extra copies as were available to distribute globally ahead of his trip. David enquired why to which Paul replied, 'No one will think I could have paid you to write this.'

His destinations no doubt included the Antipodes where initially Paul had not endeared himself to Australian booksellers. Michael Zifcak, who ran the Collins Booksellers chain (no connection with the publishers) was a refugee from Communist Eastern Europe. He had resented the fact that Hamlyn used cheap labour to print books in his native Czechoslovakia. Nor had he liked buying on firm sale because there was then no Hamlyn distributor in Australia. Matters came to a climax when Paul gave the *Melbourne Age* newspaper exclusive rights to sell a cookbook by an Aussie chef. It was advertised as being available ONLY FROM THE AGE OFFICE. Zifcak and his staff fought back by buying 400 copies at full price from the newspaper, then window-displaying them below the AGE poster, adding AND FROM COLLINS BOOKSELLERS HERE. This caused uproar in the Australian book trade but Zifcak had made his point and, thereafter, he and Paul Hamlyn became close friends, establishing a profitable working relationship. When Paul subsequently formed an Australian company he offered Michael the managing directorship but it was declined. Paul also bought Cheshires, another Australian bookseller and publisher, and the Lansdowne Press, but regretted both. They were not, according to Zifcak, right for the Hamlyn profile; Paul asked him desparingly, ' ... explain to me how it is possible to make any money in bookselling?'

Joyce Nicholson, sometime editor of the *Australian Bookseller & Publisher*, wrote in her memoirs, 'Big events for the year [1968] were the parties to celebrate the opening of the new Paul Hamlyn warehouse at Dee Why. Nobody had seen anything like it in Australia before. The Dee Why party is said to have cost $10, 000. Hamlyn arrived at the party by helicopter.'

By the time he had launched Octopus, Paul had 'rediscovered' Australia where 'the famous outdoor life-style did not exclude an equally healthy interest in the knowledge and entertainment to be found in books' (Jarvis & Thomson). There he became a media personality, appearing on the box and on radio, to comment witheringly on the Establishment in 'the old country'. Australians loved this, while retaining a potent interest in featuring on Honours Lists emanating from Whitehall.

In the Far East, Paul raised the standards of an established printing works which he used, created Mandarin publishing in Hong Kong and, in Jaipur, he subsidised through the Hamlyn Foundation a hospital manufacturing false limbs; elsewhere he turned part works into books and became game for anything. 'Early Octopus,' as Eric de Bellaigue recorded, 'was a marketing machine … never a traditional publisher.' De Bellaigue recorded the story of Octopus for both *The Bookseller* and, in book form, for the British Library. He wrote with the unique understanding of one totally versed in the ways of the City of London who had also acquired a detailed knowledge of book publishing. His account has a strong storyline with Paul playing the role of a picaresque hero constantly turning somersaults or leading a Pan-like team, piping and dancing its way down streets and airways paved with gold, his personality changing according to the part of the world he happens to be in.

Between 1975 and 1990, during which period Octopus went public, Hamlyn bought and sold like a man possessed, giving rise to the quip, made at a Bookmen dinner, that '*Publishers* can be sold like soap.' He rarely made a mistake but, when he did, could afford to dismiss it because he very soon became one of the super rich. A childhood friend from Berlin, the statistician Claus Moser, also joined the Octopus board. Both he and Gavron became directors of the Royal Opera House and were subsequently ennobled. Moser, in 2005, is still an adviser to the Hamlyn Foundation.

Yet Paul, who had turned his back on the likes of Country Life and Newnes, old-established companies foisted upon him in his *Daily Mirror* days, came to flirt with genuine literature by pedigree novelists. This occurred when Charles Pick, of Heinemann, and Tom Rosenthal, of Secker & Warburg, wished to promote some of their leading authors in omnibus form to a mass market. For all their expertise, Pick and Rosenthal could not get below a selling price of £12.50 for their envisaged nine-hundred-page volumes, each containing umpteen books by the likes of Somerset Maugham, Franz Kafka, John Steinbeck and Wilbur Smith. Paul undertook to produce them to sell at £3.95 (later, £4.95), which they did in vast numbers. The venture, code-named Operation Pickle, proved so successful that other publishers' lists had to be raided for authors. There were print runs ranging from 50,000–100,000 for most titles. Rosenthal commented that Paul actually claimed to have read and enjoyed the Graham Greene volume, a rare glimpse into the private life of the man who just occasionally revealed a desire to be literary. Robert Gavron, who thought of Paul as uneducated, possibly slightly dyslexic but with a fine mind, confirmed that he was a fan of Greene's who was a neighbour on the Riviera.

Operation Pickle worked; not all ventures did.

A decision to return to the more formal book trade in 1984 by purchasing Webster's Bookshops, which had a paperback wholesaling division and dealt in remainders – Bounty Books – sold to non-book-trade retailers, was a mistake. Paul also bought Brimax Books to produce cheap, high-quality children's books and was thus involved again in distribution. It seemed he must dabble in everything but even this supreme juggler was unable to keep all the balls in the air. Webster's had to go but there were mightier matters to hand.

Early in 1985 Charles Pick, now retired from Heinemann, joined Octopus as a consultant only to become reunited with his former company when Hamlyn brought off a deal merging the two groups. Octopus had an annual turnover of £53m, compared with Heinemann's £41m. It was a complicated deal by which Paul could lay claim to 50.1% of the voting power so long as he owned 20% of the equity; anyone wishing fully to understand it should consult de Bellaigue, pp. 104–6.

In the following year it gave Paul much satisfaction to buy back his original Hamlyn imprint from Reed International for a mere £1,000, although the purchase brought with it £10m in debts; de Bellaigue notes that with 'a turnover of about £16m' it (Hamlyn) 'had become an isolated and unprofitable unit in Reed International' which had by then amassed a vast publishing empire. Grosvenor Street could not accommodate all the imprints now owned so, in 1986, Hamlyn and Terence Conran bought Michelin House, South Kensington, where staff of the huge new group, comprised of many disparate elements enjoying only slight comprehension of what made the others tick, were required to work in open-plan offices. Many found the arrangement rebarbative.

By then Hamlyn had gained another high-powered colleague from the newspaper world, Ian Irvine, who became chief executive of Octopus and appointed Paul Richardson, ex-HEB, Macmillan and Collins, 'head of publishing development'. Richardson's role was actually to look after further acquisitions from mainstream publishing such as Methuen, Mitchell Beazley, George Philips, as well as reporting on behalf of Heinemann and Secker. Another high-flyer, Richard Charkin, with an academic background including Oxford University Press, was brought in to put the Mandarin imprint in the front rank of paperback publishing. And there was Nicholas Thompson, who had succeeded Pick and Rosenthal at Heinemann. They amounted to a lot of top people, occasionally including the unretirable Alan Hill, who shared Hamlyn's love of Australia and something of his entrepreneurial style, and whose connection with Heinemann ended only with his death.

Hamlyn's insatiable acquisitiveness was not favoured by all of his colleagues. Sue Thomson, who on becoming a mother in the late 1970s had stepped down as MD, although remaining on the board as vice chairman, was one of those who resigned. Even so, as an Octopus shareholder, she enjoyed rich benefits, as did others who had sensibly backed their employer's enlightened investment policy.

Paul's wizardry failed to transform all the literary works of the Heinemann and Secker lists into Hamlyn/Octopus-style merchandise. He was always reluctant to admit that his flamboyant style of publishing could not be applied to what was known as 'trade publishing', the process that had occupied family imprints in a mostly gentlemanly way for roughly two centuries. I think he believed that the success of Operation Pickle had proved that he could market fiction like everything else but he overlooked the fact that the omnibus volumes represented highly successful established authors whereas general literature embraced thousands of first novels, slender volumes of verse, one-off travelogues, biographies and memoirs, deeply researched studies of history, and so on – none of which could 'be sold like soap', except for the ghosted autobiographies of showbiz folk and footballers. He didn't like to be challenged about this. I was present at least twice when he walked away from an attempted discussion on the issue. I was guilty of what he called 'negative thinking'. Yet in an interview for a Sunday newspaper in 1984 he proclaimed, 'I only understand one kind of publishing and that is books of wide appeal that improve the quality of life from the stomach to the mind.'

He admitted his biggest mistake came from the comparative failure of the Mandarin paperback list. The Heinemann link had given Octopus part ownership of Pan Books, which was second only to Penguin as a publisher of mass-market paperbacks. Paul attempted to buy the other 50% of Pan shares from Macmillan under an agreement which laid down that if either of the owners sold out or merged (as Heinemann had) the other had the right to become 100% owner. Macmillan won this battle. Hamlyn, who offered to pay Macmillan more than they finally paid for 'his' interest, observed that the other publisher's MD, Nicky Byam Shaw '…was a very static gentleman'. It was certainly, as de Bellaigue observed, unusual for Paul to be outmanoeuvred. Byam Shaw insisted on Macmillan's rights under the agreement and this lost Hamlyn the profitable, established paperback list he felt his empire needed.

A ready-made entrée into this market continued to evade him, which could have been interpreted by him as a warning that he might be getting out of his depth, but he was immediately preoccupied by his biggest deal of all. In 1987, just three months before the world market crashed, he amazed the trade and the City by selling the whole of Octopus-Heinemann (including, once again, his Hamlyn imprint) for £535m to Reed, in which he retained a personal holding of several million shares. As de Bellaigue commented, he 'had an uncanny sixth sense of the right moment to strike'. Paul believed that he had ensured the future of Octopus, 'making it bigger and better', making it possible for him to do 'all the things I have dreamed of doing'. (Presumably by this he was thinking of his further endowment to the tune of £50m of the Hamlyn Foundation, because he had hardly been strapped for cash during the previous twenty years when his commercial achievements surpassed those of most of his competitors.)

Once tycoons are into the power world of super deals the actual product becomes irrelevant. Paul was now buying and selling corporations not books. How could anyone of his proven ability be expected to think in terms of outpricing a competitor by 10p, 50p or even £20? He was operating at multi-millionaire level. So were the other conglomerates who were aiming to gobble up the remaining minnows of British publishing, once among its most prestigious names. The fact that these smaller fish did not fit happily into their empires was of little consideration; it was better to net them than let them get away.

Selling to Reed did not, of course, spell retirement for Hamlyn, who remained chairman of Octopus and earned a seat on the main board along with Ian Irvine, but this was a time when mergers and takeovers were rife. Reed joined with Elsevier, of Holland, and quickly became disenchanted with the general lists of Heinemann, Secker & Warburg and Methuen, which were sold to Random House. They were not compatible with its image whereas Heinemann Educational (plus Ginn) was a prime prize, giving Elsevier world supremacy; so was Butterworth with its high-priced specialist legal and medical tomes.

Charkin succeeded Irvine before moving on to Macmillan; Paul Richardson, who had been placed in charge of children's publishing, also left to return to more academic employment. Educational and scientific publishing, including journals, became the prime concern of Elsevier, while the remaining imprints – Hamlyn, Mitchell Beazley, Philips, etc. – were placed under the Octopus umbrella along with Cassell (founded 1848) and sold, several years on, to Hachette, of France.

Paul Hamlyn's great publishing days were over, although he never ceased to be interested in the companies he had created. He was diagnosed as having Parkinson's disease, a wasting ailment which deenergises its victims. Its progress can be effectively controlled and was in his case but then

cancer struck. Despite this he continued to travel the world and to play a
public role – he was chancellor of Thames Valley University and the
Foundation provided £1m for purchase of books for the new reading room
of the British Museum – and he spent more and more time at his château
in the Luberon. (Elsewhere in France he owned a vineyard and an hotel,
run by Helen.) In 1993 he was awarded the CBE, he was given a medal by
the Royal Society of Arts and, in 1998, having been a generous donor to
the Labour Party, he became a life peer. As frequently happens to ageing
rebels, the 'Establishment' had its attractions for him and, no doubt, for his
second wife, but even so he resisted pressure, while nominal head of
Heinemann, to suppress *Spycatcher*, the memoirs of a former MI5 agent.
This embarrassment to Margaret Thatcher's Tory government may well
have pleased him, although he gagged that he would have done her bidding had she offered him a dukedom.

Hamlyn, a millionaire who believed in assisting those less fortunate than
himself, was in the direct tradition of the nineteenth-century industrialists
and benefactors, although utterly unlike them in manner. He was the least
pompous of men, his restless energy could tire others but never, until his
last illnesses, himself and, as two former colleagues wrote, working for him
'was to be on the receiving end of demands that were frequently unrea-
sonable, seemingly impossible, except that he was so often, infuriatingly
proved to be right'.

In *Who's Who* Paul did not list anything under Recreations apart from
poker; in an obituary, Sir Jeremy Isaacs recorded that he 'enjoyed theatre,
music, opera, ballet', and he was known to play poker. He did not relish
being interviewed by journalists; he made a cult of being secretive in his
private and business life, which had the inevitable effect of making him
more interesting to the media. His family, apart from Helen, were little
mentioned in his obituaries. His son Michael did not work for him as a
publisher but went into films, his daughter Jane became the owner of a
gallery. Once at a business dinner when asked about them by the wife of a
colleague he snubbed her by saying, 'We're not here to talk about family.'
In later life he and his brother Michael met infrequently. Michael and his
wife were invited only once to Paul's West Country estate where they
were shown his collection of rare, illustrated nature books 'so heavy they
could scarcely be lifted from the shelves'. Paul paid an annual visit to the
Hamburgers in Suffolk by helicopter, which was landed in a neighbouring
field. Once there the brothers had little to say to each other although a slender bond of family affection was manifested. One sister, Dr Eva Seligman,
a psychoanalyst, saw more of Paul after he had become famous and was

invited to both his French château and to a house he rented in Bali. Michael and his wife were not invited to either.

The Hamlyn Foundation is an impressive memorial to Paul, having at his death funds of almost £300m. (By 2005 it was worth over £450m.) He may not have learned how to mass-market thousands of copies of minority books but he donated a fortune to their preservation, including £3.1m to the Bodleian Library.

Paul Hamlyn, born (Hamburger) Berlin, 12 February 1926, younger son of Professor and Mrs Richard Hamburger. Married (1) Eileen (Bobbie) Watson, 1952 (marriage dissolved, 1969); (2) Helen Guest, 1970. Created Baron Paul Bertrand Hamlyn of Edgeworth, 1998. Died 31 August 2001.

Ten

ELSIE BERTRAM

The woman who did as much as anyone in the twentieth century – and far more than most – to improve the distribution of books in Britain did not make an impact on the trade until she was over fifty years old. Thereafter she became a blend of reality (mostly on the phone) and myth. What Elsie said and did was repeated by bookseller customers, many of whom never met her, publishers and their reps and by her staff in Norwich which came to number more than seven hundred.

Two years before the outbreak of WWI Elsie Hacking was born at Norton-on-Tees, in County Durham, although she liked to pretend she hailed from Yorkshire. There is a further confusion of counties from the fact that her parents, Harry and Alice Hacking, were Lancastrians. She was their younger daughter and the glad event occurred on either the 2nd or the 6th of June 1912. Harry sold medicines to farmers for treating cattle and earned sufficient to send his children to private infant schools. The family was not bookish although parents and children occasionally read to one another. Elsie gained a scholarship to the High School at Stockton-on-Tees where she was not outstanding as a pupil or at sport, although she won a prize in the sack race. This was presented to her by the local MP, Harold Macmillan. It was to prove her closest brush with publishing for a quarter of a century.

The depression was looming when Elsie, all five feet three inches of her, left school and was fortunate to find a clerical job connected to statistics with ICI. While so employed she met Edward Bertram, her future husband, who, so she told me when I profiled her for *Publishing News* in 1987, she at first instantly disliked. Eddie, like her father, sold farming medicaments.

Having married, the Bertrams moved first to Peterborough, next to King's Lynn. In the late 1930s, Elsie gave birth to a son and later to a daughter, both of whom died in under a week. When WWII began Eddie went into army intelligence; Elsie's too oft repeated quip in later life, whenever she introduced him, was, 'That's why it took so long to win the war.' She took over his job, selling to farmers in Lincolnshire and East Anglia, and, for war work, became an ambulance driver. In the latter capacity she helped to capture a Norwegian spy – a Quisling presumably, because Norway was one of the Allies; she also had the smartest team of nurses in the area, a distinction which won it a cup, received from the hands of Lady Mountbatten.

The next move was to Norwich where she was to spend the rest of her life. There she gave birth to two sons, Christopher (1944) – known as Kip – and Nigel (1948). Both were diagnosed as diabetic. Raising funds to treat that malady was to be the second most important strand in Elsie's life. Another occupation, started as a means of paying fees for her boys to attend the King Edward School in Norwich, was running a small chicken farm which was to become the best known symbol of her bookselling career. Kip gave her a hand at this but Nigel went off to university. Eddie, demobbed meantime, returned to dealing in animal medicaments, had occasional car crashes and once was responsible for sending twenty-seven trucks of timber to the wrong town. There was a Chekhovian hopelessness about the amiable Eddie but his sons adored him, even though Elsie complained that he didn't play with them when they were kids. She treated him in front of others as a lame duck held in some affection; Kip believed she was unkind to his father who was, 'a most popular man, a veritable Denis Thatcher'.

Kip had wished to become a doctor, but illness so drastically interrupted his schooling that he was not qualified for any profession. He took a temporary job with Pan Books to sell their list to holidaymakers on the Norfolk Coast and did sufficiently well to be offered a position as a full-time rep in London, while Elsie remained with her smallholding. When he transferred back to East Anglia, Elsie became *his* assistant until he went off to sell sticker books nationwide for Century 21. Then Elsie gave up her chickens and became a small wholesaler, mostly of Pan and other paperbacks, as E. Bertram Books. In her van she would make twenty or more calls a day, keeping her stock in the former chicken house. Sensing a demand for children's literature and perhaps recalling that, when an infant, she and her parents had enjoyed reading, she began to carry the Hamlyn list which had cheap, attractive books for that market.

David Hight, a young Hamlyn rep, called on Elsie and was instantly 'won over by her winning charm and persuasive salesmanship'. He felt he was being vetted by her and that she believed she was conferring a favour on the giant Hamlyn Group by selling their product. Soon afterwards he met Kip, who in the mid-1960s had tired of Century 21 and had joined his mother to form C.P. & E. Bertram Books. Encountering them in London one day, Hight's opinion was sought about starting a wholesaling business dealing in all books. Remembering the collapse of Simpkin Marshall, David warned against it. Kip ignored the advice and said he reckoned they could turn over £10,000 in their first year; in fact, they registered sales of £100,000. This was the basis for a business which over the next thirty years made them millionaires. The significance of the role they played cannot be appreciated without relating a paragraph of trade history. I have made Elsie the lead character in this particular study because Kip is still alive and well, though much of the praise bestowed on her is also due to him.

In 1955 the principal UK book wholesaler Simpkin Marshall, then owned by Robert Maxwell, went into receivership largely because publishers refused to grant discounts commensurate with keeping an efficient middle-man solvent. Maxwell survived to build an empire and cheat pensioners; publishers settled for a derisory final payment. The trade then spent more than a decade arguing about how the gap left by the demise of Simpkin's was to be filled. The subject was endlessly discussed at council meetings of the PA and the BA, at conferences when both sides of the trade met, at meetings of the Society of Bookmen, the Society of Young Publishers, the Publishers' Publicity Circle, at sessions of regional branches of the BA, in the columns of *The Bookseller*, on every bookshop floor when reps called to show their wares, at every promotional party thrown by publishers. All agreed that efficient wholesaling was essential for a healthy trade, a vital part of which was concerned with supplying single-copy orders. Wild assertions were made – 'We are essentially a single-copy trade', was one of them, and it was untrue – comparisons with the effectiveness of the German and the Dutch book trades were made, millions of words were spoken and written, all of them arriving at the same conclusion – wholesaling was too expensive an operation to be viable unless those operating it were granted a wider margin by publishers. Publishers insisted they could not afford larger discounts so for years the problem was allowed to fester while members of the public fumed about how long it took to obtain a book. (Even a highly intelligent publisher, such as Piers Raymond of Chatto & Windus, who himself backed a scheme for a single-copy house, once said to me, indignantly, 'when you order a suite of furniture costing hundreds of pounds you expect to wait weeks, even months, for delivery'. He could not see that books, as always, were different. The public knew the books it wanted were available; the item of furniture might well be produced only to order.)

Meanwhile Paul Hamlyn, although he had sold to IPC, was still expanding rapidly. He knew he could sell more books and was proving it daily, although the process was threatened by industrial disputes. The possibility

of these forcing the *Daily Mirror* to cease publication for even one day struck
terror into the heart of Cecil King, chairman of IPC. Despite which when
there was a strike at his Sunbury warehouse Hamlyn connived with the
Bertrams to break the picket lines. This was in the autumn of 1968 when
he offered them extended credit and supplied transport for their use. The
Bertrams seized their chance and never looked back. They opened numerous new accounts in all parts of the country. In the run-up to that Christmas
many bookshops would have lacked some of the Hamlyn titles they needed
if the Bertrams had not realised that the renaissance of wholesaling was in
their hands.

Booksellers who had complained constantly since Simpkin's closure
couldn't believe their luck and grabbed at the lifeline. Within months
Bertram's service, which was of a different order from Simpkin's, involving
as it did bulk supply as well as single copies, was the talk of the book trade,
and Elsie especially became an icon around whom stories quickly grew. She
wouldn't tolerate late payment of accounts (which was true); she chopped
off the fingers of staff who displeased her (which was not); she ran a sweat
shop (it was not apparent in the behaviour of her staff). She moved out of
her chicken house into what was named The Nest, larger premises on the
site of an ex-football pitch. It was opened appropriately enough by Paul
Hamlyn. Elsie held him in high affection. 'He was like dynamite,' she
recorded. 'I traded on Hamlyn's inefficiency' – meaning he had warehouse
problems. He continued to expand his business knowing his distribution
problems had improved. Bertram's established a 24-hour delivery service all
over the United Kingdom; small wholesalers, who had just survived into
the post-Simpkin era but were semi-dormant, breathed new life; others
who were fresh to the role, emulated Bertram's. None could surpass them.

Mike Butler, a trained teacher looking for temporary work until he found
a school appointment, joined Bertram's in September 1977 as 'a dogs-
body/go-between'. He remained for twenty-three years, becoming head of
buying. 'At the start,' he recalled, 'there was no staff structure, everybody,
including the Bertrams, was expected to do everything.' The working day
was from 8.00 to 16.30 but no one went home until the last order was dispatched. If that kept the warehouse open until evening, snacks were
ordered and a bar in Kip's office provided drinks. If all customer-demands
were met in the afternoon staff were sent home early. It was, wrote Butler,
'hard work, informal, fun, with reasonable pay'. In the run-up to Christmas
extra hands were not recruited, existing staff worked longer hours and were
paid overtime; one year he bought a brand new car on the proceeds of his.

Elsie became the helpful voice at the end of the phoneline who promised next-day delivery and established friendly relations while spending much of her time raising invoices with the aid of a desk calculator and keeping the hand-written ledgers; Kip organised the warehouse and, when there was time to do so, went out soliciting new custom, although much of it came by word of mouth. Fast though they grew they covered their tracks. They had won the regard of the retail trade by supplying those titles they stocked; they did not promise express delivery of every title in print but their attenae guided them in the right direction. Even as late as 1981 Elsie was writing to me, 'Our policy in limiting our range of titles but stocking in depth has proved the answer … one bookseller ordered 30 titles from us and received 29 by return (the other was reprinting) … he ordered the same 30 from a competitor and was sent only 2.'

They grew wisely but with increasing acceleration as both booksellers and publishers leaned on their service. They dealt initially only in fast-moving new and backlist titles, intelligently adding to both as demand became apparent. (Again, in January 1981, Elsie was writing to tell me they had taken on a selection of Methuen titles such as *The Wind in the Willows*, a prime seller for more than seventy years but because it regularly sold in quantity most booksellers ordered it direct from the publisher. However, when Methuen – long since a unit of Associated Book Publishers – had distribution problems it became simpler for everyone to buy it from Bertram's who were holding it 'in depth'.)

Kip sometimes stocked in extreme depth in an endeavour to corner the market in a bestseller while it was reprinting. The range held at The Nest increased and as Bertram's, or other wholesalers, became one of the largest single accounts for all booksellers, so did it for most publishers. Some of the latter complained when Bertram's demanded higher discounts but they were forced to concede them.

In less than three decades the Bertrams became rich by mastering a problem which had beset the book trade for much of the century. They earned and deserved their wealth, which was based on having made it possible for booksellers to promise their customers 'next-day delivery' for tens of thousands of titles. They insisted on minimum orders being placed (for long it was fixed at £50 invoice value) but this became easier for booksellers to bear as the range of what was available at The Nest grew. Bertram's kept apace of their own success.

In the company, formed in 1971 by mother and son, Kip was chairman and managing director, Elsie was company secretary. Both were 'boss' and each held 40% of the shares. Eddie had 10%, so did Nigel, who by then, having read Agriculture at university, had become sales manager for Monsanto, a company whose products included weed killer and animal foods. For nearly thirty years, led by Elsie and Kip (often in disagreement though not usually in front of the customers), Bertram's maintained the fantastically high standard they had set themselves. Their premises were expanded; staff grew apace. Some publishers who improved their own distribution hankered after returning to direct supply, but most booksellers preferred to deal with Norwich, which was how East Anglia, once known as 'the rep's graveyard', acquired a major call for the lucky travellers on this territory. The not-so-lucky ones had to tolerate Bertram's becoming a 'house account', looked after by the sales director himself. Bertram's led the market but there was room for many competitors; some, such as Gardner's, took over certain smaller retailers' entire supply.

Elsie was not involved in the actual buying but she got to know the reps and liked them to call and pay court to her. Trevor Moore, some time Methuen (ABP), sometime Century Hutchinson which became a part of Random House, was a favourite and she was upset when, in the late nineties, his company became a house account for Kip's buying team. Trevor recalls that she 'listened to everyone's troubles (all the "girls" loved her), had a gimlet eye for everything that went on plus a network of informers', exercised effective credit controlling and 'did more than at first seemed obvious'. Trevor called at The Nest over a long period. Even after Mike Butler, who he described as 'one of the shrewdest and most perceptive buyers I'd ever known', had officially taken over from Kip, the latter still sometimes dealt with him and a few other leading publishers' reps. (Elsie informed Trevor that after he had praised Mike, Kip was furious and commented, 'I taught him everything he knows.' Kip denied having said this and informed me this was an instance of what he had to endure from Elsie. She enjoyed having digs at her son; the mother–child working relationship is rarely an easy one.) At a celebratory lunch at the Aldeburgh Bookshop when Elsie asked to sit next to him, Trevor learned that her favourite song was 'Love is the Sweetest Thing'. Thereafter, when he called to see the buyers, 'I would stick my head around her door and warble a few bars in my best Al Bowley impersonation. She always seemed to enjoy it and would usually join in.' By 1999 when Random House had become a house account Trevor was no longer permitted to visit The Nest. Few if any reps were. Bertram's too had their own rep, a retired Collins man, bringing in fresh business.

In the early years many retail customers knew Elsie only by her voice and she was, as David Hight noted, 'a woman of many words'. It was said you didn't have conversations with Elsie, you listened. This was not quite fair, but Elsie, like Jane Austen's Miss Bates, did have a talent for digression. (When I wrote this about her she took it as a compliment, not being familiar with the work of Miss Austen.) She had also a great capacity for friendship as the Edinburgh bookseller, Ainslie Thin, recorded in his obituary of her. He and Eppie, his wife, entertained the Bertrams at home and in the Highlands, for which excursion Elsie wore 'bright red wellington boots and a floor-length mink coat'. (She also became known for her hats.)

Elsie, for twenty years and more, worked nearly a twelve-hour day arriving to open the post at 7.00 a.m. (I have a reply to a letter of mine, 'just received – 7.20 a.m. to be precise', in which she reaffirmed her secret feeling that small was still beautiful although she didn't allow this to retard Bertram's expansion.) Her day at The Nest ended at 18.30 when she would return to her detached house, with attached copse, up a steep drive in the quiet outer Norwich suburb of Thorpe St Andrew. There, after supper, she toiled until midnight on charity work in aid of diabetics, and for Norwich Cathedral.

She told Sue Bradley, interviewing her for the National Life Story Collection, that she had little time for reading but liked a particular volume of short stories; she could not remember either the title or the author but knew she'd read it three times. She was also fond of books about wildlife and birds. When I visited her house I could not see a single book anywhere on the ground floor. I saw every room because, as she was suffering from some ailment, I was asked to fetch the elevenses tray from the kitchen, where there wasn't even a cookery manual by her friend Delia Smith. Books were for selling, not reading. Kip inherited the trend, admitting that he couldn't concentrate for long enough to get through a whole book. He claimed he was not a '*book*man' but 'a *book-distribution* man'. Alison, his wife, who wrote the buyer's notes for the company's customers, was the literary one. Kip maintained a file of press cuttings and had sessions of striding about the warehouse with his camcorder preserving for posterity firsthand accounts of his staff working flat out.

Elsie spared time for socialising within the trade. She attended, with Eddie, Alison and Kip, the annual conference ('Eddie complained that all we talked about was books'). When I first visited The Nest I was permitted to take her for a brief lunch to a pub beside the River Yare. There she had temporarily to switch off because she was faced by a customer who had already placed his daily order and was now primarily concerned with food, drink and in finding out more about her. The subject appealed to my guest but she was not entirely egocentric. People in themselves, as much as people in relation to herself, interested her. I was entertained for half an hour of rambling comment, mostly unmalicious, about mutual acquaintances. She told me she had many friends but didn't like to get too close to them. She admitted to being against men who didn't remove their hats at interviews, that conferences could be boring but they were a means of picking up new custom and that Bertram's was both her life and her hobby, especially since the death of Eddie at the beginning of the year. He had died on New Year's Day 1987, when she was awarded the MBE for services to the book trade. According to David Hight, Elsie said the initials of the medal stood for 'My Bloody Effort', and it was a better gong than the OBE, which stood for 'Other Buggers' Efforts'. (She did not originate this.) She confided in me that a particular pleasure she derived from having the award was in knowing that Christina Foyle had not been similarly honoured. This was why, she said darkly, the promised invitation from the other millionaire female bookseller to visit her at Beeleigh Abbey had not been forthcoming. She further insisted that she was honoured, not for her charitable work, but for her services to bookselling.

I described her then as 'in her mid-seventies, neat, petite, still pretty, an impeccably dressed and coiffeured lady '. Her personal office was a glass-sided cubicle close to the entrance. The second time I called she insisted on taking a working lunch there where she was at the hub of the business. When it was fully operational the atmosphere could be almost nightmareish with phones constantly ringing, intercoms bleeping, staff – recording machines at the ready – in perpetual motion between offices, bookracks, loading bays, reception areas. Queen-bee Elsie loved it.

Elsie was not acccurate in describing Bertram's as her only hobby. Much of the little spare time she permitted herself was devoted to the charities already mentioned. In that same year that I interviewed her she invited Norris McWhirter (*Guinness Book of Records*), and the astronomer Patrick Moore, to launch the official Norfolk Diabetes Appeal. This raised £350,000 for the Bertram Diabetes Centre, funded partly by a donation she made from her own pension fund; it was opened by the comedian Harry Secombe. She also took the hat round in aid of a specialist eye clinic which was officially opened in 1991 by Prince Charles who, according to the *Eastern Daily News*, presented her with a basket of purple Brussels sprouts. This sounds like a gag thought up by Secombe whose goonish humour the Prince enjoyed, but Elsie declared it the 'most beautiful present she had ever received' and proceeded to auction one sprout for £1,000.

Another occasional, unexpected activity of Elsie's was watching Norwich City play football. (The Nest was built on the site of their former ground.)

She attended games with the hugely successful cookery-book compiler and television personality Delia Smith, who was a shareholder in the club.

For years Elsie insisted that Bertram's would not become computerised. Invoices and statements were handwritten and 99% accurate. (She would have said 101%.) Somehow there were never missing invoices when you checked the Bertram statement and, if there were, you paid it and argued later because Elsie was never more serious about anything than the requirement for prompt payment. Any failure she took personally. Once when an account was on the verge of bankruptcy she went, with van and driver, to the shop in question. There she insisted on removing all she could identify of 'her' stock, although before leaving she stood both her van driver and the erring customer lunch. Another offender, who was a dear friend of mine, didn't warn her in time of his insolvency. She spoke bitterly of his defection … 'After all I did for him!'

At work she was known as 'Mrs B', although Kip called her 'Else', and customers, 'Elsie'. It was Hugh Campbell, a chief executive of Hamlyn after Paul had sold the company, who rebuked me for placing so much business with her. 'They're running a sweat shop, Ian. You'd never approve of it.'

'How is it then, that Elsie gets people to work so efficiently? If what you say is true, how is it the service is unbeatable?' Hugh, who was an ex-working-class Tory, the son of an underpaid railway driver, had no answer. I saw staff in action when I visited The Nest. They were encouraged by example to positive acts of salesmanship when customers phoned in with orders. Did they also need such-and-such a title which was reprinting but 'we have stock'; how were they doing with X and Y which were fast-moving items? Elsie, in 1981, claimed 'we have a very good team here and the majority of them are on sales bonus BUT with a strict penalty clause of £2 for any mistake which directly upsets a bookseller. That penalty hurts their pride more than their pocket.'

'People stay with us a long time,' Elsie proudly recorded. Asked how pay rises were negotiated she was evasive, stating that 'there were annual increments, and they all live locally and can go home for lunch'. But that was Kip's side of the business and she hinted that she wouldn't dare to interfere. Unions were not tolerated. At least in the early days there was no salary scale. Some staff joined as temps, after graduating from the University of East Anglia, and stayed because, according to Mike Butler, they 'liked working for a laid-back central Norwich book business'.

A favourite story of Elsie's concerned a member of staff who left because he was not satisfied with working conditions. 'I'll hold the job open for you for a while,' she told him. Pause. 'He returned!' The tone of voice was the same used when she commented, 'Someone asked if I was THE Elsie Bertram. " Well," I said, "I may not be very big but I am very fierce."'

As was the case with a number of my subjects, the Bertrams veered between acts of extreme generosity and petty meanness. When Mike Butler moved, Elsie personally sent him an expensive new lawnmower as a house-warming present. Staff were taken on overseas weekend trips to mark breaking a new turnover barrier. Those who manned the Bertram stall at the London Book Fair were treated by Kip to dinner and a West End theatre; they were also adjured to save bread rolls served at hotel breakfast for their lunch.

Not long before closing the High Hill Bookshop and selling a valuable property my business was briefly in the doldrums. May was always a bad month but in 1988 Waterstone's had arrived in Hampstead as a competitor and we had lost a valuable library contract because Camden Council, close to bankruptcy, had stopped buying. Negotiations were near completion for the sale when we experienced, for the first time, a cash trickle and were behind with payments to our suppliers. Without consulting Elsie, Bertram's stopped our account. I rang to tell her we were about to conclude a deal which would leave us financially 'happy ever after'. She sounded very upset and said, 'I shall put on a black armband.' I told her a cheque would be in the post; she need not come with her van to take me to lunch.

In addition to attending annual conferences the Bertrams opened The Nest on the last Sunday in October to wine and lunch their customers amid a display of bestselling books. There was also a splendid bonanza for Elsie's eightieth birthday which was held under canvas in the grounds of the manor house at the village of Bergh Apton, south of Norwich, which was Kip and Alison's home. It was a warm, sunny June day. Elsie was reported as saying, 'Kip has a direct line to the Almighty and sent him a fax at 4 a.m. demanding sunshine.' She also thanked her son and daughter-in-law for the use of their 'allotment'. Paul Hamlyn was unable to be present but several of his former colleagues were there including sometime sales managers Bill Dancer and Penny Singleton who hadn't met for twenty years. 'In fact,' commented that lady, according to a *Publishing News* columnist, 'he sacked me.' The report, part of a special supplement to the magazine, continued with another guest's tongue-in-cheek declaration that it was now Elsie's ambition 'to spend less time with my family'. Buffet lunch was served for a huge gathering of publishers, booksellers, trade press and even retired ex-customers such as myself. At the close of the meal a medieval-style throne was unveiled and Elsie (who was said to have commented, 'I thought it was a commode!') moved shyly to sit on its edge, her tiny figure, waif-like and all but enveloped. She appeared genuinely overcome by the vast wave of affection emanating from all those around her. Bertram's was Kip's creation as well as hers – as much as hers – but she and her chicken shed were its brightest image for all of us who were present.

Trevor Moore and many others, including myself, were confided in by both Elsie and, to a lesser extent, Kip. The mother and son watched the other's every move and liked to complain confidentially of supposed misdemeanours. I had letters from Elsie's private address commenting on the inevitable technological changes which were essential to expansion, accompanied by strict instructions to reply not to The Nest but to Thorpe St Andrew. Once, at the time Bertram's was on offer, came a plaintive cry that she was in danger of being cheated. Such were the allegations she made against her family that I decided to obey her request and destroy the letter. Subsequently she did not seem to have embraced impoverishment. To the end she lived in her pleasantly situated, spotlessly clean house and there was no suggestion that anyone neglected her. Trevor Moore records that he, along with a few others, was 'used to hearing news or comments from Elsie that I was told to keep to myself, or especially not to mention to Kip'. On one occasion she had something 'very personal and/or very private' to communicate. Unusually, he says, he was invited to sit down. 'She looked at me earnestly and pausing with dramatic effect said, "Trevor, what would you do if you suddenly came into a lot of money – I mean a LOT of money?"'

That was all. Moore mumbled about giving it to family, friends, charities … and could not help wondering if something would be coming his way. Two days later the news broke of Bertram's sale to Cypher. (Some of the proceeds were shared amongst long-serving staff.)

Despite the misgivings she expressed in 1999 when told by her sons (Nigel had by then joined his brother in the firm) that a sale had been arranged, Elsie reacted, according to her NLSC tape, with the one word, 'Yippee!' She had cosseted Bertram's maternally and regarded it as 'her' child but she was aware that Kip was bearing the strain of its expansion more and more while she, now an octogenarian, was not able to give it quite so many hours each day. In fact, it was not only the stress of managing an inexorably expanding business that affected Kip. He had returned from a holiday in Switzerland with a broken femur. As he put it, 'Illness got me into the book trade, a skiing accident got me out of it.' During convalescence he realised he had not delegated sufficiently and no doubt brooded about the future. He couldn't use books as a diversion because he found it impossible to concentrate for more than a chapter. He took to tranquillisers. His condition worried Elsie who recorded that he had 'lost his enthusiasm'. The sale, she admitted, wasn't 'a complete surprise … ' and '…it was a relief'. I find that difficult to believe because Bertram's was such a vital element in her life. She may have said this because she realised the deal was a fait accompli in which she played no part.

The purchase price was £36m, which represented two-thirds of the turnover. The new owners allowed Elsie (although not Kip) to enter their old domain and be around while withdrawal symptoms were treated. She was cocky about this when I saw her. It made her feel she still mattered. Kip told me he sometimes had to bite his lip when he heard his mother in full flow; she could 'be a troublemaker'. If and when he also records for the National Life Story Collection it should make for a more balanced assessment of the Bertram achievement, but it was a fact that for most of the book trade Elsie, a formidable little woman in personal charge of an ever-expanding enterprise, was more vividly real than her son.

There was a ninetieth-birthday celebration to which I did not receive an invitation. We had gone on exchanging Christmas cards but the previous year when I enclosed a note with mine, she had replied, 'Dear Mr Ian, I know you must be a very kind person.' She could no longer place me; for the second time my account had been stopped.

Elsie's death in October 2003 was front-page news in the *Eastern Daily Press*. I was given generous space in the next issue of *The Bookseller*; the following week there was another large tribute in *Publishing News* from Ainslie Thin, David Hight and others. There was an unsigned obituary in the *Daily Telegraph*, lifting many sentences from David Hight, from the *Eastern Daily Press* and from me. I also did the *Independent*. A memorial service was held in Norwich Cathedral on 21 November. Black ties were banned and ladies were invited to wear their brightest hats, the sort Elsie adored, although not when she went to the Palace to collect her gong; then she wore a strange little bird's nest of a black titfer with an openwork veil.

The service, attended by many prominent Norwich citizens, as well as colleagues and a sprinkling of publishers and booksellers, had four hymns, an anthem, two readings and several addresses. It was followed by a champagne-buffet lunch. Elsie was seen off in style. She had done the book trade 'some service', plus the citizens of Norwich who had worked for her and 'could go home to lunch' and the diabetics whom she so generously supported.

Elsie Bertram, MBE, born Norton-on-Tees, 2 June 1912, daughter of Harry and Alice Hacker. Married Edward Bertram, 1935. Two sons. Died Norwich, 26 October 2003.

ALAN STEELE

Alan was possibly unique, certainly unusual, in having been a practising bookseller, publisher, printer and also the editor of early Penguin volumes of short stories. He was chairman of the book-production section of the British Federation of Master Printers, 1957–8, honorary treasurer, Society of Bookmen, 1948–75, served on the executive committee of the National Book League for at least twenty years and was a member of the Paternosters, the Double Crown, the Savile and the Garrick.

His name has occurred many times already in this book, he was well known to eight of my ten main subjects and a colleague of mine from 1964 until his death. He was not as eminent or influential as the others of whom I have written but he was active at the heart of the book trade for more than half a century. I include him because he exemplifies the companionship I referred to in my introduction and from the affection I feel for one who, disinterestedly, helped me and many others.

Alan was born in Walthamstow, East London, the son of a doctor who hailed from Londonderry, Northern Ireland. Educated at Felstead, a minor public school, where he met a future business partner Neil McFarlane, he did not aspire to higher education. Aged only nineteen, he and McFarlane, having each spent a year with W. H. Smith as trainees, opened a bookshop at Brighton.

McFarlane and Steele spawned several branches but the young men withdrew in 1927 to pursue separate careers. Alan bought, for £1,000, a 40% share in a company of wholesale export booksellers operating in a court close to Chancery Lane on the edge of the City. William Jackson (Books) Ltd was the creation of an oddball, Dickensian, low-life character named Frederick Joiner who specialised in filling orders from United States booksellers for English first editions and other books on which the American rights had been sold. When ordering them from British publishers he claimed they were being sent to destinations in Africa and the Far East. In many instances this meant that not only did he obtain the books but he was invoiced at 'colonial terms' carrying 50% discount. He then reinvoiced them to his American customers at 33⅓% off, plus 10% commission. Joiner was semi-literate but in no way innumerate. Publishers on both sides of the Atlantic complained bitterly of his practices (see Allen Lane, p.84) but because he paid his bills promptly he got away with it. Steele did not care to be associated with such methods because he aimed to be friendly with publishers but for a while he turned a blind eye, as I was to do twenty-five years later.

Joiner also imported banned books from Europe, such as D. H. Lawrence's *Pansies* and *Lady Chatterley's Lover*. When these attracted the attention of the Director of Public Prosecutions it was Steele, as junior partner, who was declared to be the person responsible for having ordered them. He, not Joiner, was summoned to the office of Sir Archibald Bodkin – remembered by Steele as, 'a terrifying little man with a wizened yellow face, wearing a pair of steel-rimmed spectacles' – and given a warning that there would be a prosecution if he did not desist from the practice. When an associated publishing company, featuring the names of both partners, was formed, it was Steele who faced the wrath of Mr Denny, bookseller of Ludgate Hill, who took exception to the use of the word 'knickers' in a novel subscribed to him. 'Young man,' Denny thundered, 'don't show me filth like this again.'

Alan had started Joiner & Steele partly to distance himself from the Jackson-practice of infringing foreign rights, partly because becoming a publisher appealed to him. He already moved in literary circles. Also William Jackson was the trade counter for Scholartis Press run by the Australian-born lexicographer Eric Partridge. Partridge introduced him to James Hanley and other budding novelists and remained a friend for life.

Steele spent much of his spare time at the Red Lion Bookshop (owned by Charlie Lahr, another eccentric, more literate than Joiner) which was described by the novelist H.E. Bates as 'a rabbit hutch'. There, in Red Lion Square, close to High Holborn, young writers gathered in a cramped environment, some seated on the ladder used for reaching volumes on top shelves. Charlie, of mid-European extraction, published limited editions of stories by Bates, T.F. Powys, Rhys Davies and others, known as Blue Moon Booklets because they appeared only when he could afford to finance them – 'once in a blue moon'. From them Alan got the idea of Furnival Books, slim, handsomely bound volumes which became a feature of Joiner & Steele's list. They too were published in limited editions at the then high price of ten shillings and sixpence. The authors overlapped Lahr's and included Sylvia Townsend Warner, L.A.G. Strong and David Garnett, prestigious names for the time. This was a world far removed from that of Joiner who became suspicious of young Steele, believing he was growing too big for his boots. Some of the list was printed by Butler & Tanner of Frome, Somerset.

Humphrey Tanner, then senior partner in the firm, admired Alan's enterprise but was appalled by the uncouth Joiner. He assured him that when his ancient London traveller, responsible for soliciting work from publishers to keep the presses active, retired he would offer Alan the job. Before that happened Steele had had enough. Joiner and his wife couldn't bring themselves to sack him – probably they did not have the ready cash to buy him out – so they made his life intolerable by having an inner room, lacking daylight and ventilation, constructed for the junior partner.

In 1932 Alan bade a regretful farewell to publishing on his own account, leaving the Joiner & Steele list to specialise in books about contract bridge until it gradually petered out. Inevitably, the likes of Bates and Garnett would have nothing to do with Joiner.

Alan moved to *The Times* Book Club, a large subscription library attached to the newspaper's bookshop in Wigmore Street, London W1. The terms of business guaranteed subscribers any book they wanted when required which necessitated maintaining large stocks of many titles. Inevitably, as demand for a particular title dropped, the Book Club was left with massive overstock in warehouses around Wigmore Street. Some of it was sold on to public libraries but most took up space which was expensive to rent. It became Alan's task to use his knowledge of the export market to sell them to clubs and institutions in various parts of the British Empire. This became a successful operation but due to the rising cost of transport the days of the book club were numbered. *The Times* had twenty branches across the country dispensing volumes by personal delivery to individual subscribers. Their competitors, Harrods and the Army & Navy Stores, who mounted similar operations, were able to use the same vans which carried books to convey more expensive luxury goods, thus making the whole operation viable. The average return for *The Times* on one book per subscriber was the equivalent of 4p in the pound.

Alan remained for two years until he succeeded Butler & Tanner's elderly London representative. During the five years before the outbreak of the Second World War he became a familiar figure to publishers and was so highly regarded that, as early as 1935, he was elected to the Society of Bookmen. He became friendly with Allen Lane who invited him to select and edit books of short stories for the new Penguin list. Some of these he co-edited with Joan Hancock who, after the war, became his second wife. (By his first he had a son and a daughter who played little part in the rest of his long life.)

Alan had a bad war. Having been commissioned in the 21st Light Royal Artillery he was posted to the Far East where he was captured after the fall of Singapore. He survived four years of prisoner-of-war camps in Japan and Korea before returning home, via Canada, in 1946.

He was welcomed back by Joan Hancock and, after his demobilisation, Butler & Tanner, where he resumed control of the London office, eventually being appointed a director. His first wife divorced him and he married Joan.

The position at Butler & Tanner was ideal for Alan. He had learned sufficient about the craft of printing to maintain a credible relationship with the publishers he met every day in the course of his work. They were his customers and soon in many cases his friends. He loved the trade, the gossip, the personnel; he became a sturdy branch of the grapevine. People automatically told him things; his natural curiosity, coupled to innate courtesy (I never saw or heard of Alan being rude to anyone), led him to enquire into everything; he became a fount of information.

It was a vital part of his job to be aware of all that was going on in the book trade from major movements of companies and people down to the minutiae. The principal book printers, for economic reasons, operated in East Anglia, the West Country and elsewhere in the provinces. Wages there were lower than in London and warehouse space less costly. But most of the work contracted for emanated from the capital where at least 90% of publishers were located. It was the responsibility of the London offices of the printers not only to obtain work but to ensure that it would be paid for. Alan and his counterparts at Clowes, Clay, Hazell, Watson & Viney, etc., had to keep their ears to the ground. Nothing could have suited him more. His job was as much to talk and to listen as it was to take orders. He could give or obtain advice when necessary but most publishers had their production managers and knew what they wanted. In the 1950s Butler & Tanner was already expanding. It was then that Alan enlisted Peter Cochrane from Chatto & Windus to be his deputy (See p.122).

I first met Alan around this time. I was working in Southampton Row, Bloomsbury, for Frederick Joiner who had moved William Jackson (Books) Ltd there soon after the end of the war. Occasionally a smartly dressed, bespectacled man wearing a brown trilby would come into the export department and hail Joiner. He presented a very different appearance from most of Joiner's visitors, a seedy bunch of ne'er-do-wells, with 'City' interests, augmented by a clutch of dowdy publishers' reps clad like undertakers' assistants. What business had this obviously educated and respectable middle-aged man to transact with the old rogue, attired in a food-and-beer-stained, shaggy suit, who was my boss? In due course, as Joiner came to favour me, I was introduced to his former partner Alan Steele. Later, with Joiner blind and at home, I became managing director and when Alan called we went out for drinks together and swapped experiences.

A marked characteristic of Alan's was his willingness to help others up their particular ladders. He was especially attracted, so it seemed to me, to those with left-wing political sympathies, although himself a lifelong Tory believing in 'the inevitability of gradualism'. He encouraged Alan Hill, James MacGibbon, Robin Hyman and others including myself. In 1955, with Joiner old and sightless, he was concerned about what was to happen to William Jackson and to my prospects. He and Roger Hutchinson, a senior Heinemann rep, with whom he lunched weekly, were willing to back me and a lady who worked for William Dawson, also wholesale book exporters, if Joiner would sell Jackson's. I told the company accountant and auditor what we had in mind. He instantly informed his fellow freemason, Joiner, giving him the impression that I was trying to acquire the company by stealth. Joiner was already concerned because I was questioning the rectitude of sending to America books on which the rights had been sold. Three days after my wedding in April 1955 a board meeting of William Jackson was called at which it was voted to halve my salary. The Joiners didn't have the guts to sack me; they didn't enclose my desk in an airless inner room; my 250 shares in the business were of no significance. I resigned, which left Alan feeling he owed me a job. He introduced me to Hubert Wilson who ran a small chain of retail shops based in the City plus a flourishing book-and-magazine-subscriptions export department. I was to develop wholesale exporting; Wilson also offered Alan a seat on the board. Neither of us knew that Alfred Wilson Ltd was on the verge of bankruptcy due to incompetent management by Hubert who had taken three decades to wreck his father's brainchild.

When I had been six months with Wilson's, Hubert appointed me assistant general manager in the hope that I could save the sinking ship. I couldn't. He brought in efficiency experts who forecast the worst and insisted on receiving their fees daily. Under pressure from Butler & Tanner, Alan Steele resigned his directorship of Wilson's. Soon after, I was retained by William Balleny, the receiver, to manage the Hampstead branch while he negotiated the sale of the company's tax loss to Foyles (see p.157).

In 1964, when Mavis and I sought to buy the Hampstead premises, by now High Hill Bookshops Ltd, Joan and Alan Steele agreed to back us on condition that we became majority shareholders. The decision was taken by them one evening, in under an hour, by phone. Their solicitor and

William Balleny thought they were being reckless, despite which Alan became chairman, remaining so until his death, offering me good advice and assistance. He kindly said that the High Hill investment was the best he ever made, paying Joan and himself 15% gross interest every year. He was also the catalyst whereby Trisha Nunn, his long-term personal assistant at Butler & Tanner, became a senior colleague of mine. I had hoped originally to raise the purchase money for High Hill by backing from a consortium of publishers. Ian Parsons was one who offered to come in but, when the Steeles took 40% and my parents-in-law loaned us the other 60%, I did not take up I.M.P.'s much appreciated proposal. In later years he chided me about this – 'I was willing to back you, dear boy' – but had I accepted that almost certainly would have encouraged interference from his close colleague Norah Smallwood.

It had been Alan's intention when we bought High Hill to work again himself as a bookseller once he had retired from Butler & Tanner. As the time approached – in 1968 – discussion ensued between himself and Joan, and between us, about appropriate shop attire. All his professional life he had worn a two- or three-piece suit and tie. At Hampstead we had early fallen for casual-but-clean. It was long since I had worked in anything other than open-neck shirt and slacks, plus pullover when required. Such dress did not come naturally to Alan for the working day. I didn't like to suggest he might settle for an old sports jacket with leather elbow patches and baggy trousers such as many provincial booksellers – Henry Schollick, for instance – favoured. I left it to him, so he wore formal clothes and looked slightly out of place. Then, although as alert as his new colleagues, his mental arithmetic had not been applied on a regular basis for decades. We had ancient, manually operated tills. Staff were forbidden to use calculators. We added up purchases in our heads and were invariably accurate. Alan found this difficult. Also, the war had left him with a slight infirmity in one leg which made him less adept than the rest of us at being part of a team of three working at the same till serving a queue of customers. It was not fair on a man in his seventh decade most of whose hours of employment had been spent in his own or his customers' offices.

To exacerbate the situation, though not intentionally, I delegated to him the task of servicing an annual order from University College School which involved dealing with the requirements of five hundred boys, each submitted on an individual list. Alan Steele's vision of a return to bookselling had been a rosy one in which he would talk about and sell books to literary Hampstead in a cultured ambience. For much of the time it was not like that. (A lot of our profit came from a large turnover in cookery and gardening titles, hotel guides and OU set books, though not from car manuals or DIY – dear me, no, *not* in Hampstead.)

Alan and I did not actually quarrel but there was friction. I desperately needed an effective senior working colleague; I had hoped he would be the answer but the generation gap was too wide. He quickly resolved the problem by taking a new appointment with St Paul's Press, based in Malta, an associated company of Butler & Tanner. This brought him fully out of retirement to take regular, often weekly, flights to Valetta. He remained chairman of High Hill and continued his customary visits to Hampstead. The loser was Joan who had looked forward to his energetic regular presence in their large, self-serviced garden. If she felt resentment she never revealed it to me.

The crisis was weathered thanks to Alan's realistic assessment of the situation and to the determination of our wives to prevent a rift between us. Alan remained a printer and a board-room bookseller: I found a new colleague to share my responsibilities. Thereafter Alan's role became advisory once more but he made a notable contribution by persuading Patricia Nunn to join us as shop manager. She, a close friend of the Steeles who knew me only as an occasional client of B. & T., was aware that there had been problems at High Hill and viewed the possibility of joining us with caution, although she was eager to move from printing into bookselling. Alan invited us, along with Joan and Mavis, to dinner at the Garrick, of which I was not then a member. I was well aware that I, and not Trisha, was the person present who was on trial. Luck was with me. Long after everyone else had been served their main course mine had still not reached the table. I insisted it did not matter and for once behaved calmly, impeccably, a model of good manners. Trisha decided to accept our offer and became a most accomplished bookseller and buyer. We had only one serious row in our thirteen years of working together.

As a non-executive director Alan was a wise and encouraging counsellor who never interfered with the daily running of the business. Until 1982 he was always available as a sounding board, as a shoulder on which to lean. Our weekly lunches became almost the only contact he had with the book trade in which he had played so enthusiastic a role. Some weeks we invited retired publishers or others to join us at a restaurant in Hampstead. James Hanley and Tim, his wife, also an author and now living at nearby Gospel Oak came, so did Fred and Pamela Warburg and Harry Paroissien of Penguin. Other weeks we would meet at the Garrick where Jock Murray, or another old friend, might be our guest. It was a way of keeping Alan in touch because, by the 1980s, he seldom attended a Society of Bookmen dinner. His final years were diminished by physical pain and discomfort yet the optimism and sense of humour which had helped him through the POW years were still evident. He even told funny, unsick stories about his horrendous ordeal in the Far East. As a raconteur he commanded attention by his sincerity and his refusal to be hurried. He savoured his tales, seldom, unlike Alan Hill, embellishing them to a point of near-incredibility, yet always anxious that his listener should not be deprived of them. 'I was telling Ian earlier … ', he would say to a lunchtime companion delayed in joining us … then repeat what he had said to me five minutes before. This was not boring for me; I enjoyed the repeats, noting that, like a good actor, he had perfected his pauses and climaxes.

In the Introduction I wrote that this volume grew from a desire I felt to correct and enlarge obituaries, referring to the unfortunate omissions which occur either through demands on space or ill-informed subbing. When I wrote about Alan for *The Bookseller* in January 1985 I was aggrieved that a paragraph about him as a gardener was excluded.

The garden which Joan and Alan created on their acre of land in Southwater, near Horsham, in Sussex, was an essential component of their four decades spent together. By 1946, when they married, they felt it was too late to have children. Joan, a trained horticulturist, found Alan a willing student who became highly proficient alongside her. Together they devoted themselves at weekends, and on long spring and summer evenings, to making Meadow House a haven of delight for themselves, their several dogs and many friends. The making of their richly varied garden, embracing flowers, shrubs, trees, arbours, unexpected paths through semi-undergrowth, vegetable patches and orchard, with its view over quintessential Sussex countryside, provided necessary therapeutic relief for Alan both from his POW experiences and from his arduous working days in London, giving Joan and him a common pursuit in which they were equal partners. Guests staying for the weekend were encouraged, following breakfast on Sunday, in the politest manner, to absent themselves until lunchtime; tending their acre of land was the Steeles' morning service. They were not proudly intent on making their creation look like an illustration in a glossy magazine; their garden was a place of pleasure. If you brought your children with you, you were encouraged to play at hide-and-seek without admonitions to mind the flowers. This was a reflection of their atttitude to life as a whole, one which informed Alan's approach to publishing, printing and bookselling. He could not have been as good at his job and at maintaining relations with others if he had not enjoyed the Southwater garden experience with Joan. Man, you might say, cannot live by books alone.

Alan William Steele, born Walthamstow, London E, 15 May 1905, son of Dr and Mrs Steele, of Londonderry. Educated Felstead School. Married (1) Phyllis Eldred, c.1932, one son and one daughter (marriage dissolved); (2) Joan Hancock, 19 August 1947. Died, Southwater, Sussex, 4 January 1985.

SOURCES (including Bibliography)

Texts which are peppered with small numerals, asterisks, stars and similar symbols are to me anathema. Although the intention behind them is worthy, they distract the reader and impede narrative flow; they spawn footnotes which can sometimes threaten to take over entire pages. On the other hand for the author to maintain credibility the reader has a right to be guided to the sources of the information provided. My solution involves a degree of DIY; I have indicated below the pages of particular books where some of my sources may be found. In some instances upwards of fifty or more are listed, so there will inevitably be an element of hit or miss in locating the one which is desired. However, few of these books lack an index and that could prove a help in ascertaining which of my numbers will lead to the right answer. If any readers experience difficulty I shall be happy to try to assist them. In my copious and relatively organised notes I can (usually) find exact references. When I am gone they will be found with Michael Bott, Verity Andrews and Brian Ryder at Reading.

CHAPTER ONE – BASIL BLACKWELL ('THE GAFFER')

Blackwell Archives, at Merton College and at 51 Broad Steet, Oxford

Blackwell, Basil, J. M. Dent Memorial Lecture: 'The World of Books', Dent, 1931

Blake, Lord and Nicholls, C. S., *Oxford Dictionary of National Biography, 1981–1985*, Oxford University Press, 1990

Bookseller, The, 14 April 1984, p. 1594, Obituary

Daily Telegraph, 11 April 1984, Obituary

Guardian, 11 April 1984, Obituary

Hampden, John (ed.), *The Book World*, Nelson, 1935

Norrie, Ian, 'The Gaffer Nearing Ninety', *The Bookseller* (p. 2412), 26 May 1979

Norrington, A.L.P., *Blackwell's 1879–1979*, Blackwell, 1983, pp. 16, 30, 46, 48–9, 53, 61, 66–7, 73, 78, 86, 96, 98, 100, 102–3, 140, 160

Oxford Times, 13 April 1984, Obituary and Tributes

Reid, Julian, Ricketts, Rita and Walworth, Julia (compilers/editors), *A Guide to the Merton Blackwell Collection*, Merton College, Oxford, 2004, pp. 15, 37, 55–6

Ricketts, Rita, *Adventurers All*, Blackwell, 2002, pp. xii, 10, 12, 14, 37, 43, 58, 61, 81, 87, 94, 128, 132, 142, 149, 168, 170, 179, 182–3, 197–9, 206, 214, 216, 222, 244, 246, 250, 252, 254–6

Saugman, Per, *From the First Fifty Years*, Oxford, 1993, p. 54

Schollick, Henry, 'The Gaffer Remembered', *The Bookseller* (p. 1683), 21 April 1984

Times, The, 11 April 1984, Obituary

Unwin, Stanley, *The Truth About a Publisher*, Allen & Unwin, 1960, p. 388

Letters from, personal encounters with Sir Basil, Toby Blackwell, Philip Blackwell, Richard Blackwell, Rita Ricketts, Henry Schollick, Mrs Corinna Wiltshire, etc.

The short, unaccredited quotations in this chapter are taken from A.L.P. Norrington's *Blackwell's, 1879–1979*, Rita Ricketts's *Adventurers All* or from documents in the Blackwell Collection at Merton College, Oxford. I am grateful to Julian Reid, the curator, and to Rita Ricketts for permission to study this archive and for their friendly assistance.

CHAPTER TWO – STANLEY UNWIN

Allen & Unwin Archive at Reading University

Anonymous, *Fifty Years of Publishing Books That Matter*, Allen & Unwin brochure

Anonymous, *Sir Stanley Unwin: The Celebration of his 80th Birthday and Golden Wedding Day*, privately circulated in an edition limited to fifty copies, December 1964, pp. 9, 57–8, 60

Bookseller, The, 19 October 1968, Obituary

Chambers, Ivan, 'A Man Sui Generis', *The Bookseller*, 19 October 1968

Higham, David, *Literary Gent*, Jonathan Cape, 1978, p. 175

Kingsford, R. J. L., *The Publishers' Association 1896–1946*, Cambridge University Press, 1970

Lambert, J. W. and Ratcliffe, Michael, *The Bodley Head, 1887–1987*, The Bodley Head, 1987

Lusty, Robert, *Bound to be Read*, Jonathan Cape, 1975, pp. 118–19, 156

Morpurgo, J.E., *Allen Lane: King Penguin*, Hutchinson, 1979

Mumby, F. A. and Stallybrass, Frances, *From Swan Sonnenschein to George Allen & Unwin*, Allen & Unwin, 1955

Publishers' Weekly, 28 October 1968, Obituary

St John, John, 'Ambassador of Books', *Books and Bookmen*, February 1956

Sanders, F. D. (ed.), *British Book Trade Organisation*, Allen & Unwin, 1939

Storr, Severn, *Two Young Men See the World*, Allen & Unwin, 1932

Sunday Times, 3 January 1954, Portrait Gallery

Times, The, 15 October 1968, Obituary

Unwin, David, *Fifty Years with Father*, Allen & Unwin, 1982, pp. 11–12, 27, 46–7, 56–8, 68, 83, 85, 94, 106, 112, 115–18, 120–1, 124, 126, 144–6

Unwin, Philip, *The Publishing Unwins*, Heinemann, 1972, pp. 2, 50, 54, 60, 66, 69, 73, 76–7, 80, 83, 85–6, 89–90, 92, 95–6, 130, 137, 148, 156, 158–9, 162, 167, 170, 172

Unwin, Rayner, *George Allen & Unwin: A Remembrancer*, Merlin Unwin Books, 1999, pp. 33–4, 42, 45, 49, 57–8, 72–3, 89–90, 99

Unwin, Stanley, *The Truth About a Publisher*, Allen & Unwin, 1960, pp. 15, 48, 58, 63–4, 68, 71, 75–8, 80, 84–5, 100, 106, 108–10, 112–14, 125–6, 138, 140–1, 151, 155, 159, 169, 196, 202, 216–18, 223–4, 232–3, 240, 246, 254, 285–6, 292, 301, 304–5, 344, 368, 387, 398

Unwin, Stanley, *The Truth About Publishing*, Allen & Unwin, 1926, 8th edition 1960

Watson, Graham, *Book Society*, André Deutsch, 1980, p. 88

Whiting, Ronald, British Sound Archive: Book Trade Lives, NLSC tapes, British Library

Williams, E. T. & Nicholls, C. S., *Oxford Dictionary of National Biography*, 1961–1970, Oxford University Press, 1981

Letters from Lynette Turberville-Smith (daughter of Philip Unwin), David, Philip, Rayner and Sir Stanley Unwin, Ronald Whiting and personal knowledge.

Unaccredited quotes are from Sir Stanley Unwin's *The Truth About a Publisher* and *The Truth About Publishing*. The quotation from Ronald Whiting's tape recording with the author is the copyright of the National Life Story Collection's Book Trade Lives Project.

I am indebted to David Unwin for his helpful comments and for permission to quote four short extracts from his *Fifty Years with Father*.

CHAPTER THREE – ALLEN LANE

Anonymous, *Fifty Penguin Years*, Penguin Books, 1985

Anonymous, 'Reading on the Rack', *Books and Bookmen*

Anonymous, *Penguins: A Retrospect, 1935–51*, Penguin, 1951

Anonymous, 'Twenty Five Years, 1935–1960', *Penguins Progress*

Bookseller, The, 11 July 1970, Obituary, A.L.

Bookseller, The, 27 March 1976, Obituary, Tony Godwin

Brown, Iain, 'Tony Godwin: Portrait of a Whizz-Kid', *Penguin Collector*, No. 50, p. 22

Brown, Iain, 'Tony Godwin: Bookseller', *Penguin Collector*, No. 53, p. 25

Edwards, Russell and Hare, Steve (eds), 'Twenty-One Years', Penguin Collectors' Society, *Miscellany*, 10 July 1995, pp. 9, 20, 23, 32, 37, 41, 47

Edwards, Russell and Hare, Steve (eds), 'Pelican Books', Penguin Collectors' Society, *Miscellany*, 12 July 1997, pp. 6, 36, 43, 45–8

Hare, Steve (ed.), *Penguin Portrait: Allen Lane and the Penguin Editors*, 1935–1970, Penguin, 1995, pp. 9, 12–13, 15, 29, 52, 72, 76, 89, 107–8, 132, 134–5, 152–3, 210, 219, 226–7, 234–8, 259, 262, 271, 278, 321–2, 346, 351

Hare, Steve, 'The Pevsner Exhibition', *Penguin Collector*, No. 59, p. 12

Hoggart, Richard, Lusty, Robert, etc., *Tributes to Allen Lane*, privately printed, 1970

Howard, Michael, S., *Jonathan Cape, Publisher*, Jonathan Cape, 1971, pp. 164, 285, 291

Lane, Richard, typescript of unpublished memoir, Bristol Archive

Lewis, Jeremy, *Penguin Special: The Life and Times of Allen Lane*, Viking, 2005, pp. 127, 180–1, 284. (The reason there are so few references for this excellent biography is that Lewis and I were, to a large extent, using the same sources.)

Mansell, Heather, 'Conversations with Allen Lane', typescript in the Bristol Archive, Session 1, pp. 4, 6; Session 2, pp. 1–3; Session 3, pp. 9–10; Session 4, pp. 2, 3, 5

Morpurgo, J.E., *Allen Lane: King Penguin*, Hutchinson, 1979, pp. 14–17, 19, 21–2, 50–3,

58, 64, 70, 91–4, 100–1, 104–5, 108, 113, 116, 118–20, 124, 126, 140–1, 151, 157, 159, 161–2, 164, 166, 169, 174–9, 180–1, 185, 188–90, 196, 199, 200, 202–4, 208–11, 213, 215–17, 221–2, 224, 231, 233, 235, 240, 243, 247–8, 251–2, 256–7, 261, 271, 278–9, 284–6, 294, 300, 307–18, 329, 331–2, 334, 337, 339, 346–8, 353, 358–9, 362, 367, 378–9

Penguin Collectors' Society, *Miscellany*, No. 1, p. 3.

Penguin Collectors' Society, *Newsletter*, No. 25, p. 5

Penguin Collectors' Society, *Newsletter*, No. 33, p. 32

Penguin Collectors' Society, *Newsletter*, No. 57, pp. 37–43

Penguins Progress from 1930s onwards

Pevsner, Dieter, Review of Morpurgo (op. cit.) in *The Author*, 1979

Quigly, Isobel, 'The Great Panjandrum', *Penguin Collector*, No. 45, p.23

Rolph, C. H. (ed.), *The Trial of Lady Chatterley*, privately printed, 1961

Schmoller, Tanya, 'Reminiscences', *Penguin Collector*, Nos 55, 56, 57, 58, 59, 60

Times, The, 8 July 1970, Obituary, A.L.

Webb, Kaye, 'On Allen Lane', *Penguin Collector*, No. 53, p. 22

Weybright, Victor, *The Making of a Publisher*, Weidenfeld & Nicolson, 1968, pp. 163, 169–70, 179–80, 194

Williams, E. T. & Nicholls, C. S. (eds), *Oxford Dictionary of National Biography, 1961–1970*, Oxford University Press, 1981

Williams, Gertrude, 'W. E. Williams, Educator Extraordinary', Penguin Collectors' Society, 2000, pp. 72, 77, 89

Williams. W. E., *Allen Lane: A Personal Portrait*, Bodley Head, 1973, pp. 11, 13, 15, 17–18, 20, 26–8, 31, 46, 49, 57, 62–5, 90

Williams, W. E., *The Penguin Story: MCMXXXV – MCMLVI*, Penguin, 1956

Personal letters, personal experience, interviews, talks and correspondence with Trevor Glover, John Hitchin, Clare Morpurgo, Dieter Pevsner, Tanya Schmoller and others.

One invaluable source is at the University of Bristol Library where the special Collections Section has a massive Penguin Archive, including A.L.'s personal signed copies and hundreds of files containing letters and other memorabilia connected with the company and numerous of those who have worked for it. Another lies in the publications of the Penguin Collectors' Society (PCS) which cover not only a twice yearly newsletter-cum-magazine but also individual titles on such topics as Penguin Modern Painters, the Buildings of England, Pelicans, etc.

The Bristol Archive is presided over by Hannah Lowery to whom I am greatly indebted for her assistance and forbearance. I have quoted from many documents in the archive and am especially grateful for having my attention drawn to an extraordinary memo sent by Tony Godwin to Ronald Blass.

The present editor of the *Penguin Collector* (PC) is Jo Lunt who has kindly assisted me in supplying back numbers.

CHAPTER FOUR – JOHN GREY ('JOCK') MURRAY

Adam Smith, Janet and Richardson, Joanna, Obituaries, *Independent*, 25 July 1993

Attallah, Naim, 'John Murray, An Interview', *The Oldie*, 17 April 1992

Barker, Nicolas and Fermor, Patrick Leigh, Obituaries, *Independent*, 24 July 1993

Gibbins, John, 'John Murray's 200 years' (two-part article), *The Bookseller*, 26 October 1968 and 2 November 1968

Holman, Michael, 'Tales from the Desk Top', *The Bookseller*, 25 July 1997, and comments to the author

Matthew, H. C. G. and Harrison, Brian, *Oxford Dictionary of National Biography*, Oxford University Press, 2004

Murphy, Dervla, 'A Scholar and a Gentleman', *The Oldie*, 12 November 1993

Murray, Diana, NLSC tapes at the British Library Sound Archive

Murray, John, G., *A Gentleman Publisher's Commonplace Book*, Murray, 1996

Murray, John, G., *A Poet and his Publisher*, The English Association, 1976

Norrie, Ian, Obituary, *The Bookseller*, 3 September 1993

Pinnock, Kenneth, Obituary, *The Bookseller*, 30 July 1993

Shirley, John, Obituary, the *Guardian*, 26 July 1993

Smiles, Samuel, *A Publisher and His Friends*, two volumes, Murray, 1891

Times, The, Obituary, 24 July 1993

Tyle, Christian, 'Uncorking Authors', *Financial Times*, 22 December 1990

Zachs, William, *The First John Murray and the Late-Eighteenth-Century London Book Trade*, British Academy and Oxford University Press, 1998

Correspondence and meetings with Graham C. Greene, Bevis Hillier, John R. Murray and Alan Steele, personal encounters and documents in the Murray Archive at 50 Albemarle Street.

CHAPTER FIVE – IAN PARSONS

Adam Smith, Janet and David, R .W., Addresses at Stationers' Hall Memorial Service, 10 December 1980

Adamson, Judith (ed.), *Love Letters: Leonard Woolf and Trekkie Ritchie Parsons, 1941–1968*, Chatto & Windus, 2001, pp. xv, xix, xx, 5, 90, 194, 247

de Bellaigue, Eric, *British Book Publishing as a Business since the 1960s*, British Library, 2004, pp. 132–40

Hill, Alan, *In Pursuit of Publishing*, John Murray, 1988, pp. 304–5

Howard, Michael S., *Jonathan Cape, Publisher*, Jonathan Cape, 1971, pp. 210–11, 326–8

Lewis, Jeremy, *Kindred Spirits*, HarperCollins, 1995, pp. 167, 197

Parsons, Ian, *The Progress of Poetry*, Chatto & Windus, 1936

Parsons, Ian, *Shades of Albany*, John Lane, 1928

Stationers' Company Report, 1980, Obituary

Warner, Oliver, *Chatto & Windus: A Brief Account of the Firm's Origin, History and Development*, Chatto & Windus, 1973, pp. 19, 22–3, 25–7, 32

Woolf, Leonard, *The Journey not the Arrival Matters*, Hogarth Press, 1969, pp. 112, 122, 180

Letters from Peter Cochrane, Lady Norah David, Ian Parsons; conversations with Roly Atterbury, Ronald Cortie, Graham C. Greene, Alan Hill, Norman Mackenzie, Christopher Maclehose, Alan Steele; NLSC tape of Peter Cochrane; personal recollections.

I have also quoted from *Tributes to Ian Parsons on his 70th Birthday Dinner*, Kettner's, 1976, a cyclostyled, stapled, privately distributed document of which I own one of the very few copies made. The whereabouts of the original, which was presented to I.M.P., is not known.

I am most grateful to Jo Watt, Group Contracts Director of the Random House Group, for permission to consult the Chatto & Windus Archive at Reading University and to Michael Bott, its present custodian, and his colleagues for their ever-helpful and willing assistance. I have quoted from files: 41/9; 102/3; 352/7; 359/2/1; 362/11/1; 541/6; 579/1.

CHAPTER SIX – CHRISTINA FOYLE AND THE FOUNDING BROTHERS

Anonymous, *The Foyle Story*, no date, no imprint

Anonymous, *Foyles' Fifty Years 1904–1954*, W. & G. Foyle, 1954

Bookseller, The, 8 June 1963, Death of W. F.; 6 November 1971, Death of G. F.; 11 June 1999, Death of C. F.; 18 June 1999, Obituary, C. F.

BBC Sound Archive: *Desert Island Discs*, 30 April 1962; *The Hoisters*, 20 January 1963; *Turning Points*, 23 June 1964; *Home This Afternoon*, 9 July 1964; Interview, 9 June 1971; *Bow Dialogues*, 2 April 1975; *Midweek*, 28 January 1981; *Outlook*, 10 March 1983

Daily Mail, 'Foyle's Law', 5 July 1982

Daily Telegraph, Obituaries, C. F., 10 June 1999; Peterborough, 10 June 1999; Will of C.F., 8 December 1999

Davies, Jessica, 'The Chaos Christina Left Behind', *The Times*, 31 July 2001

Eastbourne Herald, Obituary, G.F., 30 October 1971

Evening Argus, 28 October 1971, 'Bookseller Gilbert Foyle Dies'

Fabes, Gilbert H., *The Romance of a Bookshop, 1904–1929*, privately printed, 1929, pp. 11, 13, 20–1, 24–5, facing 26, 34, 40, 43

Financial Times, 1 December 2001, 'Travails with My Aunt: Interview with Christopher Foyle'

Foyle, Christina, *So Much Wisdom: A Commonplace Book*, André Deutsch, 1984, Preface and pp. 11 and 67

Foyle, Christina, 'Your Children's Career', *Manchester Evening News*, 28 January 1936

Foyle, Christopher, *The Family of George Foyle of Portsmouth*, privately published, revised edition, 2005

Frewin, Charles and Lubner, Derek, *The Bookshops of London*, Two Heads Publishing, 1993, p. 78

Guardian, the, Obituary, C.F., 10 June 1999

Guardian, the, 'Foyles Lunches', 1 October 2001

Independent, Obituary, C.F., 11 June 1999

Independent Magazine, 'A New Leaf', March 2003

Lewis, Richard, 'Foyles', *The Bookseller*, 22 June 2001

Lothar, Simon, 'How I Faced Up to Foyles', *The Bookseller*, 16 July 1999

Lusty, Robert, *Bound to be Read*, Jonathan Cape, 1975, p. 69

McAleer, Joseph, *Passion's Fortune*, Oxford University Press, 1999, p. 63

Maldon & Burnham Standard, Death of Mr W. A. Foyle of Beeleigh, 6 June 1963

Maldon & Burnham Standard, Obituary, C.F., 17 June 1999

Matthew, H. C. G. and Harrison, Brian, *Oxford Dictionary of National Biography*, Oxford University Press, 2004

Mountain, Penny with Foyle, Christopher, *Foyles: A Celebration*, Foyles Books, 2003, pp. 9, 13, 19, 21, 25, 26, 44

New York Times, Obituary, C.F., 11 June 1999

Stephenson, Diana, *Bookshops of Inner London,* Lascelles, 1981, Entry 271

Tagholm, Roger, 'Hands Off! It's a Unique Resource', *Publishing News*, 18 June 1999

This Essex, Interview with Christina Foyle, February 1974

Times, The, Obituary, W.F. 6 June 1963; Obituary, G.F., 29 October 1971; Obituary, C.F., 11 June 1999

Waterstone, Tim, 'Eccentric, Ungenerous, etc.', *Publishing News*, 18 June 1999

Who Was Who, G. F., W. F.

Who's Who, 1999, C. F.

Williams, E. T. and Nicholls, C .S. (eds), *Oxford Dictionary of National Biography 1961–70*, Oxford University Press, 1981

Private correspondence and interviews with Andrew Crofts, George Depotex, Beryl Ennion, Christina Foyle, Christopher Foyle, John Foyle, Robert Foyle, Ben Perrick, Bill Samuel, Peter Underwood, Jan Wise, news items in *The Bookseller* and *Publishing News* and personal encounters.

CHAPTER SEVEN – ALAN HILL

Beal, Tony, Obituary, *The Bookseller*, 14 January 1994

Beal, Tony, Obituary, *Independent*, 22 December 1993

Daily Telegraph, Obituary, 28 December 1993

Ham & High, Obituary, 24 December 1993

Hill, Alan, *In Pursuit of Publishing*, John Murray, 1988, pp. 1–5, 11–12, 23, 25, 36, 38, 41, 43, 52, 55, 57, 63, 66, 71, 73–6, 79, 89, 102–3, 113–14, 120, 123, 125, 128, 132, 151,

156–8, 160–2, 164–5, 170–1, 178, 181–2, 189, 191, 208, 211–12, 215–16, 228, 246,
251–3, 256, 260–1, 265, 273, 292, 295, 304, 330, 338–9, 348, 356–7, 368, 370–2

Hyman, Robin, Obituary, *The Bookseller*, 24 December 1993

Lusty, Robert, *Bound to be Read*, Jonathan Cape, 1975, pp. 158–60

MacGibbon, Hamish, Obituary, *Guardian, the*, 3 January 1994

St John, John, *William Heinemann: A Century of Publishing, 1890–1990*, Heinemann, 1990,
pp. 380–3, 477, 551

Times, The, Obituary, 23 December 1993

Who Was Who, A & C Black, 1998

Personal reminiscences of and letters from James Currey, Martyn Goff, Alan Hill, David
Hill, Enid Hill, Hamish MacGibbon, Paul Richardson and Keith Sambrook.

Tape Recording of interview between Alan Hill and the author, November 1992, now
in the National Life Story Collection at the British Library.

Unattributed quotes are, in all cases, from Alan Hill's *In Pursuit of Publishing* (see above).

Chapter Eight – André Deutsch

André Deutsch Ltd Newsletter, July–November 1962

Athill, Diana, *Stet*, Granta Books, 2000, pp. 4, 15–17, 21–4, 40, 51, 87, 101, 120–5.

Athill, Diana, 'André Deutsch: The Great Persuader', *Logos*, Vol. 14, Issue 4, 2003

Coleman, Terry, *How to be a Very Successful Alien*, newspaper interview

Cooper, Leo, *All My Friends Will Buy It*, Spellmount, 2005

Daily Telegraph, Obituary, 15 April 2000

Dally, Jan, Obituary, *Financial Times*, 15 April 2000

Deutsch, André, NLSC tape in the Sound Archive at the British Library

Lewis, Jeremy, *Kindred Spirits*, HarperCollins, 1995, Chapter 3, 'Deutschland Uber Alles'.
Note: Jeremy and his millionaire publishers failed to provide an index to this incompara-
bly entertaining memoir of working in publishing.

Maschler, Tom, *Publisher*, Picador, 2005

Mikes, George, *How To Be Seventy*, André Deutsch, 1982, pp. 143, 162–3, 223, 236

Norrie, Ian, 'Seventy Not Out', *Publishing News*, 20 November 1987

Norrie, Ian, 'André Deutsch as I Remember Him', *Publishing News*, 11 April 2000

Oxford Brookes University: the André Deutsch Archive, comprising André's personal
library, memorabilia and effects which were not sold with the company archives to Tulsa
University Library. Chris Fowler, the curator, kindly mounted an exhibition of them for
my benefit.

Letters, interviews, meetings with Piers Burnett, George Depotex, Graham C. Greene,
Bill McCreadie, Trevor Moore, Paul Richardson and T. G. Rosenthal and personal experience.

CHAPTER NINE – PAUL HAMLYN

Barker, Nicolas, Obituary, *Independent*, 22 September 2001

Bevan, Judi, in the *Sunday Telegraph*, February 1984, quoted in de Bellaigue

Calder, John, Obituary, *Guardian, the*, 3 September 2001

Clee, Nicholas, Obituary, *The Bookseller*, 7 September 2001

Daily Telegraph, Obituary, 4 September 2001

de Bellaigue, Eric, *British Book Publishing as a Business since the 1960s*, British Library, 2004, pp. 91–9, 102–3, 107–10, 113, 115, 119, 126

Jarvis, Philip and Thomson, Sue, 'Paul Hamlyn: "There Must be Another Way…"', *Logos*, Vol. 14, Issue 3

Jones, H. Kay, *Butterworths: History of a Publishing House*, Butterworths, 1980, p. 233

Leventhal, Lionel, *On Publishing*, Greenhill Books, 2002, pp. 29, 30, 32

Thomson, Sue, NLSC tapes, British Library

Whiting, Ronald, NLSC tape, British Library

Correspondence with Bill Dancer, Michael Hamburger, Philip Jarvis, Paul Richardson, T. G. Rosenthal, David Whitaker, Ken Wilder and Michael Zifcak, personal recollections and meetings with Lord (Robert) Gavron and the subject.

CHAPTER TEN – ELSIE BERTRAM

Culot, Caroline, 'Energy and Passion in a Life Lived to the Full', *Eastern Daily News*, 28 October 2003

Daily Telegraph, Obituary, November 2003,

Hight, David, Smith, Delia and Thin, Ainslie, Obituary, *Publishing News*, 7 November 2003

Jones, Philip and Stone, Andrew, 'Cypher Group Paid £36m for Bertram's', *The Bookseller*, 15 October 1999

Norrie, Ian, 'Elsie Bertram, MBE', *Publishing News*, 1 May 1987

Norrie, Ian, Obituary, *The Bookseller*, 31 October 2003

Publishing News, June 1992, The People Column

Times, The, Obituary, 5 November 2003

Walber, Eve, 'Mrs Elsie Bertram, MBE', *Norfolk Journal*, May 1987

Meetings, conversations with/letters from Elsie Bertram, Kip Bertram, Mike Butler, Hugh Campbell, David Hight, Trevor Moore, John Prime and personal experience.

POSTSCRIPT: ALAN STEELE

Notes by and letters to the author and personal experience.

INDEX

Nowadays it has become customary for an index to comprise, under individual entries in detail, a summary of the contents of the whole book. Where a full length work has one principal subject this is often desirable but, in this instance, the publisher believes that because there are eleven main subjects, each taking up an average of twenty-three pages, this will not be required by the general reader. However, to assist biographers and researchers into book trade history, an extended index is available by e-mail on request to the publisher (gmo73@dial.pipex.com) or may be obtained direct from the author in computer print out form. This more detailed index is based on one prepared by Hazel Bell which proved of inestimable value to the author, as an aide-memoire, during long periods of revision.

First published in Great Britain by

Elliott & Thompson Ltd
27 John Street
London WC1N 2BX

© Ian Norrie, 2006

ISBN 1 904027 49 0

First Edition

Book design by Brad Thompson

Printed and bound in the UK by Athenaeum Press